D1218538

WORD-MUSIC

WORD-MUSIC

The Aesthetic Aspect
of Narrative Fiction

James Guetti

RUTGERS UNIVERSITY PRESS
New Brunswick, New Jersey

PERMISSION TO USE EXCERPTS FROM THE FOLLOWING WORKS IS GRATEFULLY
ACKNOWLEDGED:

As I Lay Dying by William Faulkner. Copyright © 1930, 1957 by William Faulkner. Reprinted with the permission of Random House, Inc.

Bend Sinister by Vladimir Nabokov. Copyright 1947 by Vladimir Nabokov. Used with permission of McGraw-Hill Book Company.

The Car Thief by Theodore Weesner. Copyright © 1967, 1969, 1971, 1972 by Theodore Weesner. Reprinted with the permission of Random House, Inc.

A Clockwork Orange by Anthony Burgess. Copyright 1962 by Anthony Burgess. Copyright 1963 by W. W. Norton & Company, Inc. Reprinted with the permission of the author and W. W. Norton & Company, Inc.

The Collected Poems of Wallace Stevens. Copyright © 1923, 1931, 1935, 1936, 1937, 1942, 1943, 1944, 1945, 1946, 1947, 1948, 1949, 1950, 1951, 1952, 1954 by Wallace Stevens. Reprinted with the permission of Alfred A. Knopf, Inc.

Feeling and Form by Susanne Langer. Copyright 1953 Charles Scribner's Sons. Reprinted by permission of Charles Scribner's Sons and Routledge & Kegan Paul Ltd.

Heart of Darkness by Joseph Conrad. A Norton Critical Edition, edited by Robert Kimbrough. Copyright © 1971, 1963 by W. W. Norton & Company, Inc. Reprinted with the permission of W. W. Norton & Company, Inc.

Opus Posthumous by Wallace Stevens. Copyright © 1957 by Elsie Stevens and Holly Stevens. Reprinted with the permission of Alfred A. Knopf, Inc.

The Red Badge of Courage by Stephen Crane. Copyright © 1975 by the Rectors and Visitors of the University of Virginia. Reprinted with the permission of the University Press of Virginia.

The Sound and the Fury by William Faulkner. Copyright © 1929, 1956 by William Faulkner, 1946 by Random House, Inc. Reprinted with the permission of Random House, Inc.

Tales of Adventure by Stephen Crane. Copyright © 1970 by the Rectors and Visitors of the University of Virginia. Reprinted with the permission of the University Press of Virginia.

V. by Thomas Pynchon. Copyright © 1961, 1963 by Thomas Pynchon. Reprinted by permission of J. B. Lippincott Company.

Library of Congress Cataloging in Publication Data

Guetti, James L
  Word-music.

  Includes bibliographical references and index.
  1. Fiction—Technique. 2. English fiction—20th century—History and criticism. 3. American fiction—History and criticism. I. Title.
PN3355.G8   823'.9'12   79-9468
ISBN 0-8135-0883-5

THIS BOOK IS FOR NICHOLAS,
HIS "HOUSE IN A FIELD"

Contents

Extracts

there was great listening
which was the music.

—Ed Roberson

A man listening to a story is in the company of the story-teller; even a man reading one shares this companionship. The reader of a novel, however, is isolated, more so than any other reader. . . . In this solitude of his, the reader of a novel seizes upon his material more jealously than anyone else. He is ready to make it completely his own, to devour it, as it were. Indeed, he destroys, he swallows up the material as the fire devours logs in the fireplace.

—Walter Benjamin

—A girl who craves the interesting becomes the trap in which she herself is caught. A girl who does not crave the interesting believes in repetition. Honor to her who is such by nature, honor to her who becomes such in time.

—Sören Kierkegaard

Poetry too came to me through my father. At first, of course, I did not understand the words. But why should words be understood? Perhaps the idea of understanding words in poetry is a mistake. Perhaps poetry stands for what Bernard Shaw . . . called "word music."

—Jorge Luis Borges

One

Visual and Aural Motives
in Fiction

"NONE OF THEM KNEW the color of the sky":[1] the story begins, as usual, in the realm of knowing and seeing. This is in fact so much as usual that we may not even notice it. We are accustomed to what I want to call fiction's "visual motive," and most often we take that motive for granted; we assume that the natural way, even the only way, to begin a story or a novel is with a naming of seen or seeable parts.

Nor—given the presumed connection between sight and knowledge—does the choice of that sort of beginning seem at all narrow. For in our experience of reading, as well as in our experience of language more generally, "seeing" is not an action only of the mind's eye. To "see" through words is conceived not as one of the functions of the mind, but as the main function, that of understanding itself. It seems natural that any act of seeing—whether in reality or in fiction—will either amount simultaneously to knowledge or be followed quickly by it: as if visualizing always meant, sooner or later, conceptualizing, as if seeing were always attended by Seeing.[2]

But hearing this, one is liable to say, Who would have thought otherwise? For this inseparableness of seeing and knowing is so presumed as to amount to a tyranny. As far as our verbal imagination is concerned, there seem not to be five senses, but one: seeing, in permanent association with knowing, appears to include and to dominate the rest, so much so that it may seem the only important business of words and the mind. This connection between visibility and intelligibility is fundamental in that it forms the very basis for what we think of as the literal use of language, with all its

actions of pointing and showing so as to explain and to figure.
Indeed, in the "real" world, any act of seeing that is not also an
act of knowing may be felt as a waste of time.

At the same time, however, in the world of our reading, the
association between seeing and knowing is fundamental to the
dynamics of narrative sequence in fiction, especially in the case of
"realistic fiction." The progress from seeing to knowing is felt to
be perhaps the most important aspect of reading fiction, and even
to justify it. What it justifies as well, or rather compels, is the main
action we take in our reading, where seeing becomes knowing by a
constant process of accumulating and digesting images on the way
to some ultimate reduction or abstraction of them. We follow from
image to image to arrive at a "larger," more comprehensive image
that will rule them all. The relation between seeing and knowing
in verbal sequences thus takes the form of a constant demand or
pressure to number and to total the parts of an imagined world as
we move through it to its end. Such a process insistently requires,
of course, that the parts of this world be various. Imaginative
progress requires for its medium a continual sequence of imagistic
change. In this way, the commitment to the universe of seeing and
knowing is also, and perhaps above all, a commitment to novelty.
In order for the visual-intelligible condition—or the illusion of it—
to persist, things have to keep changing. And this, of course, is
exactly what happens in realistic fiction:

> None of them knew the color of the sky. Their eyes glanced
> level, and were fastened upon the waves that swept toward them.
> These waves were of the hue of slate, save for the tops, which were
> of foaming white . . . (68)

The illusion of imagined life, of something actually happening,
depends crucially on our progress as readers from one thing or condition or action to another; the illusion of realism requires continual
verbal variation because such variation is necessary to imitate the
conditions of the seeing-knowing process that is usual with us in
actual life. So long as those conditions seem established, there is
little felt difference between the way we treat fiction and the way

we treat real experience. We do not need, then, to be told epigraphically that this story is a "tale intended to be after the fact," for even if the men and the sky and the sea are not facts, while their variation continues they are grist for the process from visibility to intelligibility, and so we treat them just as if they were facts.

But in "The Open Boat," this variation does not continue unabated; it is itself varied with something else:

> None of them knew the color of the sky. Their eyes glanced level, and were fastened upon the waves that swept toward them. These waves were of the hue of slate, save for the tops, which were of foaming white, and all of the men knew the colors of the sea. The horizon narrowed and widened, and dipped and rose, and at all times its edge was jagged with waves that seemed thrust up in points like rocks. (68, my emphasis)

"And all of the men knew the colors of the sea" seems to generate an imaginative reflex very different from what precedes and follows it. The tone of the prose momentarily becomes echoing and sonorous. We become aware of a measured rhythm, distinct and sententious, and this—when we compare it to the clicking progress of the paragraph as a whole—amounts to a decided change of the imaginative conditions.

Such a change of the fictional conditions is perhaps easy to notice, but it seems difficult to describe with any intensiveness. If we suppose that realistic fiction imitates life largely by establishing the same sort of progress through imaginative variation that we associate with the action of literal language in life, then we may understand, at least in abstract, that any sort of repetition or sameness will, in either case, have drastic effect. In everyday explanations, for instance, or in arguments, or even in giving travel directions—in any use of words to make something understood—if we repeat ourselves we may seem to have failed. The corollary of our assumption that words are used essentially for purposes of communicative intelligibility is our assumption that any repetition within this use is a fault. This feeling goes deep: at the sound of words repeating, dissatisfaction and boredom and embarrassment are stock responses;

3

we write "rep" on students' papers with the assurance that it will be understood as an obvious and justifiable criticism. In all cases where the seeing-knowing motive dominates, and most of the time this apparently applies to all cases of language use, repetitions appear to thwart our progress to intelligibility just because they abrogate the accumulative variation of images that such progress depends on. So repetition amounts, in literal usage, to default, to a cancellation of the entire verbal game.

Fiction, of course, is not argument or explanation, but nonetheless it is most often felt to operate on the same scale: if any literary form approaches the uses of language that we think of as literal, that form is the novel, for in its pretension to history and social comment and regional realism, the novel declares its visual motive and commits itself to the progress from visibility to intelligibility. And while narrative repetition does not flatly cancel or invalidate these expectations for a narrative sequence, it does effect a dramatic conversion on them—or even a metamorphosis, where the imaginative action of following and accumulating images is transformed into a totally different process and result.

Here, from a reputedly realistic, and thus visual, writer, is an extravagant example of this sort of conversion:

> In the late summer of that year we lived in a house in a village that looked across the river and the plain to the mountains. In the bed of the river there were pebbles and boulders, dry and white in the sun, and the water was clear and swiftly moving and blue in the channels. Troops went by the house and down the road and the dust they raised powdered the leaves of the trees. The trunks of the trees too were dusty and the leaves fell early that year and we saw the troops marching along the road and the dust rising and leaves, stirred by the breeze, falling and the soldiers marching and afterward the road bare and white except for the leaves.[3]

The commitment to visibility here, as the passage begins, can hardly be exaggerated. This does not mean, of course, that there is no attention to the sound of the sentences at that point; but it does mean that rhythmic motives are totally in the service of visual ones, a lubricant for the visual wheels. The prose insists on its variety of detail, upon relatively small imagistic units that sustain a changing course toward some composite picture. And that continues for three sentences. But what happens to this picture, or to any picture, when its parts begin to repeat? What happens when our visual-conceptual progress is stayed, when, instead of more images, we get the same ones in the same use over again?—as occurs here, after "and we saw": again the marching and dust and leaves falling and marching and the road and the leaves.

We may imagine a moving picture, a film, running the same sequence over and over again. But even that is not accurate for this effect. For if we consider our experience of reading here I believe we find that, at least by the end of this paragraph, we have stopped "seeing" almost entirely; instead, we have begun "hearing" the words. It seems also that this act of hearing words interferes with their visual efficiency.

But to say anything more precise about this shift from the visual to the "aural" motive seems difficult. The imagination of words in fiction may seem so dominantly a matter of the eye that the shift to the mind's ear may be figured as a cancellation and a blank, something that cannot be thought about fruitfully. We know, for instance, how impatient we may become if—in the middle of some literary conversation—someone starts talking about the music that he hears in a narrative. Still, that is what we seem to have here. The recurring images and rhythms of this prose make a music, and the visual-intelligible effect is subordinated to something else.

One of the effects of this music, and of this subordination, is the staying of imaginative progress. The recurrence of images and rhythms not only seems to make the pursuit of new images impossible, it also suggests that such a pursuit is no longer important. The imaginative action of following has been halted here and perhaps may even seem satisfied. The pressure toward intelligibility has eased. In this way, the "aural motive" in fiction seems just opposite to the visual: instead of progress, it engenders stasis; instead of pressing movement, rest; and instead of an appetite for ever more varying images, it appears to create a confidence and even a complacency that no further images are necessary.

What this amounts to is the breaking of one sort of spell and the weaving of another. Certainly the illusions of realistic fiction are dispelled here. We no longer feel that we are dealing with the parts of a world, for it has become difficult, perhaps impossible, to see them. The conversion to aural motives and energies says to us that we are not seeing something but hearing something. It sounds like a simple difference, but it is a crucial one.

For seeing has to do, once again, with worlds and their parts and with what we ourselves can make of them. And any such visual world must be one of continuous variation: nothing in its particular and available space can ever be there twice; nothing in its ostensibly pure and successive time can repeat. This is why repetition—of images or of sounds into rhythmic patterns—is so effective. For the repetition tells us immediately that the space of the fiction is not real, that the time of the prose does not come to us untouched: that it has been altered, measured, formed. And to become conscious of that measure and form is to become aware that what we are perceiving is no open reality—no world that we might operate on as if it were such a reality—but a fiction, made by someone other than ourselves.

If the illusion of realism in fiction may thus be said to depend upon the accepted pretence of unaltered time, then the perception of altered time as we read is, simply, identical to the hearing of words in a rhythm, a rhythm whose source is not in ourselves. Thus, such an experience is not real in the way that visual experience may be. It involves the dominating awareness of an overt fictional action and of a fictionalizer beyond ourselves. It involves feeling that we are being told a story.

To understand this better, we may again consider music. Although in listening to music we do all sorts of things, at least one of them, probably, is to feel strongly, perhaps overwhelmingly, the presence of an artist—the composer himself, maybe, or the conductor, if he is especially good or bad, or the player of a particular instrument. And so one feels the immediacy not of some kind of life, as in a realistic experience, but of a kind of art: one experiences

a performance, by someone else, and that someone else is undeniably there in a way that the self-restrained and even invisible
narrators of realistic stories never are. In reading such stories, and
on our way to more and more seeing and synthesizing, our own
imaginative authority dominates. But in listening to music, some
other authority is undeniable, and what we can do with the music
for our more aggressive imaginative purposes is narrowly restricted,
possibly excluded. In listening to music, we must entertain a presence, an imagination, other than our own, and thus the self-fulfill-
ing urge for more visibility and intelligibility is set aside. Instead
of the one important player, we become the played upon.

To put this in a more particular relation to fiction: when we hear
the words of a narrative, we hear a voice. We therefore cannot continue to feel that the parts of a world are being assembled and
established, as if by an invisible creator, for our own appetite and
manipulation. We can no longer respond to the fiction as we can
to the facts of our lives. When we are made to hear someone else
telling it, it becomes avowedly and unquestionably a story that we
are listening to, told by someone who holds—and to whom we
relinquish—all the active imaginative power of the situation. The
illusion that by seeing it we could make this story into a world of
our own fades, and we sit back to enjoy the sound of someone else's
making, to enjoy the story in relation to its telling and its teller.

That makes it all sound easy, and also inconsequent. Which is
normal, for the conversion in fiction from the visual to the aural
motive is always deceptive in at least two ways. On the one hand,
it may seem so easy and obvious as not to amount to much of a
change: the ear is just a few inches from the eye, after all, and hearing just another sense in the service of vision: "What *if* someone else is telling it? It's still a story." On the other hand, and
more important, in our bias any talk about aural imagining seems
also, paradoxically, to be subversive. We are so much more at home
discussing visual and conceptual experience that a decided shift to
the aural may seem, again, just a dead end: "If someone is *talking*
here, then it's not a *real* story at all. I don't want to hear it."

Both perceptual difficulties arise, I think, because the aspect of
aural processes is so overtly and rootedly the aspect of play. While

the visual experience of fiction can be documented and discussed much as facts and ideas can, and so go hand in hand with our efforts to make practical use of all of our time—even the time of a fictional sequence—the aural experience is conspicuously nonprogressive and nonproductive. So it may seem childish.

Indeed, such experience is childish, just as it is primary to us: it is most likely the first sort of experience that we have with stories —and even with language itself—and it remains involved in that experience for the rest of our lives. This helps to explain, I believe, whatever readiness we show to be "played upon" by a storyteller, and it helps also to define that readiness as a relinquishment of imaginative authority, the same authority that we rather exercise and sustain when we more actively try to see and know for ourselves. The visual motive in fiction is an invitation to author the story ourselves; the aural motive insists that the story already has an author and that therefore a reader is relieved of such obligations. In this way, the aural motive may seem to involve our return to a much less willed and more innocent kind of imagination.

The deep-rootedness of aural experience also suggests that our probable irritation at remarks about, for instance, the "wonderful sound of Faulkner" springs perhaps from our conviction that such subjects are somewhat too special, or even too private, to talk about. Even so, the aural motive—or something apparently like it—does have a critical tradition in poetry, especially lyric poetry; we have been willing to talk about things like sound and music there.[4] But nobody ever used the phrase "realistic poetry." Poetry is at least presumably a more special and private form, and even a less serious form, than fiction, in part just because it is assumed to play more regularly to the ear. And poetry that does so emphatically—that insists upon its sound in a dominating way—is felt to be even less serious than poetry that is more visual or ideological or both. (How much does one hear, for instance, about Dylan Thomas these days, or even Hopkins?) This in turn follows from our presumption that the visual-conceptual universe must dominate and that the most that sound should ever be is a decoration for sense.[5]

With fiction, this presumption is much stronger, or perhaps just much more ostensibly reasonable. For fiction, of all literary forms,

8

has the greatest overt commitment to the visible-intelligible, to historical reportage, literal comment, moral inference, and all other
sorts of public knowledge: the preconditions of its form seem to
rule singing right out. And that is why the imaginative situation
that results from the "music" in fiction is so complex and energized. Listen to Hemingway:

> There were mists over the river and clouds on the mountain and
> the trucks splashed mud on the road and the troops were muddy
> and wet in their capes; their rifles were wet and under their capes
> the two leather cartridge-boxes on the front of the belts, gray
> leather boxes heavy with the packs of clips of thin, long 6.5 mm.
> cartridges, bulged forward under the capes so that the men, passing
> on the road, marched as though they were six months gone with
> child.[6]

This movement is full of imaginative variation and of the sort of
progress through it that realism involves, as well as recurrences
within the variation that arrest it and create an experience that we
might associate with the stilled action of ritual. Mists, river, clouds,
mountain, trucks, mud, troops—all that leads us on, seeing and
wanting to see more and different. But against that invitation and
pressure rides the feeling that with every new act of seeing here
we are somehow doing the same thing. It is a feeling that is stimulated first by the recurring rhythm of phrases—over the river, on
the mountain, on the road, in their capes—and of a grammar that
is largely that of a list. But it is confirmed and established, and comes
to dominate the situation, when the visual images themselves begin
to repeat along with their rhythm: "the troops were muddy and wet
in their capes; their rifles were wet and under their capes . . ." And
when "under the capes" itself is later repeated against the grammar
of the sentence, then we may know we are listening to music.

It is an interweaving and an oscillation which makes this effect
so strong. For much of the way the prose continues to pursue its
sense and to progress: first it is the troops that are wet in their capes
and then the rifles are wet and something else under their capes,
and so on. We are thus presented with images to see and to work

with and urged along through them. But at the same time, by the emphatic rhythms of their presentation and by their particular repetition and apparent interchangeableness, we are reassured that there is no hurry, that these same images may return and return again, as they would in music or in a story that was not real and so could take its own time and be told over again and again. So we seem to be following and finding things out, but also to know them already: encountering a real world with all its attractions and, simultaneously, a story with all its securities.

It should be clear that the dynamics of repetition here do not effect, as they would in ordinary communication, a total failure of the intelligible. The aural action of fiction usually does not completely cancel its visual commitments. In the example just cited, the realistic progress of the story continues—in a gesture typical of Hemingway—right out of the movement, by means of a dramatically new image: "marched as though they were six months gone with child." But the conversion to aural motives and back again—which, at this frequency, is felt as an oscillation—seems both to create movement and energy and to still and secure them. Our progress through the imagined world is thus converted from anxious to sure, as sure as only fiction and our awareness that what we are experiencing is fiction, can be.

Even in Hemingway—where the rhythmic energy seems so marked and primitive in relation to the monosyllabic sparseness of his language and the simplicity of his grammar—the conversion to the aural motive seldom appears to result in a new domination, but rather in a balance or, again, an oscillation. For Hemingway is always returning to or beginning again with the visual, at least until the end. Ironically, however, even such decided conversion and reconversion may be hard for us to see, because the pressure of the visual is so strong in us and any deviation from it may threaten an overthrow. So long as our attitude is this drastic, we shall have difficulty seeing what we have yet to see consistently about the relation of visual to aural motives in fiction: seeing, for instance, that there may be more complex relations than the one I have described as "oscillation," moments in fiction when the opposed pressures and pleasures of the visual and aural seem simultaneous and when as readers we are doing two things at once. At such times it may seem difficult, critically, to determine what motive is governing a movement in fiction and our response to that movement: whether it is the various and progressive sense of the words or the immediacy and intensity of certain familiar and anticipated rhythms.

Thus what often appears, in Hemingway, to be motivated by a demand for realistic plausibility may instead be seen to spring from a more aural design:

> Nick's father always assumed that this was what would happen [that is, that the logs would be left to rot], and hired the Indians to come down from the camp and cut the logs up *with the cross-cut saw and split them with a wedge to make cord wood and chunks* for the open fire-place.[7]

Like many of his stories, this one—"The Doctor and the Doctor's Wife"—has begun efficiently. The three paragraphs that precede this one establish quickly and variously the parts of the imagined world, its characters and its conditions. And in contrast to that sort of efficiency and the kind of realism that results from it, the section that I have emphasized moves very slowly indeed. In fact, it seems here that all that detail about making firewood answers not a visual but an aural requirement. The need to go on so extendedly would not seem to visual purpose, especially in contrast to the rapid progress of the narrative up to this point. These added images seem rather to answer a need for more words in the sentence, for a certain fuller cadence. But at the same time, satisfying that rhythm undeniably produces an added visual fullness as well, a realism so detailed that—as often in Hemingway— it seems almost technical writing (how to cut firewood, how to fish high water, how to make camp, how to fight a bull, and so on). Thus, what may well be aural motives here result in a lack of visual haste and engender an imaginative patience that may expand visual effect.

Yet in a way this isn't so, for our very feeling that the aural motive is their source compromises our seeing of these additional details. Their stated visualness, dense as it is, may seem slight beside the cadences they satisfy. This is a complicated action with a complicated effect; the aural dictates a form that seems to further the visual, but the initial dictation remains felt even in the visual action and progress, stilling and ritualizing it.

Of course, this verbal action is more complicated for purposes of literary criticism than for our experience of fiction, where we are accustomed to such doubleness. I have spoken so much about Hemingway here just because, for critical treatment of this narrative action, he is an obvious if not a simple case, because the visual-aural conversions in his prose are so plainly marked, because he has such obviously strong and continuing commitments in such opposing directions, and because, as a result, his interweavings of the visual and the aural occur so frequently. Such frequency may be seen to follow obviously from certain technical aspects of his language—its plainness, its monosyllabic and repetitive economy—and from his grammar—with its lack of subordination or of any other formal arrangement that might compromise its access to heavy rhythms.

But even in such a strong and clear example as Hemingway, this recognition may be complicated both for a reader and, especially, for a critic. For our own motives are involved, and the imaginative stakes for resisting or accepting the conversions that I have described seem high, just because the imaginative changes connected with them are drastic: from business to play, from what seems serious to the frivolous, from the illusion of independent and adult action to that of a dependent and responsive and childlike passivity.

Thus when repetition implies a shift to the aural in a heretofore visually imagined world, that shift may be resisted and recognized only as a fault in that world[8] upon which we need to take further action, to translate it into a context that allows us to maintain our visual concentration:

> Nick was happy as he crawled inside the tent. He had not been unhappy all day. This was different though. Now things were done. There had been this to do. Now it was done. It had been a hard trip. He was very tired. That was done. He had made his camp. He was settled. Nothing could touch him. It was a good place to camp. He was there, in the good place.[9]

When a narrator goes on like this, and so closely to his character, we may simply attach the chanting, formulaic language and the overdetailed and extended ritual action to that character. We may say that the strangeness of the prose is a function of Nick's consciousness, even of his psychology. In this instance we are at least half right; the story may have fuller effect this way. But the fact that such an adjustment or translation seems fruitful in "Big Two-Hearted River" is more a matter of luck than judiciousness. We make the obstinate rhythm here a product of Nick's imagination, and so convert the aural back to the visual, not so much because it seems appropriate to the design of the story but because it is in line with a larger motive: because in doing so—and in continuing the story's sense—we continue our own sense and maintain our authority over the imagined world. Such a translation, in other words, allows us to continue exerting our will and agency. If this chant were to be recognized as part not of Nick's imagination but of the narrator's, then we would begin to feel the story as told, begin to feel it as fiction, a very strange fiction. In that case, we would either lose our agency and yield our imaginations to this strangeness, to the manipulations of the story's teller, or reassert our agency by insisting that if such weird talk is not a dramatized psychological symptom then the story is no good.

Again, in the case of "Big Two-Hearted River," and in much of Hemingway, such translation of and resistance to more purely aural imagining may seem legitimate, especially if we ignore all the moments in his fiction when similar verbal process is *not* connectable with any character's psychology. But this resistance is both narrowing to Hemingway's own range and prejudicial for the cases of certain other novelists. It may result, for instance, with a novel like Faulkner's *Absalom, Absalom!*, in a partial and negative view, where all we can talk about is the narrative's failed attempts at intelligibility, or its dramatization of a failure to compose history, or its critical awareness of its own form—which is to mistake, as I see it, the force of what Faulkner is doing and not to understand why he so often refers, explicitly, to "the old tales and talking." In short, such a perspective does not allow for the probability that aural motives and effects are Faulkner's first priority and that he gravitates so often to failed and fragmentary stories only because it is those whose incantatory repetition may seem justifiable to our visual conscience, as if—as he so often claimed outside them—he were telling them over and over merely in an attempt to "get them right."

What prevents our balanced view of Hemingway, of Faulkner, and of many other novelists—what encourages our unrecognition of their aural motives—is largely our hold upon our own imaginative autonomy. Though at rare times we are content to relinquish, momentarily, imaginative authority, much more often we demand that our imaginations continue dominant. And for that purpose, whatever fiction we are reading must continue realistic, as basis and material for the process and progress. Considering that imbalance, and considering also that aural experience apparently seems too special or private to describe with any success, aural motives, especially in fiction, may seem forbidding as a direction for inquiry. For fiction is the most intelligible and public of literary forms, and any treatment of it not designed to generate meaningfulness of that sort may seem suspect.

The aural energies of fiction, however, are much more prevalent in it than this bias allows and run counter to the pressures and efficiencies of "seeing through." They work always, as I have tried to show them working in certain particular passages, to effect imaginative patience and to allow a kind of seeing that has much less to do with ultimate intelligibility—a seeing that participates in an order of perception quite different from the realistic and that is much more frequent and more powerful, even in our day-to-day imagining, than we are accustomed to acknowledging. If we begin to recognize that perception more fully and explicitly, we may begin to have a better idea of what our imaginative priorities really are, or ought to be. Such a recognition is what I am attempting in the inquiry that follows.

Two

The Sense of the
Terminology

THE TERMS *visual* and *aural* may remind us of the much more traditional categories for narrative fiction and poetry—written and oral. But between the two sets there is only a superficial likeness, and they are entirely unlike in their respective capacities to illuminate the dynamics of fiction. We should not suppose then that because oral narratives were, after all, heard, and written ones seen, that continuing with these terms will cover any territory that *visual-aural* might attempt to explore. For *written* and *oral* appear narrowly limited for the examination of narrative action; indeed, they even appear intentionally restricted and perfunctory.

In the first place, the *oral-written* dichotomy is implicitly a literary historical conception: it is used almost always with the assumption that as a distinction it is no longer current, since oral narrative as a literary form has lapsed in our literature. Oral-written, in short, is a circumstantial terminology whose circumstances have passed. Because its original purpose seems that of characterizing how narratives used to be performed, it has at best a residual and metaphoric value for describing narrative that is all performed written. *The Odyssey*, for instance, surviving as it does in writing, is said to reveal the traces of its oral origins: its rhetorical action resembles that of narratives either known or supposed to have been spoken.[1] But are we as likely to remark the oral characteristics of Hemingway, or Faulkner? For—perhaps because of its historical and circumstantial sources—the oral-written distinction seems a crude one; it functions only when we expect to be confronted with obvious unwritten characteristics in a narrative. The fact that all our narratives are now written puts us to sleep, and so long as the alternative categories for narrative are written and oral, we shall likely be unaware of the current and complex dichotomy of fictional processes.

In its concentration, furthermore, upon the conditions of a narrative's performance or delivery, which may be obvious, the oral-written distinction can make us think we know much more than we really do. Because it is easy to see how a narrative has been performed, it may seem easy to draw certain inferences about the experience of that narrative—for instance, that a narrative we speak will have oral form, with which one associates stylistic formulas, repetition, and a disregard for narrative progress, suspense, and discovery. But this is obviously false. We may speak all sorts of stories —to our children at bedtime, to our friends, and so on—and one can as easily imagine the oral delivery of a realistic story—with its continuing emphasis on variation, accumulation, and surprise—as of a story that repeats and resonates and soothes in the oral manner. And it would surely be too dutifully metaphoric to sort this out by saying that some of the stories that one tells are really written.

For the examination of narrative fiction—or of any art—we must consult the experience of reader or audience. That is where the study, if it is to be truly inquiring, must begin. Written versus oral not only does not consult that experience first but also may prejudice our view of it, or make it seem far simpler than it might be: "In an oral culture this problem [of the relation between the author's world and the reader's world] does not exist. Singer and listeners share the same world and see it in the same way."[2] From this we might suppose that the teller and the audience of, for instance, Beowulf were in total accord, sharing a world view that was universally established, agreeing on what could be told or not told, and that Anglo-Saxon culture was thus uniformly oral—all homogeneous and clear.

The perpetual attractiveness of this sort of idea to the literary or linguistic historian would be reason enough to doubt it: it seems we are always imagining a time when meanings were clear and communication perfect, when everyone knew just what everyone else knew. This is a version of pastoral.[3] In it, the relation of past cultures to our own is figured as the relation of a childhood to an adulthood; the old, simple, successful time as opposed to the new, complicated, and failed one. (Such an idea depends, of course, upon our losing, or forgetting, what childhood was in the first place.) This conception indulges ourselves and insults our imagined antecedents. It is transparently self-flattering: we are not as successful at communicating and knowing just because we know more, or are wiser and larger, or because we have grown. What we have lost is innocence, and that is not something lost at all, but something added, even gained. Our ideas fail us because we are better.

But as dubious as such a model may be, we can see in the case of oral narratives the problem it is meant to answer. It is hard to suppose that the audience of *Beowulf* responded to its telling as we would respond to our more realistic fiction. Its formulas, its repetitive grammar, its disregard of what we would consider necessary continuity and revelation and variation and sequence all preempt the following, accumulating, solving action that we perform with most of our novels. In this writing culture, furthermore, we tend to imagine all our reading as a process of questioning and answering, as a progress toward a meaning, and therefore, since the form of *Beowulf* precludes that sort of action, what could the audience have been doing but agreeing or sharing? There is a vacancy here, in short, that literary criticism and history feel obliged to fill. Faced with what for us is the strangely inactive attitude of the oral narrative's audience, we ascribe it to shared assumptions and attitudes, to general agreement—perhaps because we suppose that were we to sit and listen to anyone else for so long, it could only be because we agreed.

But if my inferences about aural motives in fiction are relevant here, then the Anglo-Saxon audience's agreement had little to do with their listening attitude. For aural processes in narrative may achieve such utter domination of the imagination that they cause us to relinquish completely our very right to agree or disagree. However the Anglo-Saxons saw their world all around the singing experience of *Beowulf*, that view is both indeterminate and irrelevant to that experience. I suppose that when they sat down to listen, they knew what they were doing, that like us—and perhaps better —they knew the difference between their world and a sung story within it and that they allowed with pleasure the imaginative domination that the aural narrative experience entails. By the same token, I cannot imagine such passivity and self-effacement if what was in question was not a story but an entire and continuous world view. If we explain the oral audience's inaction by declaring that their imaginations always worked this way, then we are imagining a culture of simpletons.

What I am suggesting, then, is that the experience of oral narrative—like the aural experience of any narrative, spoken or written —involves a deliberate and temporary imaginative submission, where all the more active rights of one's individual intelligence are surrendered for the sake of another sort of pleasure. To suppose that this is characteristically done only culturally wholesale and that the proper attention to oral narratives can only occur where people think (or don't think) orally all the time is to mistake entirely the special qualities of literary occasions, either oral or written, and of literature itself.

It is the historical implications of the *oral-written* terminology— the fact that we now have only the written and so suppose that the oral must have been very different—that may lead to such mistakes. And so we compose a fiction of cultural homogeneity to account for the fact that people actually sat and listened—often, perhaps, for hours—to a narrative that was not various or suspenseful, listened without questioning and following and summing up, without exercising all the free intelligence that we may exercise and associate with reading written narratives. But both oral and written narratives may involve two markedly different and even opposed kinds of experience. It is possible to tell all sorts of stories, and one can imagine another storyteller in the hall where *Beowulf* was being sung, crouched in a corner away from the fire with his seduced handful of dissident listeners, telling them stories of a more realistic sort. More important, we may by the same token see—for this takes no such fantasizing—that our own written narratives often play not to our active, following, and solving mind, but to other motives and capacities and, therefore, that to say that they are written does not separate them from oral—or aural—experience except in a historical and circumstantial way that is both trivial and misleading.

But if *written*, in its traditional opposition to *oral*, misleads us about the action of fictional forms, it must be admitted that we are willing enough to be misled. For with our written texts, we may exercise our commonest imaginative power—our capacity to follow and find, to accumulate and solve, to derive by our own independent action the meaning of a story. This free pursuit of meaning may seem nothing less than democratic, and realistic fiction itself— the form that allows this freedom most—even politically legitimate. However that may be, our stake in this sort of action is high, just because we seem to be so dominating in it. And in this way, *written* may come to be much more than a merely historical label. We take it as a sign, often, that our main concern with narratives ought to be their prospective intelligibility, their deciphered meaning. Not only does that seem to be, culturally and historically, where we are: it seems also to be where we morally ought to be.

The result of this prejudice, in literary criticism, is twofold: it may be seen first in the preoccupation with the sort of fiction that plays to the problem-solving intelligence, with realistic fiction— whose successive variety must be synthesized—or with oddly structured and open-ended narratives for which we may even have to construct the proper succession, so as to wind up with realism. I am not arguing that these, or any other, sorts of narratives necessarily must be treated as puzzles, but simply that this is the way we tend to treat them. Not all novelists align themselves on the side of difficult deciphering as the main activity of the reading imagination; but most literary critics do so. The second result of our bias in favor of intelligibility, then, is that many narratives that might be considered differently are measured only on the scale of intelligibility, or—to use my preferred term—the scale of the visual.

I shall return to this demand in literary criticism for intelligi-

bility in literary form, but for the moment we may focus on one of
its simpler manifestations, in a fairly typical discussion of the
meaning of narrative. *The Nature of Narrative* allows that "to
begin with, not all narrative works are seriously concerned with
meaning at all," but adds that the ones that are not so concerned
will be "best understood after an attempt to confront those works
which definitely do aspire not merely to 'be' but to 'mean' as well."[4]
One can perhaps see the deck being stacked with that "not merely
to 'be' "; for I was unable to find—after the extensive discussion of
varieties of narrative meaning—the promised discussion of nonmeaning narrative processes. This may have been my oversight, but
if not, the situation is quite typical. For criticism often promises to
consider literary energies other than the meaningful, only to find
itself going on, as the authors of *The Nature of Narrative* do,
about the various simple or complicated ways that narratives may
mean and to discover that these ways can in fact be stretched to
include any problematic cases. Scholes and Kellogg get at—or
around—it this way:

> The connection between the fictional world and the real can be
> either *representational* or *illustrative.* The images in a narrative
> may strike us at once as an attempt to create a replica of actuality
> just as the images in certain paintings or works of sculpture may,
> or they may strike us as an attempt merely to remind us of an
> aspect of reality rather than convey a total and convincing im-
> pression of the real world to us, as certain kinds of visual art also
> do. That kind of art, literary or plastic, which seeks to duplicate
> reality we will designate by the word "represent" in its various
> forms. For that kind of art which seeks only to suggest an aspect
> of reality we will use the word "illustrate." In art the illustrative
> is stylized and stipulative, highly dependent on artistic tradition
> and convention, like much oriental painting and sculpture, while
> the representational seeks continually to reshape and revitalize
> ways of apprehending the actual, subjecting convention to an
> empirical review of its validity as a means of reproducing reality.
> The illustrative is symbolic; the representational is mimetic. In
> the visual arts illustration ranges between almost pure meaning—
> the ideogram or hieroglyph—and almost pure pleasure—the non-
> representational design.[5]

The distinction between representational and illustrative meaning is of course one form of a very old distinction in literary criticism, if one considers that various other adjectives have been and will be substituted for *illustrative* while preserving the basic opposition of a text that means by continuous correspondence to the real world and one that means by occasional, or oblique, or covert reference to that same world. There are problems enough here, to be sure, in the notion of meaning as a kind of correspondence, in the first place, or, in the second, in the idea of some imagined "real world" as mimetic model or criterion. But such questions are perhaps too radical here, and if we allow Scholes and Kellogg their assumed basic dichotomy, we may see that it seems to make sense for a while. Typically, it makes sense just so long as representational narrative, its characteristic form and continuous action, is considered. But regarding the illustrative—which "seeks only to suggest an aspect of reality"—we may wonder what else it is doing when not "suggesting" its "mere" and occasional "aspect." And the characteristics of that illustrative mode, furthermore—"stylized and stipulative, highly dependent on artistic tradition and convention" —sound suspiciously like those of oral narratives in the authors' own terms—or like those of forms perhaps not concerned with achieved meaning at all. But the "illustrative," we are told, "is symbolic": it "means" "symbolically." But any form perceived to be not intelligible in its given context may be said to be symbolic —that is, intelligible in some other context not so evident. That sort of imaginative switch is basic to symbolic action; it is one of the necessary conditions of that action. But it is not a sufficient condition. Forms that are unintelligible in their immediate context may be symbolic—intelligible when transferred to another context —but they also may not; such a transfer may not be appropriate or even indicated. "Symbolic meaning" in narrative is too facile and catch-all a category to be trusted, especially when "representational" and "illustrative" are at stake.

But one can understand the temptation to trust it, even to revere it. For if an unintelligible, or nonmeaning, narrative is not symbolic, then what is it? Literary criticism either does not have categories for such narratives or the categories it has are so obviously dead ends in terms of meaning—like oral narrative—that they may be dragged out and employed only reluctantly. Criticism's bias for meaning of some sort in literary form is in this way both strict and apparently necessary. It traces, as well, to assumptions about language that are seldom questioned—that meaning and communication are its main business, and any other functions are special or artificial.

This prejudice, of course, ignores all sorts of situations. In the case of literature's meanings themselves, for instance, it is often possible to infer that verbal constructions that have resulted in surprising or subtle implications were not originally conceived to do so. Writers describe all the time—and experience, I suppose, even more often—unintelligible motives and energies in their composition. The fact that Hemingway and Conrad, for example, talk about their "luck," while Yeats spoke, at one time, of mystical "Instructors" and other poets of the Muse is not so important a difference as the similar thrust away from deliberately intended meaning and communication. And anyone who does much speaking before audiences knows that many of his happiest phrases were not constructed by reference to a predesign of meaning, but fell together from various other causes and then, after the fact, turned out well so far as meaning was concerned. This is known; but it might not be admitted, for it all comes to a matter of imaginative credit. Only those who are, at least, more interested in the nature of writing than in capitalizing on it will admit to the presence of luck, or something else other than intended meaning, in the writing process. Most often one hears from a writer that, of course, he designed and meant it all, as in Ford Madox Ford's pretentious claims in the "Dedicatory Letter" of his fine novel, *The Good Soldier*.[6]

But I am not so interested here in the nonintelligible sources of hypothetically intelligible narrative forms as I am in those forms that do not appear, in the end, intelligible themselves and in what such forms offer us other than meaning, in what their imaginative process involves. Before pursuing that interest at length, however, it may be helpful to further define my terminology, to make clearer what sort of narrative action I am not talking about.

One sort, for instance, is described by Ralph Freedman in *The Lyrical Novel*:

> Lyrical fiction, then, is not defined essentially by a poetic style or purple prose. Every novel may rise to such heights of language or contain passages that contract the world into imagery. Rather, a lyrical novel assumes a unique form which transcends the causal and temporal movement of narrative within the framework of fiction.[7]

The sort of narrative with which Freedman is concerned, to put it simply, is conceived as out of, or even against, novelistic time. Conventional narrative sequence, as he argues, is quantitative, whereas lyrical fiction aims for a "qualitative progression" (9), "ordering all parts retroactively in a total image" (6).

I do not mean to denigrate Freedman's argument when I say that the fictional model he imagines so vigorously may be a familiar one, especially to readers of literary criticism. It is one in which the narrative elements cluster rather than follow, where such elements may arrange themselves spatially—to put it generally—rather than temporally, where narrative is "used by the perverse poet as the object of his deformations" (10). But even in the sharpness of Freedman's view, the formal action that he describes is not so "perverse" as all that, for the "deformations" of the lyrical novel are nonetheless motivated by a desire for intelligibility—or, as he says himself, for a "different concept of *objectivity*" (1). The massing of images out of sequence—the "spatializing" of them—constitutes the reduction of the fictional world "to a *lyrical point of view*" (8) that may communicate instantaneously, or with more immediacy than conventional narrative process.

From this we may gather that the "lyrical novel" as Freedman imagines it shares the motives of the narrative form that it departs from, that like the more conventional narrative, its aim remains communicated knowledge of some sort. As Freedman argues, this is knowledge of another kind than that yielded by novels at large. But its difference seems a matter of mechanics rather than motives. The important thing for my purposes is that it is articulable knowledge of some sort and that the drastic variations of narrative form that may be associated with the lyrical or spatial novel are not supposed to remove that novel from what I call the "grid of intelligibility." The lyrical or spatial clustering of images that we associate with unconventional narrative remains a visual effect, by which one sees and understands, or at least struggles to do so. And the "lyrical novel" still seems to want to be "the novel," with all the commitment to meaning that that implies.

Perhaps because this is so familiar a critical stance, it makes one suspicious. Nonsequential narrative form has been traditionally considered as a violation of form but not of purpose, as a different path to the meaning one has a right to expect from any novel. I think that this view can be questioned at large, however, and from example to example, one may find the energies of nonsequential narrative forms working for purposes other than achieved understanding. I am not ready now to expand on this further, nor do I want to fault, at this point, Freedman's model of the "lyrical novel."[8] Rather, I want to grant for the moment that this model is accurate, so as to establish that the narrative effects that I shall consider are not covered by it.

For the ends of what I call aural effects in fiction are not those of Freedman's lyrical novel; these effects participate in a different set of motives, where it is not assumed that ultimate intelligibility is the goal of a fictional action. That action itself, furthermore, is liable to be obviously, superficially different in its technical features from the sort of nontemporal massing and clustering that we might associate with lyrical or spatial form. For the narrative form that I am interested in here does not typically ignore time or deform narrative sequence into conspicuously nontemporal patterns. Rather than the dynamic of images arranged around in space, aural energies in narrative depend upon pronounced narrative rhythms that—at least initially—are felt in relation or contrast to linear sequence and successive time: whereas in the lyrical novel, time is set aside in the interests of a certain sort of more immediate and more simultaneous perception, in the aural process, time is conspicuously present and marked, and the formal action depends on the perception of altered time.

In this way, Freedman's lyrical novel is in its obvious technical features farther away from the realistic novel—with its insistence on linear sequence—than is the aural form with which I am concerned, even though lyrical and realistic would seem to share the motive of meaning. For aural processes depend upon a felt conversion of conventional narrative time, which first may appear as natural or unaltered but then, through rhythm and repetition, is felt as the marked time of music. And this is far from a formal dynamic in which time is felt to dwindle and even to disappear in the interests of visual immediacy.

Therefore the model of the lyrical novel—as well as our more general conception of spatial fictional form—does not really bear upon the imaginative areas in which I am interested. I would say further that most often in critical treatments of irregular narrative forms, we may discover the consistent assumption of a regular motive: though critics apparently cannot deny that narrative varies from some steady, linear, temporal, historical model, they continue to suppose that this variance is superficial and merely a matter of means and that the purposes of any novel—no matter how strange its shape—are the same as ever, or the same as the "ever" they imagine. If the model of narrative action has had, then, from time to time to change, the model of narrative motives has remained pure. No amount of formal variation, as I see it, has been able to persuade us that there is more to fictional action than knowledge of "reality," or that we should measure that action on some scale other than that of the modes and degrees of intelligibility. And this is the force of our visual bias.

There is evidence, however, that it can be as misleading to insist—at least ostensibly—upon motives different from the visual-intelligible—what I call aural motives—as it is to ignore them. The example of such insistence that I have in mind is Marshall McLuhan's *The Gutenberg Galaxy;*[9] I think it can be shown that McLuhan's interest in aural perception—or as he is much more likely to say, "oral media"—and his attack upon the visual is only "ostensible," that what he means by *aural* is insufficiently distinguished from the visual, and that, furthermore, he is himself an intelligence of extravagant visual bias.

The difficulty in dealing with McLuhan, however—apart from the generally erratic nature of his way of arguing—is that he is not always wrong. At moments, he establishes the opposition between visual and aural processes both accurately and fruitfully. He considers the visual emphasis in general as linear, successive, and quantifying and, in this regard, as a special and even artificial imaginative bias. More often than he opposes this by describing aural processes, however, he inclines to the *oral* category. The difference need not be crucial, perhaps, but in McLuhan it is, for it entails a focus upon modes of performance—or "stimulation"—rather than upon modes of perception—or "response"—and so it is liable to cause him ultimately to ignore the radical motivational and experiential differences between visual and aural processes. But, again, at moments his contrast of visual with oral seems suggestive in relation to the lines that I am following:

> To the oral man the literal is inclusive, contains all possible meanings and levels. . . . But the visual man is impelled to separate level from level, and function from function, in a process of specialist exclusion. The auditory field is simultaneous, the visual mode is successive. (111)

Where such observations lead McLuhan, however, is to a historical discovery. The visual specialization that he laments begins, he decides, with the invention of printing and the resultant ascendancy of the phonetic alphabet: "And quantification means the translation of non-visual relations and realities into visual terms, a procedure inherent in the phonetic alphabet . . ." (160). The trouble with this view—as we shall see—is that it is deterministic and, in McLuhan's hands, apocalyptic; nonetheless, in outline it bears useful relation to the imaginative processes I shall associate at length with the action of visual, realistic fiction. I have already suggested how such narratives invite a reader's independent action with them, even his domination over and appropriation of them. McLuhan traces this to the technological fact of print itself: "It was as if print, uniform and repeatable commodity that it was, had the power of creating a new hypnotic superstition of the book as independent and uncontaminated by human agency" (144)— "uncontaminated," I would say, before it got into a reader's hands, where its "independence" from other humans became the invitation to possession. And though McLuhan seems not sure exactly why, he notes that "print intensified the tendency to individualism as all historians have testified" (176). Whether or not they have indeed so testified, the "tendency" would seem to follow from what McLuhan remarks as the very "anonymousness" of print itself, which would seem to promote a reader's own "authorship" of what he was reading, to suggest that his own acquisitive action with a text was the action of the text itself.

I have suggested—and shall continue to consider—how in some narrative fiction this "anonymity" is disestablished, how in the aural processes of such fiction, the presence of the author is felt just as surely as it was, in McLuhan's view, by the readers of manuscripts. That sort of discrimination does not concern McLuhan himself, of course, and I am not sure that it should. But his tracing of changes in reader attitudes to historical and technological changes positively rules it out. Gutenberg is seen not only to have made one kind of reading possible, but also to have destroyed another. McLuhan is intent upon showing us that after print people had to respond imaginatively only along certain channels, just as he is intent upon demonstrating that the new electronic technologies restrict us to the opposite bias.

But at moments he has to admit that the cycle he has in mind is not completely covered or explained by technological change:

> But here our concern is to understand how *before typography* there already was a powerful drive towards the visual organization of the non-visual. There grew up in the Catholic world a segmenting and also a sentimental approach in which, writes Bouyer, "it was taken for granted that the Mass was meant to reproduce the Passion by a kind of mimetic reproduction. . . ."[10]

It is plain that there was in liturgy precisely the same drive towards cinematic reconstruction by visual segmentation that we have seen in Huizinga's story of *The Waning of the Middle Ages*. . . . (McLuhan, 138, my emphasis)

As I see it, it is crucial to our understanding of both the opposed and the reciprocal actions of visual and aural motives that we consider that they exist—now, certainly, and perhaps always—outside of deterministic historical schemes. If before typography "there already was a powerful drive towards the visual organization of the non-visual," there may indeed also have been a drive toward aural modes and processes after typography. What I am concerned with showing is that, contrary to McLuhan's revolutionary perspective, which supposes and requires wholesale cultural conversions, the capacities for both visual and aural imagining are always current and possible for us. The probabilities as to how they will be exercised, and in what proportion, depend upon all sorts of factors, including, but not restricted to, such large-scale generators as technological development and cultural bias. But to be fair, it is not a historical story that McLuhan is telling, but an apocalyptic one. His sense that the invention of printing generated a wholesale imaginative transformation is necessary to his pronouncement that another star has now risen and that electronic media have created another such transformation, this time to the oral.

The first problem with the celebration of the oral mode is to see what it means, and McLuhan is no more informative on that than are the literary critics who have declared for the sort of new meaning that turns out to be different only in its means of establishment. Like them, also, McLuhan is much better on what the oral is not than what it is. He understands very well the force of visual specialization:

> Imagination is that ratio among the perceptions and faculties which exists when they are not embedded or outered in material technologies. When so outered, each sense and faculty becomes a closed system. Prior to such outering there is entire interplay among experiences. This interplay or synesthesia is a kind of tactility. . . . (265)

What is "prior" to this specialization, this "outering" and fixing, is thus difficult to understand: it is an "interplay" or "synesthesia" or "a kind of tactility." These labels, especially as they accumulate, are not clear, though they of course suggest that the oral process is another, conglomerate sort of perception. But the more McLuhan elaborates on the conditions of that perception, the more recognizable it becomes as something we have seen before. "Mosaic" configurations, which he associates with the oral and which he appears to be trying to imitate in the argumentative and typographical disarray of his books, are in his view those figures which allow for freer understanding, for kinds of intelligibility more participatory and collaborative between responder and stimulator. He even calls such a configuration a "do-it-yourself-kit" (217).

From such phrases, it seems evident that Marshall McLuhan, for all his proclamatory insistence upon the oral, is not talking about a perceptual mode or motive distiguishable from the visual processes he declares defunct. The oral turns out to be merely a kind of multiple and simultaneous and spatial visual, where the same understandings indigenous to written words are mixed and speeded up, to the viewer's delight or frustration. Again, it appears to be the circumstances and conditions of the "stimulus" that dominate his own imagination—so much so that he has not really considered imaginative responses beyond the visual or how radically dichotomous the division he notices in our perceptual motives may be. He does not consider that *visual* implies the successive progress toward intelligibility most usual for us and that the oral may not be intelligible at all as such a progress. This is evident again and again in his judgments about particular perceptual cases and phenomena, which are often illogical. For example, he does not understand that any code—no matter how it is constructed—demands by definition linear deciphering and is therefore a visual phenomenon: thus he has no idea where to place numbers, for though he declares that they are code, and though they are obviously quantifying, a function that he associates with the visual, he continues to insist—presumably because numbers lack evident visual substance?—that they are "audile-tactile." In the same confusion, he constructs definitions of ostensibly oral phenomena that are, simply, absurd: "Song is the slowing down of speech to savour nuance" (200).

It might be suggested to McLuhan that slowing down or speeding up has very little to do with it, that relative velocity is not a sufficient means of distinguishing between visual and oral phenomena. To put it crudely, touring along a road is still touring whether one goes fast or slow—until one stops. But we should not be surprised to find that in this last example McLuhan's own imaginative bias is visual-intelligible to the extent that it figures even music as merely a different pace of linear visual sense. This bias has in fact been obvious all along. He has remarked and condemned the "Gutenberg drive to apply knowledge by translation and uniformity" (172), but to his reader, it is clear that this is also the "McLuhan drive." For he is rabidly translative; he cannot quote Shakespeare without insisting on what the passage must mean to us; or cite a humanist without reminding us, "More is saying that . . ."; or refer to the behavior of an African tribe without declaring what it amounts to. He treats all the world of evidence as a code to which he has the key or as a miscellaneous babble that he will have to translate.

Of course, any arguer must do something like this to some extent, and so, in the abstract, it may seem only a fault of argumentative excess or extravagance. But in particular relation to the visual-oral inquiry at hand, this fault is crucial, just because McLuhan's extravagance is itself visual: his perspective is so narrowly and intensely visual that one cannot see how he would even be interested in—much less sensitive to—aural motives and processes—unless one remembers that he is interested in them as something whose current ascendancy he can proclaim as the core of his apocalyptic program. The declared dominance of the oral in electronic culture is really a function of McLuhan's translative and linear—and visual —domination of his evidence and of his requirement that the oral must triumph over the visual, as if the ear could beat the eye at its own game. What he does not understand is that, unlike the eye, the ear is not fixating and hierarchical: it does not control what it perceives nearly so much as does the eye, but is itself controlled by that perception. The irony here is that if McLuhan's oral revolution really were to occur, to such an extent that even his own visual bias were overcome, neither he nor anyone else would proclaim it or capitalize on it. There would be nothing to say; everyone would be too busy listening.

It remains here to make one further distinction or exclusion to clarify what I mean in describing the fictional processes and energies I am considering as "musical." In a study called *Verbal Music in German Literature*, Stephen P. Scher defines a verbal dynamic that I am not considering:

> The term "word music" has wide currency in literary criticism to denote a type of poetry or prose which primarily aims at imitation of the acoustic quality of music. Experimenters with such "pure" poetry or prose of intense sound attempt to evoke the auditory sensation of music by composing verbal structures consisting predominantly of onomatopoeic words or word clusters.[11]

Aural motives are for me a matter of wholesale imaginative bias and tendency; they have nothing to do with particular auditory sensations striking the ear and cannot be said to be either generated or restricted by such special stimuli. Speaking more generally, there is perhaps nothing more imaginatively enervated than onomatopoeic processes. They are corresepondent to what in music is called *program music*, which attempts to reproduce by imitation the sounds of reality, such as the sound of a steam engine. (Wilson Coker cites Arthur Honegger's remark that his *Pacific 231* was intended "to express in terms of music a visual impression and physical enjoyment.")[12] Perhaps it is merely and flatly the crossing of contexts and motives, from aural to visual, that—for me at least —is so unattractive to the imagination. But it seems more likely that this crossing is objectionable because, as Coker goes on to show, it depends upon "patent mimicry"; it is "dead metaphor":

> The merit, or lack of it, in particular cases of musical mimicry is frequently questioned, but it seems that it is the aptness of use that really matters. The use of dead metaphor in music can be adequate or skillful or charming or humorous or inept or trite and so on just as verbal use of idioms can. The main danger implicit

in overt imitations has been duly noted by a composer well qualified to speak to the point. Richard Strauss observed that ". . . one can paint in tones and sounds, particularly motives expressing action, but there always remains the imminent danger of relying too much on the music and falling into the trap of a boring imitation of nature."[13]

The trap in question is a yawning one, and the artistic liabilities of mimicry far outnumber the assets. Its implications as a particular and local technique, furthermore, bear relation to the more general issue of aesthetic imitation, something that we are given to suppose art often attempts or accomplishes. Though I do not want to pursue that issue at more length here, the aesthetic criterion of imitative accuracy—given the way we tend to resist or shun mimicry—is suspect, and it would seem necessary to look elsewhere for the way art, and fiction in particular, generates feelings of "realism."[14]

But to be fair to Mr. Scher, he is not talking about local onomatopoeia or that sort of word music, for his subject is "verbal music," by which he means "any literary presentation . . . of existing or fictitious musical compositions: any poetic texture which has a piece of music as its 'theme'" (Scher, 8). I am not sure that I understand this distinction, for his *verbal music* seems to imply works where the mimicking process is simply larger, a matter of the entire form rather than of increments within the form. But I do understand that this is not what I mean by pursuing aural or musical motives in fiction. For what *musical* describes for me, here at the outset, are energies not specifically and superficially melodic but processes that counter the more familiar visual and intelligible energies of fiction, that alter radically the imaginative attitudes of the reader and the quality of his relation to narrative. In my terms, the effects that Mr. Scher, like most other literary critics interested in music, considers are not aural at all, but depend upon the active recognition of patent significations, and that, whether one calls it "musical" or anything else, is strictly a matter of ordinary intelligibility, strictly a visual business.

Three

Noncognitive Images:
Wallace Stevens

ECAUSE THE MOTIVE of literary criticism is knowledge, it is
perhaps to be expected that the varieties of literature itself
are most often described in terms of their intelligibility and imagined as various forms of knowing. The knowledge that literature
communicates is of course supposed to be less obvious, or more
complex or oblique or delicate, than is the case for nonliter-
ary, or perhaps "ordinary," language, but it is held to be knowledge nonetheless, and its value as such is held the ultimate measure
of the literary form that produced it. Perhaps such an attitude
seems crude when described so baldly, but I think the description
is accurate: far more frequently than they ask, of a poem or a narrative, what is it doing, what is the energy of its action, critics, as
well as general readers, want to know, what does it tell us and
where does it get us—what do we know by it?[1]

It may go without saying that such an approach is far better suited
to some literary forms than to others, that, at least in the abstract,
we can easily imagine literary processes that would be distorted or
just mistaken by an insistent attempt to know something by or
through them or even by a too forcible effort to understand them.
But it is much easier to take so balanced an attitude in a discussion
of rational principles than it is in practice, just because we are so
much better equipped to talk about processes that mean something
than about those that may not. Our methods for describing varieties
and degrees of intelligibility in literature—for describing "levels"
of "irony," for instance—are far more sophisticated than those we
employ to consider its less obviously cognitive aspects. And it is
restrictive to our critical judgments and, more important, to our

33

aesthetic capacities to continue supposing that energies that do not function toward intelligibility in literary form cannot, or need not, be described.

Therefore, in this chapter I shall attempt to describe, in the case of Wallace Stevens, literary action that we may consider "noncognitive," to show how it proceeds and what it amounts to, what kind of images it produces. No single writer provides a better example of this dynamic than Stevens, even in a discussion that confines itself otherwise to prose fiction. His characteristic form, despite the fact that it is a poetic form, is also very often a narrative form, in which sequential action is crucial. This may be so because he is so often, at least superficially, an argumentative and even a "philosophical" poet. As I have suggested, the intelligibility of narratives in fiction itself depends fundamentally upon the process of various and cumulative sequence. But argumentative sequences are even more highly pressurized than those that may occur to keep a story and a reader moving and realistic, and so Stevens' special usefulness by analogy with prose fiction is that sequential process—and its noncognitive conversion—is more concentrated in his poetry than in any fiction, and thus one may see in a few lines the run and culmination of a dynamic that in fiction may require hundreds of pages.

At first imagining, also, Stevens seems a good example of noncognitive energies in literary form because he is a surprising one. For if his poetry does indeed seem philosophical to us—and few poets have been taken more philosophically than he—then how can he be a rich mine of the noncognitive? His poetry has been consistently supposed to play more, not less, to our intelligence and understanding than does other poetry; are we then to suppose that, in reading him, intelligence is consistently frustrated? Yes and no: for although argumentative sequence is crucial at certain stages in his poetic movements, it does not remain so. Stevens' poetic movements characteristically involve a change of motive, a change in the direction of the noncognitive. At the same time, we are perhaps not quite so liable as I have implied to be sharply challenged by problems of intelligibility in Stevens. For, unlike this essay, those poems never begin with a declaration that understanding them is often impossible and irrelevant. Rather, they begin with a confidence of eventual intelligibility and only change their direction later. Stevens thus avoids raising a reader's hackles, since the prediction of unintelligibility, if presented to our fresh and energetic attention at the outset, would be received as a challenge that we had better not fail, and given such a challenge, we would very likely set out to understand something in the poem, regardless of its difficulty. But in the second place, and much more important, the noncognitive energies that I am considering require a more positive sort of opening, require the invitation to and expectation of understanding, and spring from its exercise and its exhaustion.

Stevens' poetry abounds with these invitations: titles and first lines and first stanzas ask questions and pose problems that are metaphysical and that deal frequently with the problematic processes of imagination and perception, both aesthetic and "ordinary." Encountering them, we may suppose that they promise answers, or at least we may assure ourselves that they do. But what we get, much more often than an answer, is a countermovement. Here is a simple example:

METAPHORS OF A MAGNIFICO

Twenty men crossing a bridge,
Into a village,
Are twenty men crossing twenty bridges,
Into twenty villages,
Or one man
Crossing a single bridge into a village.

This is old song
That will not declare itself . . .

Twenty men crossing a bridge,
Into a village,
Are
Twenty men crossing a bridge
Into a village.

That will not declare itself
Yet is certain as meaning . . .

The boots of the men clump
On the boards of the bridge.
The first white wall of the village
Rises through fruit-trees.
Of what was it I was thinking?
So the meaning escapes.

The first white wall of the village . . .
The fruit-trees. . . .[2]

This poetic progress is characteristic of Stevens. We begin with a metaphysical question, continue on a course that is decidedly argumentative, and are given to expect some solution. But, as is also usual with Stevens, the "problem" is not solved. Instead, the "meaning escapes," and we fall away from what seemed the all-important question into what had been its scenery, its mere backdrop. Or rather, we fall upon this scenery, for the movement seems quite pleasant: "The first white wall of the village . . ./The fruit-trees. . . ."

But that very pleasantness, since the poem has appeared to default on its expectations, is odd: why aren't we disappointed at the development? We might think it is because we are relieved. The poem's direction turns from the metaphysical to the physical, from philosophic questioning to unquestionable, sensuous commonplace, and such a diminishment may be pleasing of itself. But to hold to such an explanation is to ignore two of the poem's conditions. The first is that to begin by wanting to answer some large question—here one about the relativity of perceptual facts—and then to end with distraction into the sensuous is to appear to fail. In that case the hypnotic quality of the last two lines might seem narcotic, sinister. Stevens didn't have to risk that, if the ascendancy —and perhaps the happy ascendancy—of sensuous facts was his end. He could have stopped with "so the meaning escapes"; he does something like that in other poems with unmistakable cheerfulness. That brings us to the second ignored condition, which is that these last two lines function not merely as realistically sensuous images but as a refrain: they repeat a part of the poem and turn us back on the poem. For despite the apparent repetitiousness of its elements, the poem has never really repeated until now. Each term of its argument, because obviously part of an argument, seemed to be an advance. And the force of the refrain is not only to arrest that advance, not only to tell us that we no longer have to proceed so strenuously, but also to give us good cause, as I shall try to explain, for stopping, apart from the particular aspect of what we are stopping with.

Of course, if we hold tight to the sort of brisk philosophical alertness with which the poem begins, then these last lines—in their drowsy repetition—are negative. If we insist on the beginning, then the poem has failed in its direction, and the comforts of the final lines are both sensuous and stupid. But I don't think that we can remember that beginning: it seems that Stevens prevents us from maintaining our interest in metaphysical understanding in two ways. The first is the insistent sequentialness of the poem itself—the very action that supports its promise of ultimate understanding. For the successiveness of the poem is so determined, most of the way, that in its very exercise it enervates its initial purpose. That is, we travel far enough with it that—like its speaker—we may forget where we began. In this way, the last images of the poem may not amount to a failure to answer a remembered question because, again like the speaker, we may not remember the question. These images, indeed, may not seem to be part of any scheme, but to be simply where we are when the poem ends.

Their autonomous quality is partly generated, then, by the stringing out of the sequence in which they occur; but it is insisted on by the fact that these last images are repetitions, and as such, they are outright violations and denials of that sequence—the argumentative succession of the poem's movement. We arrive at them with our inquisitive energies flagging and are confronted by their repetition, an action by which they remove themselves from a movement of which we were weary anyway. Thus, they seem as stationary and permanent as the previous images were progressive and temporary: they seem far more "real."

Another way of describing this change of imaginative state—for that is what it is—is to say that the movement from sequence to final repetition, from narrative to refrain, amounts to a change from argument to song. And now the sections of the poem that I have been ignoring may become more clearly relevant. For the second stanza declares that even the initial question of the poem—its metaphysical problem—is a "song," "old song/That will not declare itself. . . ." It is song, I suppose, because it is not new, even as a question; one has heard it before and, hence, might know that the novelty it promises from its argumentative progress is in fact a fiction. It "will not declare itself" not merely because as a problem it is so difficult but because—and here is where its very continuance as a problem and its cancellation as such through repetition are intimately related—it has repeated in the imagination so long that it cannot "declare": because it is "song," and song declares nothing. And so, though it is "certain as meaning," it is "certain" in a very different way from "meaning." It is "certain" in its separateness from meaningful processes or schemes; "certain" in that it is beyond inquisitive tampering, off the scale of the intelligence.

"Metaphors of a Magnifico" is a demonstration. Stevens is always to some degree telling us what he is doing, but this short poem has become so clearly such a telling for me that I could not even say whether I think it a good poem. If that is a disservice to the poem, I hope it is a service to Stevens' motives and methods. For as I see it in "Metaphors" Stevens shows us the process through which the images of narrative—of both argumentative and, by inference, realistic sequence—may be transformed into "song," into "musical images," images that, though they are obviously elements within a process of understanding, and then alterations of that process, are finally established with another sort of imaginative substance entirely, a substance that seems to set the understanding aside.

This imaginative conversion happens most often at the ends of poems; the formal dynamic that I am describing often creates a great deal of pressure upon the final images of Stevens' sequences. Thus, at times it may be difficult to know how to receive them. This is true in part, of course, because the sequences leading to these images are often themselves so problematic. In "Thirteen Ways of Looking at a Blackbird," for instance, the twelve "ways of

looking" that precede the thirteenth are difficult to make sense of
in their individual, independent action and even harder to combine. Mostly, they do not seem to be ways of looking at a blackbird at all. A blackbird or blackbirds are involved in each of them,
to be sure, in various ways: it may be central or peripheral, literal
or figurative, in dreams or riddles or wise sayings or jokes or pretty
images or premonitions. But the ways in which the blackbird figures
from stanza to stanza are in fact so various that "involved" is perhaps too strict a term: sometimes the blackbird is there in a way
that seems most uninvolved.

But one may be resourceful, or stubborn. One may try out all
sorts of patterns on Stevens' sequence, to fit it together, to
transform it to something other and smaller—and more convenient
to the mind—than itself. And if one is engaged in a classroom
discussion or a critical essay—both cases where produced intelligence is supposed to be crucial—he will try even harder to reduce
the poem's sequential variety to something simpler and smoother.
So, once more, he may look very sharply at the last verse, which it
all comes down to:

XIII

It was evening all afternoon.
It was snowing
And it was going to snow.
The blackbird sat
In the cedar-limbs. (95)

But one of the troubles with this last way of looking at a blackbird
is that it is quite different from the rest. It may seem very flat and
static to us; because, for one thing, it is the first time in the poem
that the bird has not been engaged in some sort of movement and,
for another, because of the harsh insistence of the image's arrangement: "the blackbird sat." At the same time, the image of the bird
here seems simpler than in earlier stanzas. It is not oblique or melodramatic or evidently metaphoric, as earlier images have been; it
is not even obviously problematic, which is the absence of another
sort of motion. This stillness of the thirteenth blackbird is the more

39

striking, too, as part of the internal sequence of its stanza. In the first part of it we encounter a kind of magical continuity, in which things as they happen contain within them their following stage or state so obviously that they are dominated by it, and onward movement seems compelled. And then, against this momentum, there again is the blackbird.

This abrupt change of rhythm in the thirteenth stanza is crucial in a reader's own motion, for he cannot "go on" with this last image as he has been going on through the sequence of images preceding it. This is not simply because it is a last image, for often the final stage of a problematic fictional sequence allows us our imaginative continuation: one can imagine a kind of blackbird here that we could take right out of the poem with us and, looking back, use to refigure the poem. But Stevens has not given us that, but an image much more intractable. Unless we can figure something out—and I don't think it possible—our own imaginative action will be stopped: we will have to see that we cannot do anything with or make anything of this last blackbird.

The question then is how we will bear this news. What effect will our difficulties—even our powerlessness—against this final image have upon the way that we receive it? One would expect, of course, something unpleasant. If the only sign the last blackbird gives us is that it is not going to signify—even in the complex and fragmentary manner of the twelve previous stanzas—that it will resist our intelligence even more completely than they did, then its quality will be felt as threatening or, at any rate, as something bad.

That is indeed the way this last image may work. I have heard readers declare such feelings, and I surely have had them myself, in this poem and in Stevens more generally. But I have also had others: one may finish this poem with this image quite pleasantly. Its intractableness, in such a case, is rather a kind of quietness, not a frustration of an attempt to understand but some sort of reassurance, seeming to settle us and the poem completely.

But how is this possible? We have not found the poem's answer, and the thirteenth blackbird in its emphatic resistance to our efforts ought to be unrelievedly irritating. The possibility that it may not be suggests that something may have happened to these efforts themselves, that our design with and for the poem has changed, along the way of reading it. If its sequence has not answered any of its presumed questions about perception or perspective, if, indeed, it has not even raised them clearly, and yet we end it all happily, then our motives must have changed. I think they have, and in essentially the same way that our motives change through the sequence of "Metaphors of a Magnifico." Something has happened to the argumentative promise and energy of the sequence even as it has been exercised. To be aware of this, of course, we must read the poem in sequence: to open the book to the thirteenth stanza and ask directly about its meaning will abort the overall rhythm of the poem and make the question of final intelligibility much sharper and, so, more frustrating than it appears as the end of the entire poetic movement. If we have followed the course of the poem, our inclinations to the final image will be in no way so fresh and perhaps not so curious. This change of energy and motive—and, as I shall explain later, it is a loss of visual energy and motive—that results from following a difficult imaginative sequence is something of which I believe Stevens is well aware, for at times it seems itself to be the very scene and subject of a poem:

Man Carrying Thing

The poem must resist the intelligence
Almost successfully. Illustration:

A brune figure in winter evening resists
Identity. The thing he carries resists

The most necessitous sense. Accept them, then,
As secondary (parts not quite perceived

Of the obvious whole, uncertain particles
Of the certain solid, the primary free from doubt,

Things floating like the first hundred flakes of snow
Out of a storm we must endure all night,

Out of a storm of secondary things),
A horror of thoughts that suddenly are real.

We must endure our thoughts all night, until
The bright obvious stands motionless in cold. (350–351)

This poem illuminates the change of imaginative attitude that I am considering both by enacting it and by appearing to make a statement about it. Its first stanza is as apt for "Thirteen Ways of Looking at a Blackbird" as it is famous as a poetic rule: "The poem must resist the intelligence/Almost successfully." Perhaps so, except that there was no "almost" about the thirteenth blackbird nor, therefore, about the other twelve; their resistance of our intelligence was a complete success.

The same is true, I think, of the illustration—in "Man Carrying Thing"—of the poem's very premise: this "illustration" itself does not seem to make sense. The "figure" and the "thing he carries," we are told, "resists/Identity." So they are both to be "accepted" as "secondary," "parts not quite perceived/Of the obvious whole, uncertain particles/Of the certain solid, the primary free from doubt." So far so good: readers of Stevens will be familiar with the importance of "primary" and "secondary" in such cases and with the vague Platonism of the argument here; but then the parallel parts of this illustration seem to confuse: "Things floating like the first hundred flakes of snow/Out of a storm we must endure all night." Those "first hundred flakes," to preserve the previous rhetorical order, would be the "secondary," and the storm they presage, the "primary." There is a shift of feeling here, for the pleasantness of the "obvious whole," the doubtless "primary," turns into an all night storm to be endured; but still the sense, at least, seems preserved. Until the next stanza, where it turns out that the storm is itself a "storm of secondary things." Should we have reversed the order? Was it the "first hundred flakes" that were "primary"? It would not seem so. And so both "flakes" and "storm" are "secondary"? Where then is the lapsed primary?

Thus the sequence, like so many of Stevens' sequences, loses us. Its difficulty seems—as also often happens—to be its own fault and not ours; it cannot be solved because a crucial logical parallelism is not sustained. As we continue the poem, we see that the "secondary" is all we have as yet, and that we must accept as such the "man" and the "thing he carries," accept "a horror of thoughts that suddenly are real." Not so "real," apparently, as "primary," but real in the sense of immediate, of needing to be dealt with and cleared up: a "storm" of "reality." And like enduring that "storm," "we must endure our thoughts all night, until/The bright obvious stands motionless in cold."

But submerged as we are in the "secondary," in this "storm," this "horror of thoughts," we may wonder how this will happen. The "obvious whole," the "primary free from doubt," has dropped out of the poem's immediate sequence. It does not follow upon the "uncertain particles" and has become neither "obvious" nor undoubtable, but something that will just come later. Its assured metaphysical connection was suggested in the poem by a close rhetorical connection, which has dwindled into the indeterminate "until." And so a reader may wonder what is the closing connection between "secondary" and "primary" that makes the "bright obvious" appear, since it is not a regular, logical track. In other words, what sort of sequence is it that Stevens is describing here? What does it mean that "our thoughts" must be endured all night "until" we get what appears to be an answer to them or at least some relief? Why is it in the presumable early morning, after "all night," that this "bright obvious" appears? Is it that the long process of reason must be that long, that so many steps or stages have to be taken to it? The image of the all night "storm" or "horror" suggests nothing so orderly. It suggests instead that this is all more a matter of time—"until"—than ordered progress, and that, after a time, things will change. The only scenario that I can imagine for that sort of shift is one in which the imagination achieves the "obvious" not by "success" but by "failure," not by conquest but by default. It is a situation in which the desired "certainty" comes not from accomplishment but from exhaustion, from the played out unwillingness to ask any more questions or to entertain any more possibilities: this "obvious" is produced not by intellectual rigor or by tenaciously following the sequence out, but by an abrupt and emotional desire to settle, by a breaking off or out of sequence. The last image—the "bright obvious"—becomes the last just because one is unable to go any farther.

"Man Carrying Thing" enacts the process it describes, at least to an extent. We are told that something appears "bright" at the end, and even if that is not clearly visible (is it the man and the thing he carries, or something like?), even if we do not quite understand it, we may be ready to believe it, just because to do so is such a relief from the arduous intellectual succession of the poem up to its last motion.

This relation between effortful imaginative sequences and the last images that relieve us of them is, again, typical in Stevens. Seldom does the final image solve the sequence: it is seldom an answer to the questions the sequence maintains. Its substance comes not from our discoveries and designs, not from understanding it, but from a blanket readiness to receive it that proceeds, if not from the exhaustion, then at least from the thorough exercise of the intelligence that needed satisfying.

Now we may see more clearly the important difference between considering Stevens' final images in isolation and asking quick questions of them, and considering them as they occur at the ends of difficult imaginative processes. The sequence of "Man Carrying Thing" is less long but more blankly difficult than that of "Thirteen Ways of Looking at a Blackbird," for the former poem practically declares an exhausted dead end to intelligibility, while the latter, over a longer movement, is rather an exercise of the intelligence through which the intelligence may weaken. But in both cases, the approach to the final image prepares us for less intelligibility rather than for more; it weakens, rather than strengthens, our inquiring attitude.

When Stevens says, then, that "the poem must resist the intelligence/Almost successfully," he may mean by the "almost" that in the end a reader gets something, something like the "bright obvious" at the end of this poem. And it may not matter that usually, as in this poem, that something is not the achieved product of intelligence, that—if we had to say exactly what it was or meant —we would have to admit that there was no "almost" about it and that the poem has resisted us completely. It may not matter, because by the time such images are given, after imaginative sequences that are usually difficult and often long—as it were, after an all night storm of thinking—we are ready to receive them, no questions asked. For, although such receptiveness results from the exercise and even the weakening of the intelligence, the process seems less pejorative than that as it occurs, especially when we consider all the poetic processes beyond the exercise and faulting of sequence that support it. It should rather be conceived, therefore, as a natural change of motive—as if, after exercising one faculty, we were then prepared to exercise another.

This relation between Stevens' argumentative sequences and the images that they ultimately achieve thus involves a simple but crucial distinction for literary theory, a distinction between sequences whose results follow from their intelligible process and are produced by a reader's continuing that process within and beyond them, as opposed to sequences whose results are discontinuous with their process and are produced only by the breaking off, the exhaustion, of that process. When literary criticism has considered such a distinction, it has done so pejoratively. The relation between sequence and product that we encounter in Stevens would be called at best "indirect" or "inverse," but more usually, and at worst, "failed." Because of the demand for intelligibility in literary form, something that is generated by the lapsing of intelligible process may seem a desperate thing and more a loss than a gain. Yet this is not the feeling of such images in Stevens at all. In his poetry, once more, the exhaustion of the more rational imaginative powers seems always—much less negatively—an exercise of mind that readies us to participate in a different sort of perception and energy. In Stevens, to run out the string of intelligibility is enabling.

OF MERE BEING

The palm at the end of the mind,
Beyond the last thought, rises
In the bronze distance,

A gold-feathered bird
Sings in the palm, without human meaning,
Without human feeling, a foreign song.

You know then that it is not the reason
That makes us happy or unhappy.
The bird sings. Its feathers shine.

The palm stands on the edge of space.
The wind moves slowly in the branches.
The bird's fire-fangled feathers dangle down.[3]

First, some summary may be useful: Stevens is explicit about the palm's location, "at the end of the mind/Beyond the last thought," which apparently does not mean that it is some ultimate stage or extension of the mind's sequence, but somehow off the scale of sequential imagining itself. And the following stanza insists on the unintelligibleness of the image even as it articulates it: "without human meaning,/Without human feeling, a foreign song." What is most interesting here is that, characteristically, the image seems generated by virtue of an evident lapsing of the reason; this lapsing is necessary and enabling for the image's substance, a substance that seemingly could not be denser or brighter.

It is from this poem that Holly Stevens takes the title for her own selection and ordering of her father's poetry, with what, in my view, are the best of reasons.[4] For I see "the palm at the end of the mind" as the most accurate of all possible directives into Stevens, the best of all possible cues to his poetic action. "Of Mere Being" describes the result of a poetic process—a process in which mind and the reason must play a dominating part until they flag—and assures us that such a result is always imminent. We may need the assurance, for the process itself and what it achieves may all seem predicated on a loss, a loss of the mind that reasons and follows and questions and answers and works sequences out, an exercising out of the motive of intelligibility in favor of something after it. That seems, again, important: the approach to these noncognitive images in Stevens is an exercise, and this process does not imply the abdication of all intelligence at the start. The characteristic motion of Stevens' poetry is always to begin with the problematically intelligible; there is almost always a question asked and a sequence to be followed as if to be understood, and it is only at the end of that sequence and after the intelligible motive has been tried and tried again that the palm and the bird may appear. Although the "being" in this poem is "mere" then—bared, perhaps, or stripped, which are also the necessary aspects of the imagination

46

that would perceive it—that phrase is ironic, for there is nothing easily "primitive" about this "being." If it suggests purity, that purity seems after, and not before, the fact of intelligence; its "innocence" is accomplished, not a condition prior to thought and action, but consequent.

This figure for the establishing of being may be seen as a complete reversal of our usual way of thinking about it, where the greatest imaginative clarity and density is always predicated as something that must occur before imagination. Thus, being is conceived nostalgically, as beautiful but somehow childish or, again, as primitive, something that one must lose as one gains the mind. The obvious corollary is that in order to achieve such visions, the mind must be abandoned at the outset—and we know we cannot do that. But Stevens' poetic action shows us that there is no "abandoning" in it, that palm and bird and song are not "back there" somewhere but on ahead of us, the unlooked for fruit of the intelligence's fruitless action.

This is a nice prospect, but may also be a threatening one, and some readers may be irritated and frightened by it and by the figure of imagination that it establishes. For such readers, perhaps, the loss of mind is crucial, and they are not willing to imagine anything beyond it. And they will not continue with Stevens, for without such willingness, he cannot be read for long, and will not see what in Stevens' terms is gained from the loss, what these noncognitive images are and do, nor how their quality is always so full and energized, nor why Stevens always seems so happy to have reached them.

These images possess an imaginative autonomy that promises unending articulation: at the end of the mind there is a palm and in the palm a bird and the bird sings and its feathers shine and the wind moves in the branches of the palm and, possibly, on and on. Perhaps because the image is out of any sequence that might direct and so restrict it, it has the potential to multiply within itself forever. It can spread its parts, and even more important, it can repeat its parts without any loss of visual power, because unlike intelligible perceptual sequences, it does not depend upon progressive novelty. We are not going anywhere with it, but remain with it, dwelling on it, and the more we dwell, the more we can see. That feeling of dwelling, too, is a feeling of reassurance and of a dense solidness. It is a feeling of intense energy, and at the same time, as the "fire-fangled feathers dangle down," it is a feeling of rest:

> Score this anecdote
> Invented for its pith, not doctrinal
> In form though in design, as Crispin willed,
> Disguised pronunciamento, summary,
> Autumn's compendium, strident in itself
> But muted, mused, and perfectly revolved
> In those portentous accents, syllables,
> And sounds of music coming to accord
> Upon his lap, like their inherent sphere,
> Seraphic proclamations of the pure
> Delivered with a deluging onwardness.
> Or if the music sticks, if the anecdote
> Is false, if Crispin is a profitless
> Philosopher, beginning with green brag,
> Concluding fadedly, if as a man
> Prone to distemper he abates in taste,
> Fickle and fumbling, variable, obscure,
> Glozing his life with after-shining flicks,
> Illuminating, from a fancy gorged
> By apparition, plain and common things,
> Sequestering the fluster from the year,
> Making gulped potions of obstreperous drops,
> And so distorting, proving what he proves
> Is nothing, what can all this matter since
> The relation comes, benignly, to its end?
>
> So may the relation of each man be clipped.
> (*Collected Poems*, 45–46)

The course of "The Comedian as the Letter C," Crispin's course, is the course of intelligible sequence at large in Stevens' poetry, which always may come to the "sounds of music," whatever the "pith" of the "anecdote" and whatever phrases like "not doctrinal/In form though in design" may ultimately mean. And even if the "music sticks," perhaps if it seems itself compromised by the failure of the sequence, by the fact that all the "philosophy" is "profitless," "concluding fadedly," as the intelligence in Stevens so often does, the conclusion nonetheless is happy, just because it is the conclusion: "what can all this matter since/The relation comes, benignly, to its end?"

The final benignness that Stevens declares here is typical of his poetic process, and it is just what a reader who is put off by "the end of the mind" misses. In part, it is simply the joy of imaginative action ending, regardless of its result; it is the exhilaration of devoting all one's powers to a movement, exercising those powers to their limit, and getting out. This achievement in the fullness and end of the exercise, of having it all over with, is where "Comedian" stops, and this is benign enough. For as a resolution it is specifically musical: it sounds exactly like the happiness that one may hear at the end of certain pieces of music, as a celebration of their completion. But as an imaginative condition, at the same time, it is not merely melodically and unspecifiedly pleasing, as one might argue that "pure" music is. For in Stevens we may discover that the very exhaustion of the intelligence as it converts to the musical also enacts, in literary process, a kind of seeing beyond the intelligible. In poem after poem, we have both music as something heard, whose perception seems a pleasing end of the mind and, at the same time, music as the precondition for images that are realer, denser, more luxuriantly visible than the images of intelligible sequence could ever be. Stevens begins and ends, then, as a poet of high visibility. At the outset of his poetic movements he is visible in the way of argumentative succession, where seeing is inseparable from wanting to see more, dependent upon our following and understanding, and where the objects of sight are metaphysical or even philosophical answers. But the exercise and the exhaustion of this sort of vision provides the ground for what seems to me a truer form of seeing, ground from which rise images pure and monolithic, images now so resistant to our minds' efforts that we can do nothing but set our plans and schemes for them aside and really see them, with a visibility that is at once more concentrated and more relaxed than mere understanding could ever provide.

49

Thus, the intelligence is necessary to the end of intelligence. Stevens does not discard the mind. His view of the real does not depend upon a nostalgic model of a world without intelligence but upon the continuing dynamic of the intelligence exhausting itself in order to achieve images beyond itself. In his poetry, that intelligence is always acting; but he is not—at least as he has been considerered and even legitimatized—a philosophical poet. His end is not intelligence achieved but spent—spent to prepare and allow the uprising of things arresting beyond our intelligence of them.

I once saw, in the house of a collector, a crystal of calcite in its matrix. I was told that crystals-in-matrix are much more valuable than those that have been mined out, and I thought I could see why. The calcite itself seemed both clear and milky, and its geometry was nice, but against the dark randomness of its base and source it was brilliant and startling, as if it were not a metamorphosed extension of the matrix but another substance entirely, even of another world. Just so, the intelligence is there in Stevens' poetry as the matrix that in its processes ultimately produces its opposite, as something necessary to and yet nothing beside the images that ride upon and within it, images beyond our powers to know them and thus fully within our sight.

What I have been doing here, for one thing, is using Stevens to make a rule for reading him. From that, one might say that I have turned him out, after all, as a philosophical poet. But with that particular inference I have no quarrel, for I believe that Stevens both dramatizes and describes the aesthetics of poetry—and of literary imagining more generally—with a pointedness found nowhere else. Yet, as with the making of any point, the recognition of this one has served my arguments better than Stevens' poetry, and my treatment of him has been efficient rather than amplifying. A wider reading, even merely as a test for the rule I have derived, has been sacrificed to a statement that here must be made economically and, as it were, quickly: that there is such a thing, in his poetry and in the literary imagination, as the noncognitive image and that it is furthermore not primitive—requiring the initial overthrow or abandonment of the intelligence—nor achieved merely by not thinking. And I can only contend, since I have attended to the dynamics of such images in but a few poems, that these dynamics are general in Stevens and that a wider reading of him discovers them consistently.

By the same token, the force of *noncognitive* is itself, of necessity, somewhat too restrictive here: that adjective covers only one aspect—albeit the essential one—of the image in question. I have concentrated upon that aspect because it needs establishing, both in this inquiry and, to a larger extent, in literary theory. But I hope that it has been clear also that there is nothing negative—except in our initial way of describing and discovering it—about the noncognitive image, both in its achieved imaginative substance and in the processes that establish that substance. For the most part I have considered how such images are generated negatively out of the exercise and exhaustion of argumentative sequence and have largely neglected all the various rhetorical gestures and poetic techniques that accompany and catalyze this generation. And I have done so because it is the force of their relation to sequence that is crucially important for my main concern, narrative fiction.

Stevens himself, once more, is an unusually sequential and narrative poet—that in part is why he may be so illuminating with regard to nonpoetic fictional processes. But he is a poet, and this means that the devices he employs to convert argument to music, to catalyze, again, the exhaustion of sequence and the lapsing of cognition into the musical condition, are far more numerous and subtle than those we have observed so far in the process of narrative fiction. At the same time, those devices in Stevens and in poetry at large are much more conventional. It would seem crude, therefore, to say that of course the heart of the dynamic by which argument becomes music is repetition, because repetition in poetry, as in music, is such a fact of life, and the point in such cases is not simply to declare its general presence but to articulate its particular and ingenious forms.

But my interest here, again, is narrative fiction, and in fiction the imaginative process in question seems simpler, if only because it has been so much less explored than it has in poetry. There the conversion of sequence into music, both by the sequence's lapsing into specific repetition or by its exercise to exhaustion, is new ground. And therefore it seems justifiable, at least at this point, simply to note that this process we have observed in Stevens' poetry does indeed occur in fiction and to anticipate a more detailed consideration of the specific prose techniques that *repetition* might cover, while neglecting presently the more subtle formal techniques of Stevens' poetry.

But one technique that these include should be remarked here, because it seems generally a surprising one and because it arises so particularly in Stevens' poetry and in narrative fiction. We have seen in "Metaphors of a Magnifico" how the most unanswered and itchy sort of metaphysical inquiry can become music. The "old song" in that case is simply a set of philosophical alternatives, a question that has existed and perturbed the mind a long time and, thus, that has repeated in the imagination a long time. So it would appear that all that is necessary in this case, and in others, to turn the question into music is to draw adroit attention to its perpetualness. This in turn may illuminate what it means in Stevens, and elsewhere, to exercise one's intelligence through a difficult and unanswered sequence; for it is as if there is a music implicit in one's efforts the moment one notices their repeatedness. This figure, I believe, is most relevant to the process of narrative fiction, a process that may involve attempts at intelligibility even more lengthily strenuous, if not usually so immediately difficult, than that of "The Comedian as the Letter C." In fiction, any revelation that such a wearying imaginative progress was not real, that it was itself a perpetuation or a recurrence, would, quite logically, release the most intense energy toward the musical—an energy proportional, as it were, to the visual effort that had just been denied.

But there is a further, and perhaps even more important, inference to be drawn from the relation of Stevens' poetry not only to narrative fiction but to imaginative perception at large. The establishing of noncognitive images in Stevens, images "at the end of the mind," is—as Stevens himself describes it—a matter of music, and this music is not restricted to pretty or soothing sounds and, thus, is neither a mere cancellation of the intelligence nor an ornamentation of it, but is in fact an order of general perception, a particularly patient and articulated action of seeing itself. What this means in relation to my terminology of *aural* and *visual* is that these categories describe not particular perceptual actions, but different, and even opposed, motivational contexts in which these actions may occur. The visual context is so named because seeing most often implies the dominating action of the seer through a sequential and cumulative series toward some intelligible product, because such action seems conventionally indigenous to visualness. But one may of course hear or listen in this process and with this motive as well or do anything else to visual purposes. More important, the general receptivity associated with the aural motive is not limited to hearing, though again, listening is the perceptual act that seems most fundamental to that motive. This is a laborious but a necessary discrimination, and it should be kept in mind whenever visual and aural motives and effects are considered. For if both of these terms are remembered to entail not specific perceptual senses but the dominating motives for, in each case, an entire perceptual range, then clumsy phrases like "aural seeing" or even the more familiar "visual resonance" may seem forgivably necessary attempts to deconstitute our usual assumptions about imaginative perception, to the purpose of giving a fuller and more balanced accounting of literature's own range of energies and of musical perception itself—of whose presence and process all through our imaginative lives the poetry of Stevens reminds us.

Four

Voiced Narrative:
A *Clockwork Orange*

THE EVIDENT ASPECTS of voiced narratives are musicalness and a resultant unintelligibility—that is, these narratives are not understandable in the way that unvoiced, visual narratives are and do not yield to the same treatment. Still, voiced narrative has both images and sense, and these, within their quasi-musical context, are treated by a reader in some way. We might even say that they are seen and understood, so long as we remember that they are not seen or understood, as visual images are, by following and reducing them or by contesting and proving them—by knowing what they "mean" in the usual sense. For describing both of these aspects of voiced narrative—its music and the feeling that the experience of its images does not depend upon ordinarily communicated meaning—Anthony Burgess' A *Clockwork Orange* is for me the best possible example.

The music of this narrative may seem immediately obvious. The opening line—"What's it going to be then, eh?"—repeats as a refrain through the opening pages of each of the three sections of the novel. Phrases like "O my brothers" and "your Humble Narrator"—which might be called oral formulae—constantly punctuate and frame the story's movements, reminding us always that this is a story being told. And in that story, words are repeated, musically, three times, four times, five times. At the earlier stages of the narrative, such words tend to be simple and exclamatory: right right right, out out out out! But later they become more visually articulated: the crack crack crack of an egg, the kashl kashl kashl of a cough. Yet all of these specific aural effects may seem relatively weak beside the musical energy of the dialect that Alex, the "Humble Narrator," speaks throughout.

Like any foreign language, this one—"nadsat"—is heard by us much more than a familiar language would be. We are much more aware that the words of it are words and that they have a sound—that, in fact, as words in a language we hear, they are sounds in a rhythm. And the rhythms of Alex's nadsat narrative are so strong as to seem infantile. It may be that all insistently rhythmic speech is somehow childish, but Alex's seems specifically so in both its playful and its dictatorial energy. This quality is usually most obvious in the words of his language that are not of Russian origin: words like baddiwad, skolliwoll, eggiweg, jammiwam, guttiwuts, and so on; words that seem generated from a wonderful self-exuberance and self-complacency, the whimsy of one who holds such whimsy to be his right and power. To say, furthermore, that this rhythmic verbal mutation in A Clockwork Orange—or anywhere else—is childish is not to deny but to recognize its force. The energy it produces is extraordinary:

> Our pockets were full of deng, so there was no real need from the point of view of crasting any more pretty polly to tolchok some old veck in an alley and viddy him swim in his blood while we counted the takings and divided by four, nor to do the ultra-violent on some shivering starry grey-haired ptitsa in a shop and go smecking off with the till's guts. But, as they say, money isn't everything.[1]

This language makes a music far beyond its evident melodicness, though there is plenty of that. It is not so significant, for instance, that "some shivering starry grey-haired ptitsa in a shop" has obvious phonetic consistencies as it is that a formula so obviously musical—again, in the simple sense of melodic—is not strained here. It comes as no surprise; whereas "But, as they say, money isn't everything" is surprising, and funny, which may tell us how far the run of this narrative takes us from ordinary words in commonplace order.

The relative extendedness of Alex's sentences and the relative weakness of his grammar—by which I mean his tendency to compound rhetoric and coordinate constructions—are important here and by themselves would create—as they may in Hemingway—musical effects. But unlike Hemingway's, such effects in A Clockwork Orange seem instantaneous, not built up through a series of overextensions and repetitions and not converted from any more visual processes active in the narrative. These effects are generated as aural right from the start, and this makes A Clockwork Orange a quite special narrative even within the special context of aural fiction.

Its thorough musicalness springs in part from the musical potential of the smallest units of the narrative language, from the felt sonorousness of the words themselves and their resultant facility for harmonious combination. But such combination—and the power of the narrative music overall—is not merely a matter of easy and handsome sound. For because nadsat is so foreign to us, its combinations may seem right. Alex's teenage talk thus seems to make two kinds of sense. There is, first, the evident logic of its rhythmic necessity and fluidity, which seems compelled by the power of its speaker. And second, there is the logic that we suppose it has, the logic we grant to any foreign language, any language of apparent and audible symmetry that we do not really understand. On the one hand, the narrator's phrasing seems utterly easy and free to a listener; it seems—as might be so with any new language—that the one speaking is doing just anything he wants and, therefore, that the language is always serving his immediate individual motives, always subject to his will. So one who speaks a foreign language may seem to dominate it and us as we listen, as if without effort and for no intelligible causes. At the same time, and on the other hand, we may suppose that the speaker knows what he is saying just because he sounds so good. Confidence in—or intimidation at—his rhythms breeds a more general acquiescence, and his rhythmic momentum and smoothness seem both justified by and indicative of another consistency, an assumed intelligibility. He apparently can say anything he pleases and yet still be held to be making sense. Even Alex's dim droog Dim can do this:

"What natural right does he have to think he can give the orders and tolchok me whenever he likes? Yarbles is what I say to him, and I'd chain his glazzies out soon as look."

"Watch that," I said, as quiet as I could with the stereo bouncing all over the walls and ceiling and the in-the-land veck beyond Dim getting loud now with his "Spark nearer, ultoptimate." I said: "Do watch that, O Dim, if to continue to be on live thou dost wish."

"Yarbles," said Dim, sneering, "great bolshy yarblockos to you. What you done then you had no right. I'll meet you with chain or nozh or britva any time, not having you aiming tolchoks at me reasonless, it stands to reason I won't have it." (29)

For one thing, Dim's pathetic and wonderful grammarlessness creates overconsistencies that are densely logical by their redundancy: "chain his *glazzies* [eyes] out soon as *look*"; "*not having* you aiming tolchoks at me *reasonless*, it stands to *reason* I *won't have it*" (my emphasis). For another, the repetitive symmetry of his speech as nonsequential and nonsensical makes it obviously musical. But much more important is the way the language that Dim uses can grow, freely and yet certainly, in such a way that we grant it further sense: "Yarbles . . . great bolshy yarblockos to you." As from "yarbles" to "yarblockos," the narrative language of *A Clockwork Orange* has always this capacity to transform and increase itself before us without our questioning. And to say that these transformations bespeak a rhythmic motive—that they result from the constant extension and multiplication of the narrative melody—is not to deny that at the same time they seem absolutely right. Dim knows what he is saying here; there is no doubt of that. But, more strangely, so do we. We know that it makes sense to go from "yarbles" to "yarblockos," and our approval may seem hard to understand.

Of course, one might say, again, that this feeling of knowing Dim's language here well enough to approve the way he uses it proceeds simply from feeling his rhythmic certainty; one might say that rhythm is all there is to it. But such an account seems contradictory with our feeling that there is in fact more than rhythm in the verbal process, that we recognize in Dim's words a kind of sense that we cannot be said to understand. This matter should therefore be examined further, for the questions here are general and important: How do such purely voiced narratives "mean"? What sort of intelligibility do they achieve? In what does our knowing them consist?

Such questions ignore the possibility, of course—and I think they do so justifiably—that our understanding as we read A Clockwork Orange is of the usual, visual sort, that what we practice when we read it is some sort of translation. At the back of the edition of the novel I am using, for instance, there is a list of nadsat words translated into more ordinary English, placed there not by Burgess but, "unauthorized," by the critic Stanley Hyman, who found that he "could not read the book without compiling a glossary" (182). Probably some of us do not share the literary critic's occupational appetite or anxiety for meaning of this sort; probably if no glossary had been appended here, we should not have made one. But given that it is here, should it be used? Or should we ignore it in favor of the narrative's own, stranger terminology? There is no "should" here, because the appetite for ordinary intelligibility—the visual appetite—varies both from reader to reader and from reading to reading for a single reader. So too, it is difficult to know whether or not a typical reading of A Clockwork Orange would involve a somewhat less rigorous action of translation, in which a reader would be content to go along guessing meanings from their context, and so making a less formal but still intelligible glossary. And if a reader did not do even that—if he wanted even less or even no meaning of the translated sort—would that be a sign of self-indulgence or laziness? The answers to questions like these may be approached by attempting to describe the dynamics of the two sorts of reading I have mentioned, by concentrating upon the imaginative actions that each seems to involve.

We may place the imagination of the literary critic, with its need for glossaries and a steady flow of intelligibility, at one end of a possible scale. We can thus conceive of a reading of this novel that never lost sight of its meaning, a reading that was in fact a continuous act of translaton of the language of the novel into a terminology more normal to the reader. This is an extreme example of the sort of reading that we practice all the time with realistic fiction, a matter of treating a narrative visually. But it is not really important whether I think such a reading mistaken or not here, nor even whether I think it likely, since it is obviously possible. What is important, again, are the conditions of such a reading.

The most fundamental condition of this translative reading is compelled ignorance of the music of the narrative. Busy-ness with a word's meaning will cause the word—its sounded presence—to disappear: one just looks right through "yarbles" to the glossary at the back of the book—or the back of one's mind—and says "testicles."[2] Though upon consideration such a procedure seems, even logically, faulty, for if "yarbles" means "testicles," then what does "yarblockos" mean? If we say that it is just another word for testicles, then we seem to be denying the narrative language's evident and particular detail and change; we seem to be arguing for a reduction and a redundancy that we do not feel in the amplified potential of the words themselves as they occur in the narrative. Similarly, when Alex says, to an old woman he is about to rob, "you stinking starry old sharp" (61), the energies of sound—and thus the potential meaning—seem contradicted by translation. If "starry" means "old" (or "ancient," as Hyman guesses), then the utterance becomes both redundant and, if we pursue it, utterly clumsy.

We may not, of course, pursue translation so thoroughly; we may use the narrative language more gently, so that such obvious illogic and awkwardness is not felt, but the dominant narrative conditions of fluency and immediacy will still to some extent be set aside by translation. Any interest in meaning is pursued here only at some cost to those conditions. For example, a line that I find, for no obvious reason, memorable occurs when Alex is at a record shop to buy himself Beethoven's Ninth and encounters two girls much younger—"couldn't have been more than ten"—than himself. And they have, as he tells us, "their own way of govoreeting": " 'What you getten, bratty? What biggy, what only?' " The glossary tells us, and we may guess, that "bratty" may be understood as "brother," which is very well, though we may feel that it has many other implications also. There is nothing at the back of the book, however, about "biggy" or "only," perhaps because the real question here is not of the words' isolated meaning but of their combinational usage. "Biggy" may sound like the slang of our own disc jockeys, however, and from that, "only" must be supposed to refer to what Alex is "getten": the "only" record possible at this time, the one and only. But there is another set of possibilities. For since these girls are younger than Alex, and smaller, and since their address may run on so exuberantly, "biggy" might refer to Alex rather than his record, and so too with "only"; and thus the line becomes a kind of mocking yet flattering greeting, even a come-on, to our "Humble Narrator."

Admittedly, the conventional probability of the first meaning is greater here than that of the second, but as I read I do not want to define that probability, nor do I want to choose between the two meanings. In fact, I do not even want to recognize the ambiguity. Now one might protest that the ambiguity was there all along; that it has to be recognized, it is self-indulgent not to. But I don't think so. Something was there all right, but it was a sounded complex of potential meanings that only became articulated even as an ambiguity—or even as potentially meaningful—in the process of translation and, as it were, visualization. The fact and existence of potential or ambiguity itself, no matter how delicate or subtle it may be, is a rigidification of an energy in the phrasing that is both prior to and greater than such potential.[3] The music of the line in this way seems to hold meaning both in the sense of containing it and in that of resisting it, and it is this containment and resistance, this feeling of content and denial of content, that we may feel to be so energized in musical narrative. In this way, the fluid energy of the language of A Clockwork Orange in its own form exceeds the more fixed imaginative substance that we may achieve by translating it—or even by beginning to translate it—for meaning's sake. But such a comparison is only partly to the point here, and one would like to know more about the experience of this musical language itself, about what its energy amounts to if untranslated, about the imaginative action of participating in this fictional world as such.

In the first violent incident—and I shall return to the idea of violence in *A Clockwork Orange* later—of the narrative, Alex and his droogs accost an old man who is apparently returning from a library with some books on crystalline structure. They tear up the books, beat him, and rob him:

> and then we began to filly about with him. Pete held his rookers and Georgie sort of hooked his rot wide open for him and Dim yanked out his false zoobies, upper and lower. He threw these down on the pavement and then I treated them to the old boot-crush, though they were hard bastards like, being made of some new horrorshow plastic stuff. The old veck began to make sort of chumbling shooms—"wuf waf wof"—so Georgie let go of holding his goobers apart and just let him have one in the toothless rot with his ringy fist, and that made the old veck start moaning a lot then, then out comes the blood, my brothers, real beautiful. So all we did then was to pull his outer platties off, stripping him down to his vest and long underpants (very starry; Dim smecked his head off near), and then Pete kicks him lovely in his pot, and we let him go. He went sort of staggering off, it not having been too hard of a tolchock really, going "Oh oh oh," not knowing where or what was what really, and we had a snigger at him and then riffled through his pockets, Dim dancing round with his crappy umbrella meanwhile, but there wasn't much in them. (6–7)

To describe what the experience of reading this passage is, one has again to consider what it is not. First, the feeling of it is not violent; probably it is not even sad. For I have already misdescribed the case: this is not an old man, but an old "veck," and it is not his false teeth that are torn out and crushed, but some "zoobies." And so on: not punched in the mouth, but "fisted" in the "rot," not kicked in the stomach but in the "pot," "tolchocked." Here, however, it might be objected that the man is a man and that we know he is kicked just as we have known throughout the movement that violence was going on. But what is the force of such knowing here? It is true that our translative awareness can be insisted on and summoned up, before or after the fact, but my own feeling is that it recedes in the actual and immediate reading, that this movement in the narrative, quite typically, takes on an imaginative autonomy where veck and zoobies and rot and tolchock are themselves only, and not what we could make of them. The action of the prose thus creates its imaginative isolation.

This isolation or autonomy is not only a consequence of the strangeness of the scene's furnishings: it is not only that "rot" and "zoobies" and "tolchock" are different from "mouth" and "teeth" and "blow," but also that the dynamic within which they occur, their form and rhythm, maintains and insists on that difference. The rhythm here, for instance, is not the rhythm of a beating, but the rhythm of play. Whatever happens here happens easily and without tension or climax, happens as easily as if assumed. To put this another way, the rhythm here is not the rhythm of a realistic event, but of a fictional voice: it is Alex's rhythm, and if we feel it, we shall not be likely to feel anything else.

The autonomy here, then, is the autonomy of voice. Within this voice something is going on; or rather, the voice is telling about something—"fillying" with an "old veck"—and while under the spell of the voice, while participating in its experience, we accept its terms. It is as if no one is being roughed up here; this is "fillying," and how could so pretty a sound describe anything unpleasant?

But that may tell us something about the action of the entire narrative. For the prettiness of "fillying around with him" is a single detailed instance of a more general and compelling prettiness that we are thinking of when we say that this entire narrative process is musical. Our awareness or even worry about what the story means is thus continually damped and muted; it is mused, not simply by the prettiness of the music but by the fact of it, which is the same as to say that this is, in the first place, a voiced narrative and that we do not so much see it as hear it.

In the simplest sense, this means that many "scenes" in A Clockwork Orange—even the most dramatic ones—do not have much that is seen in them. The episode from which the story gets its title is a case in point. Alex and company break into the writer's house, beat him, destroy his work, and then hold him looking while each rapes his wife:

> So he did the strong-man on the devotchka, who was still creech creech creeching away in very horrorshow four-in-a-bar, locking her rookers from the back, while I ripped away at this and that and the other, the others going haw haw haw still, and real good horrorshow groodies they were that then exhibited their pink glazzies, O my brothers, while I untrussed and got ready for the plunge. Plunging, I could slooshy cries of agony and this writer bleeding veck that Georgie and Pete held on to nearly got loose howling bezoomny with the filthiest of slovos that I already knew and others he was making up. Then after me it was right old Dim should have his turn, which he did in a beasty snorty howly sort of a way with his Peebee Shelley maskie taking no notice, while I held on to her. Then there was a changeover, Dim and me grabbing the slobbering writer veck who was past struggling really, only just coming out with slack sort of slovos like he was in the land in a milk-plus bar, and Pete and Georgie had theirs. Then there was like quiet and we were full of like hate, so smashed what was left to be smashed—typewriter, lamps, chairs—and Dim, it was typical of old Dim, watered the fire out and was going to dung on the carpet, there being plenty of paper, but I said no. "Out out out out," I howled. The writer veck and his zheena were not really there, bloody and torn and making noises. But they'd live.
>
> So we got into the waiting auto and I left it to Georgie to take the wheel, me feeling that malenky bit shagged, and we went back to town, running over odd squealing things on the way. (23–24)

Although this movement is potentially sensationally visual, and though it is arranged in the deliberate temporal sequence—then this, then that—that would normally facilitate the illusion of fictional seeing, it has an odd visual reticence. Alex tells us that he "ripped away at this and that and the other," for instance, but not precisely what. Then Dim "should have his turn," and then "Pete and Georgie had theirs." One feels here, in other words, that the narrator does not really describe what is going on, that Alex is somehow not interested in doing so. And when he does describe it in his own vocabulary—"plunging, I could slooshy cries of agony" —the effect remains, curiously, visually reticent. It is almost as if Alex is blind and numb to anything but the terms of his own experience and the sound of his own voice.

Now we are closer to defining the processes of musical narrative. We can see here that one of its actions is to deemphasize and mute visual detail in relation to aural energy. This happens here simply when events and things go undescribed, but it happens also in a slightly more complex way, when those events and things are described consistently and only in the narrator's single and private terminology. The particular act of saying, at the woman's breasts, "real good horrorshow groodies," then, is in immediate imaginative effect not to name them at all; and in general the things in this narrative, the actual ingredients of this fictional world, are thus both there and not there. If we see them, we must see them as Alex does. But in our terms that may not amount to seeing them at all. We credit their existence without seeing them then, and we do so, once more, for a complex of contradictory reasons.

First, we credit them without really seeing them because Alex sees them. As I suggested earlier, the rhythms and energies of the narrative voice—the very elements that prevent us from seeing— are evidence that the narrator does see, and they immediately persuade us to go along with his vision. And second, because the vision is his, because this is his story, we are content to go along: our own visual motives or appetites of necessity relax or decline as we are taken with the narrator's voice. One way to explain this is to call it a condition of imaginative domination, where our own motives for independent imaginative action are overpowered. But this action does not feel so embattled as that would imply. At times, in fact, it seems a kind of relief, as if, so long as someone is doing the seeing, we do not have to. Or, we do not have to see because there is no seeing really going on. And the curious thing here is that we seem to treat both cases the same way. For us, someone else's seeing is the same as no seeing going on: if we ourselves are not somehow participating in it, it becomes not real and not the sort of thing we might challenge or discredit.

64

The result is that voiced narratives are credited with a visual substance, a substance that we grant and feel but that we do not see and test for ourselves in the way that we do in unvoiced narratives. We may see how this originates in the perceptual autonomy of a narrator, how it depends upon our feeling and allowing his compelling rhythms as both insistently present yet separate from our own imaginations, and so both considerable and not considerable.

The undeniable force in such narratives, however, of voice itself may tempt critics to describe what is an aural dynamic in the visual-intelligible terms of psychology. Alex's voice is so much a factor in our motives for his story that one may want to solve it; it is so beautifully resistant to our attempts to translate it that we may only do so by psychological discount—we may say that Alex is such and such a sort of case and discredit his voice and vision, thereby re-activating our own. And then we may say just about anything we please about the relevance of A Clockwork Orange to our own lives, remarking its violence, its political significance, and so on. I shall say more about this sort of mistake later, but it should be clear even now that it is a mistake, simply because it is to take Alex as a kind of vision only, to ignore the rhythms he makes, to ignore his voice. For while we hear that voice, it is impossible to say that his vision is wrong or narrow or perverted. To do that we would already have to be exercising our own, presumably wider, visions, and while we are listening to him, we will not do that— again, because he is so different from us and thus dominantly important and yet not important at all.

That paradox is necessary, though like all necessary paradoxes it is annoying. It may become less so, however, when we understand that this importance-unimportance aspect, this way that a voiced narrative and its narrative voice have of both mattering only and not mattering enough to challenge, has to do with its evident separateness from our own imaginations and with how we feel about anything so separate. The separateness of voiced narratives—as a function of the visual autonomy of their narrators—is at the same time a function of their told aspect. We tend not to insist on our own independent imaginative activity when we know that we are being told a story. The awareness of a narrator who always reminds

us, either explicitly ("O my brothers") or implicitly in his pronounced rhythms that this is both *his* story and his *story* results in
a relaxation of our imaginative efforts. Whether this means that
we regard all life that is truly separate from us—that is, all life that
at the moment there is no question of controlling—as fiction, I am
not sure, but I believe so. But it more evidently means that this is
what may happen in our reading and that the very action of establishing a voice truly separate from our own gives that voice the
power and the powerlessness of fiction, the reality and substance
that we credit freely because it is obviously not ourselves or our
reality, and so not crucial, because it is so clearly hypothetical and
temporary in the way that fiction is.

This response depends, once again, not upon a felt weakness or
a perceived insubstantialness in the fiction but upon the opposite,
upon the strength and presence of the voice in voiced narrative. We
see what we do not see and know what we do not know in *A Clockwork Orange*—we feel the substance and reality of a world we do
not understand—because someone else, our "Humble Narrator,"
so evidently sees and knows and feels. We relinquish our right to
challenge and prove the details of the narrative—something we
would never do with realistic fiction—we pause in our more or less
constant process of making everything intelligible, because someone
else is pursuing that course with a demonstrated energy that pre-
empts our own efforts. Thus we acknowledge the existence of a
knower other than ourselves, and we assume what he knows and
sees, and the base of our assumption is the strength of his voice.

This sort of response may be compared with other literary actions
where assumed knowledge—or something like that—is involved.
In the dynamics of irony, for example, a reader seems often to be
aligning himself with another knower, a speaker or even an imagined
figure beyond or behind the text who knows more or other than
anyone in the immediate fictional world. And in the subtlest
irony, what is actually known may be vague. We may look askance
at a character or smile at a movement not because we are sure we
can see around him or it but because we are sure that somebody—
such as the author—does. But in this case, the look or the smile
itself is a kind of attempt to discover the other knower: it is a

moment in a process by which we share or expect to share the knower's position. This is obviously, therefore, not a relinquishment of our individual imaginative powers, but an insistence on them. The experience of irony in literary situations is a matter of imagined partnership, whereas the experience of voiced narrative, as of music, is a matter of allowed domination. In irony, too, it is the other knower—for instance, again, the author—who has to be invented as an order for the evident fictional tension, a key to its code; in voiced narrative, however, the knower is what is undeniably present, and we come to assume what he perceives just because he is so present. Irony is thus a condition that is active and hopeful; the experience of the realities of voiced narrative is passive and assured.

The same is true, more generally, of a reader's relation to the movement or sequence of voiced narratives as opposed to his relation to the sequence of unvoiced narratives. In either case he may be said to follow a sequence of details, images, words. But in unvoiced narrative this following is expectant and unsatisfied as it proceeds. It might even be said to be a process of getting even with or catching up to both story and author, a process that involves the constant anticipation of sharing the imaginative end of things. It is also a solving and reducing process. In voiced narratives, on the contrary, one follows and even accumulates narrative detail with much less anxiety about ultimate understanding. In A Clockwork Orange, a reader moves through tolchocks, chellovecks, litsos, devotchkas, lewdies, and so on, and soon enough may be said to recognize them, not as blows, men, faces, girls, or people, but as themselves. The following that occurs in voiced narratives seems an interior matter, where the parts of the fictional world are related to each other rather than to their counterparts in our own lives and languages. The images of voiced narratives, in their purest action, do not extend to correlatives in the reader's imagination.

But talking this way about the situation makes it sound much more stable and formulaic than it is. For whether a narrative is voiced or unvoiced is after all a matter of a reader's perception of it, and obviously there is more to that perception than the nature of the work itself. Which is simply to say that whether we are susceptible to visual or aural energies at a given time depends not only upon the formal dynamics of what we are seeing and hearing but also upon our own perceptual tendencies, either habitual or occasional. It is hard for me to imagine that one would want to "see" A Clockwork Orange, to make it all intelligible, to render it out in translation, to correlate it with the facts and incidents of one's own life. But we have already seen at least one literary critic's efforts to do this. We might say that he was mistaken, that his motives were counter to the consistently expressed motives of the narrative, but—for the sake of additional clarification—let us take a more difficult case: A Clockwork Orange was also the basis for a film.

The issue here can be centered on the violence of the story. Unlike the novel, where what occurred was "fillying," "ultra-violence," "twenty-to-one," "red red krovvy," and the "old in-out in-out," and where Alex's voice kept assuring us that these were what was happening, the film showed us brutality and blood and rape. Alex's voice was there, still, riding over the scenes; but since it was a movie, these were scenes—all the action was visualized for us. But whether it was visual in effect or not is another matter. For most of the audience it seemed to be: their silence in the theater, their grim or solemn faces when they came out into the lights, suggested that they had recognized what they had seen, that there had been a connection between the violence on the screen and the violence that they knew existed all around them.

But for others it was different: some were laughing when they exited and had been laughing aloud throughout. This difference in perception may be illustrated by a scene I have already considered, where Alex and his droogs rape the wife of the author of "A Clockwork Orange." The rape—or what can be shown of it—occurs on film; there is no doubt of that. But while it is going on, the boys, especially Alex, are dancing soft-shoe and singing "Singin' in the Rain." Put crudely, the question seems to be this: What does a spectator do here, see a rape or listen to a song? Does one see a real action or the ritual, stylized action of the dance? Does he think he is seeing the truth or life, or does he know that he is seeing a fiction? These, I think, are the poles, and how we position ourselves at or between them is the question. For my case, I was listening to the song and seeing the dance and laughing, and some of the people around me were giving me dirty looks. And it may be that my response was mistaken. It may be that the motives and energies of the film were, as one would expect, visual and realistic and that my own taste for heard rhythms and for fiction was distorting them. It may be, in short, that others of the audience had a better eye than I had; but in that case it may be also, of course, that I had the better ear.

What this means, however, in relation to aural-visual motives or voiced-unvoiced imaginative form, is that we cannot assume that anything seen—or even meant to be seen—will be visual, nor that anything heard—or meant to be—will be aural. It means also, I think, that certain awkwardnesses of phrasing will be inevitable—at least until we discover a better terminology—when we attempt to define the imaginative effects of a given form, and we shall have to say "aural seeing" or "visual hearing" and the clumsy like. And even these compound terms are of little use when we try to characterize the intenser perceptions that seem to occur in aural or voiced forms, even when our real or intelligible or clear senses seem to have been either preempted or exhausted.

But the example of the film of A Clockwork Orange raises other issues about the novel's form. My own relative unawareness of or numbness to the movie's violence entailed my insensitivity to it as social or moral or political comment; or, that numbness entailed my sensitivity to its musical, fictional isolation from other contexts. Either way, I did not do anything with the experience of it; I did not relate it to anything else in my experience, or rather, to anything in my real experience. And though it is also possible for one to see in the fictional world of the novel a reflection of our own violent times, or a ramification of present world politics, it should be clear that all such responses would involve linear extension of the novel: they would depend upon realistic connections between our own experience and the novel's now not so fictional world; they would assume a continuity between two sets, and two sorts, of imaginings. At the other end of the scale, however, a reader's experience of A Clockwork Orange is not continuous with reality:

all that violence never escapes the circumference of the novel's own world, and a reader perceives nothing that can be recognized with any realistic force. From this perspective, the fictional world of the novel is absolutely self-contained and self-limiting, and one's response to such a world is not to go on talking about it so as to extend it into this or that other context.

Just as some viewers of the film were laughing, on the jacket of the edition of A Clockwork Orange that I am using, William Burroughs is quoted as saying, "The fact that it is also a very funny book may pass unnoticed." This could be taken to mean that Burroughs and all the rest of us who laugh as we read it are thugs, either insensitive to or lusting for violence, or that we are aesthetes, unresponsive and irresponsible to moral-social-political considerations. In either case, I think, our not seeing violence is mistaken for our approving it and our relative unawareness of moral implications mistaken for a lack of conscience. But obviously if what is transpiring in the narrative is beatings and knifings and rape and murder as they could occur in our own experience, there is nothing funny here. And so anyone who laughs would appear—at the moment he or she laughs—to be assuming a discontinuity between the world of the novel and the other worlds that surround it.

It may follow from that discontinuity that the laughter itself does not spring from the sort of comedy that depends upon point-to-point disjunction or awry-ness between fictional and real worlds, but rather from the wholesale lack of connection between the two. Laughter in this case expresses elation, exhilaration, and joyfulness in response to the concentrated, exuberant play of the world within itself; it expresses continual relief, also, at the constant reminders the form gives that it is not our form or our world, but a construction independent of all that and, as such, a temporary release from it.

But to say that laughter—or at least, happiness—is our characteristic response to what is obviously fictional is not to say that it is the only response. My simplified account of the polarized responses to the film of A Clockwork Orange—and such polarization tends to occur in public situations above all—emphasized the overriding "funniness" of the fiction in contrast to the seriousness of more realistic forms and perceptions. We should infer from this, I think, that the self-limiting, isolated aspect of fiction usually or even always involves a sort of joy or gaiety. But we should also see that this joy does not restrict a range of responses, as it were, within or upon it. At a sad sequence in a fiction, for instance, we may be sad at the moment and also, simultaneously, pleased in our awareness of the fictionalness of the sequence. What this suggests more generally is that our response to fiction as such may be always somehow double, that it involves an emotional complex; whereas conversely, realism and the perception of it invites perceptions more single-minded, and sad moments are just sad, and—once more —violence is the violence of our everyday imagining.[4]

The ground of this complex response is aural energy in general and music in particular. In *A Clockwork Orange*, the heard or voiced narrative reminds us constantly that what we are seeing is something told, a story, an entertainment, reminds us constantly that we are experiencing fiction. In one set of terms, this is not seeing; it is not an experience at all. But in another, it may amount to perceptions fuller and more detailed and luxuriant than any possible in the world of intelligible reality.

What I am trying to mark here, then, are the ends of a scale, and I do not mean to suggest by the strength of the contrast between these two sorts of experience that they are practically immutable from reader to reader or even formally changeless within a given work for a single reader. For there are at least two sorts of imaginative variation possible here. There is the sort of formal oscillation in which a single form shifts its energy from aural to visual, fictional to realistic, voiced to unvoiced, and back again and again, where, assuming a more or less constant and consistent and balanced reader, we can observe variance in the motives of the form itself. But there is also the much more unstable variation possible in a reader's own motives, for one does not have to hear music, even when it is pure: one can read *A Clockwork Orange* for its violence or its politics or whatever other significance one wishes.[5] But the force of this dichotomous definition—the force of the scale I am imagining—is not compromised by the particular imaginative fluctuations that are possible within it; the definition holds even though, within its contrasting possibilities, we shall do as we will.

The imagination has its range even when listening to the purest music or pursuing the most various sequence of images, and the figure of aural versus visual energy allows us to mark that range and to describe points within it. It should not be felt automatically to prescribe for any imaginative situation. Consider, for instance, the common case of listening to music and remembering some other occasion when we heard it. What is heard might thus be transformed into intensely visual associations and experiences. It would be possible in such a case to say that the perceived experience is not in primary accordance with the motives of the form, but in some oblique or secondary relation to it. But that would not be to deny the pleasure or even the value of such a response. It might not even be to deny its legitimacy, for such responses gain legitimacy simply by their frequency and so may always be on the way to becoming primary.

Still, there are extreme cases where we might want to make a firmer decision, and one of these is perhaps the case of our "Humble Narrator" himself. Because for me the one "meaningful" aspect of A Clockwork Orange bears directly on my arguments about it; it has to do with Alex's own general response to music, which, in purple prose and broken rhythms, is consistently an example of formal misappropriation and mistaking, and even of perversion:

> Then, brothers, it came. Oh, bliss, bliss and heaven. I lay all nagoy to the ceiling, my gulliver on my rookers on the pillow, glazzies closed, rot open in bliss, slooshying the sluice of lovely sounds. Oh, it was gorgeousness and gorgeosity made flesh. The trombones crunched redgold under my bed, and behind my gulliver the trumpets threewise silverflamed, and there by the door the timps rolling through my guts and out again crunched like candy thunder. Oh, it was wonder of wonders. And then, a bird of like rarest spun heavenmetal, or like silvery wine flowing in a spaceship, gravity all nonsense now, came the violin solo above all the other strings, and those strings were like a cage of silk round

my bed. Then flute and oboe bored, like worms of like platinum, into the thick thick toffee gold and silver. I was in such bliss, my brothers. Pee and em in their bedroom next door had learnt now not to knock on the wall with complaints of what they called noise. I had taught them. Now they would take sleep-pills. Perhaps, knowing the joy I had in my night music, they had already taken them. As I slooshied, my glazzies tight shut to shut in the bliss that was better than any synthemesc Bog or God, I knew such lovely pictures. There were vecks and ptitsas, both young and starry, lying on the ground screaming for mercy, and I was smecking all over my rot and grinding my boot in their litsos. And there were devotchkas ripped and creeching against walls and I plunging like a shlaga into them, and indeed when the music, which was one movement only, rose to the top of its big highest tower, then, lying there on my bed with glazzies tight shut and rookers behind my gulliver, I broke and spattered and cried aaaaaaah with the bliss of it. And so the lovely music glided to its glowing close. (32–33)

The misappropriation here is not merely a matter of translating the music into lushly visual terms, nor is it evident only in the fact that the writing—or rather Alex's speaking—characteristically at such moments in the narrative, is so bad. Both of these aspects of his response—and they are related or, perhaps, identical—are embarrassing and possibly even irritating, because they suggest that Alex is not really responding to the music as such at all, as Burgess emphasizes ironically when, after what has been conspicuously not music, Alex says, "and so the lovely music glided to its glowing close." We may feel very differently about his response here than we do when, while listening to Bach, he talks about "the brown gorgeousness of the starry German master," which seems to me a lovely and appropriate image. And the difference appears to lie in the extension of the visual metaphor in relation to the musical experience. The "brown gorgeousness" metaphor indicates a kind of imaginative submission; and as a description, it admits that it cannot describe. But the long passage just quoted is quite the reverse. It is a domination and a manipulation of the music. The most

73

obvious sign of that manipulation is simply the rhetorical extension of the response—the way Alex goes on and on—and that is
fitting, because the extension that he enacts is not only rhetorical.
Alex's own experience of the music is itself linear. He does not
merely see through it to "such lovely pictures"—and so transform
heard energies into those of sight and touch—but extends it straight
into violence.[6]

That is a transformation, and a translation, indeed. This "lovely
music" is no music at all, but only a vehicle for other use. Because
Alex's use is violent and sexual, it is clearly and particularly mistaken. But we should also see here that any use of a form whose
energy is self-contained and static, any extension of that energy into
other contexts—even, for instance, righteous indignation at the
violence of the narrative or dour political prophecies based upon
it—may be seen from one point of view to ignore its fundamental
and primary motives. Once again, how we define those primary
motives, and how we decide to respond, may be difficult to determine in certain cases, since it will depend upon our immediate and
individual imaginative requirements. For me, the narrative of A
Clockwork Orange in particular is more musical, more voiced, than
any other I have read and takes its place at the far end of the scale
I have used it to describe. Perhaps more important, however, its
action allows the imagining of that scale in the first place and allows
us to speculate about a set of fictional motives that are not widely
recognized, motives for an imaginative form that is self-limiting
and self-substantial and, therefore, of no use for social commen-
tary or moral incitement, since it cannot be taken away from itself
or put to uses beyond itself. Whereas unvoiced or visual forms, at
the opposite pole, insist upon their correlation with and extension
into the contexts of experience that surround them, the aural action
of voiced narrative isolates itself to its separate and interior reality.
Thus one might say that aural fiction, when it occurs for us, is the
most truly fictional of all fiction, where we do not take or mis-take
a narrative sequence for our own imaginative sequence or incorporate the imagined other into our imagined selves. It is the only
form, therefore, in which there is anything really, durably, novel,

in which an active imagination can continue to feel experience quite separate from its own. And, somewhat on the other side, this is also to say that voiced narrative, in its purest state, will be limited in motive and effect to the merely decorative—that it can only be beautiful.

A *Clockwork Orange* is an unusually pure enactment of voiced, or aural, fictional motive, and in its thorough musicalness, it is rare. This does not mean that there are not other such novels, but that there are few as compared to the many examples that reflect mixed motives. The action of narrative form—where aural motives are involved—is much more characteristically an oscillating action in which fictional energies are converted from visual to aural and back at some frequency.

On the one hand, this means that the pleasure one takes in A *Clockwork Orange* is rather more one-sided than one's experience of visual-aural combination; in my view, that pleasure approaches as closely as is possible for fiction the pleasure of music. Of course it is a novel, and not music, and the verbal presence of language even in such a musical case generates a special sort of visual imaginative force that we might call "residual." But there is nothing in its formal process that might otherwise reconnect it with or extend it into realistic experience—save, perhaps, its melodrama and violence, and I have already indicated that, for me at least, these are not sufficient to break into its formal self-enclosure. In this way, it is an extravagantly unified and single-toned narrative, in comparison with other novels that participate in aural motives. The feeling that it gives, the single feeling, is for me the happiness of farce or burlesque, a feeling that may be most intense, but not, at least in comparison with cases of mixed motives, complex.

The imaginative force of visual-aural mixture and conversion in narrative fiction may be stronger upon a reader than the purer music of Burgess' novel. Such conversion, whatever its frequency, may be said to create continual bursts of energy as one shifts from one sort of perception to another. There is no such effect in A

Clockwork Orange, no such fluctuating function of narrative process. The pulse of its energy is much steadier than would be possible in a context of mixed motives. It surprises us, then, not by its rising and falling, but by the force of its regular and compelling continuation, by the self-determined extravagance of its extension into itself, by how luxuriantly it can grow within itself, how far it can carry its own, single imaginative course.

Five

Unvoiced Narrative

To PUT IT THUS in the negative and say "unvoiced" narrative rather than "visual" or "realistic" narrative may seem inappropriate. For in our time, the taste for realism among audiences—and the related taste for intelligibility among critics—seems dominant, the rule and not the exception, and it would seem to make more sense to maintain that priority. What I am claiming by the reversal, however, by putting realism in the negative and calling visual-intelligible narratives unvoiced, is that this is the way that they are experienced—their most fundamental aspect is felt as a need, a pressure, a demanding insufficiency upon which a reader must take action. Visual narrative form is experienced as an absence of form; its felt substance seems in obvious ways not merely to depend upon but to be inseparable from what a reader does with it. And at the same time, it is a resistance to form; it can only maintain itself by resisting for a certain time, for whatever its imaginative duration, one's efforts to see it, while simultaneously making the seeing of it the crucial imaginative issue. So at the outset we might expect a visual or realistic narrative to deal in surprises:

> Again today Alex Housman drove the Buick Riviera. The Buick, coppertone, white sidewalls, was the model of the year, a '59, although the 1960 models were already out. Its upholstery was black, its windshield was tinted a thin color of motor oil. The car's heater was issuing a stale and odorous warmth, but Alex remained chilled. He had walked several blocks through snow and slush, wearing neither hat nor gloves nor boots, to where he had left the car the night before. The steering wheel was icy in his hands, and he felt icy within, throughout his veins and bones. Alex was sixteen; the Buick was his fourteenth car.[1]

"Alex was sixteen; the Buick was his fourteenth car"; the force of that sentence is generated in its novelty, in the fact that we have never heard of such a thing. And usually the initial action of un-voiced narrative is to insist, even melodramatically, that it is some-thing we don't know about, one we haven't heard. Such insistence is characteristically supported, furthermore, by narrative processes that continue surprising from moment to moment; they involve the quick and compelled variation of relatively small, densely pro-liferating rhetorical units—the Buick Riviera, coppertone, white sidewalls, the model of the year, the 1960 models, upholstery, wind-shield, heater, warmth, Alex, chilled, and so on. Moreover, the uniform grammar that arranges these elements is never strong enough to prevent even the most casual or incidental variation. In fact, the grammar of *The Car Thief*—changing subjects followed by the verbs they most closely entail—is as flat and self-effacing as possible, acting to present new additions but never to form them out of their novel force. It is a grammar that allows a continuous run of imagistic variation, a grammar that consistently prevents the imagistic settling and solidification that would finish its meaning and put an end to our interest.

The usual course of *The Car Thief*, then, is along a straight and level track through varying scenery. At times the narrative seems to rise to a moment where something more seems about to be—or could be—expressed, but that expression never comes:

> The shreds of snow parachuted onto the water, shriveled gray and disappeared; his mind was ranging off as if in judgment of things the size of life itself, and of himself, but of nothing he could see in particular.
>
> Turning his neck down, looking directly into his reflection, he found he could see through his face into the water. He worked his reflection to reveal the bottom. It was still autumn down there, brown and green, the sand blond, moss hair wavering black from green stones, from the dock piles. Two nearly translucent fish, no thicker or longer than a finger, hovered unconcerned. He glimpsed the sweep of his trouble and it was so wide and unknown that his head began trembling while his mind told him nothing. (15–16)

Even where some realization on Alex's and the reader's part seems imminent, the narrative characteristically holds to its uncommitted course. The prose moves through a wide variation, of things (its changing nouns) and their conditions (all those colors) and their motions (the looking down and through, the wavering, the hovering). Such variety may in itself, without the narrator's more explicit urging, give us to expect a larger statement or image, but contrary to both, Alex's glimpse yields only unknowns and tells him nothing.

At the same time, a passage like this by its very irresolution holds an eventual promise; its varied motion seems the sign of settled meanings to come, its resistance to intelligibility places it firmly within the context of intelligibility. But *The Car Thief* is an unusually pure example of visual process; for all of its key moments, there is no key. The narrative action, especially at the most dramatic points, is relentlessly random. When his father commits suicide, near the end of the story, Alex's response—and ours—is particular, multiple, and open:

Whether the skin was warm or cool, he did not notice. He *then* touched his father's wrist, picked it up as if in imitation of something he had seen in a movie, and tried to feel his pulse. His father's hand was heavy. *In just a moment* Alex laid it down again. His father lay still. Alex knew that the man had left now; he knew that he was gone.

Turning, undecided about leaving or staying, he looked at the rifle lying on the floor. . . .

Alex stood quietly in the kitchen, next to the wooden table. He did not know quite what to do. *For a moment* hardly a thought or a feeling seemed to rise within him. *Then, for a moment*, a visionary and strange moment, as if none of this were true, he felt a desire to see his father, to seek shelter within his father's strength against something troubling and frightening and unknown.

He glanced around the kitchen, lighted at twilight. He stood there.

Outside, in front of the house, he stood on the sidewalk *for a moment*. A car passing had its lights on in the dusk. He went up the steps *then* to the landlady's front porch . . . (356–357, my emphases)

Alex keeps moving, and that is figured—as I have tried to show by my emphases—in strictly temporal sequence. And he keeps thinking, but his thoughts are marked only as commonplace ("Alex knew that the man had left now") or nearly nonexistent ("hardly a thought or feeling seemed to rise") or fantastic ("a visionary and strange moment, as if none of this were true") or just unknown.

In this way, the only doubtless substance of this narrative is "factual." Again and again, the more ambitious moments of *The Car Thief* write themselves off as fantasy, a fantasy, furthermore, that always dissolves quickly, issues back to an insistence upon the random facts, with an "as if" or a "seemed" denying any larger feeling or imagining at the same time that the possibility of it is suggested.

Even from his father's death there appears no significant consequence. Alex goes into the army, where he was going anyway—an intention that may, and only may, have been involved in his father's motives for committing suicide. Soon after this, the story stops. It is not an ending. Alex looks at himself in the mirror, feels his father in him, and feels "a new heart beating in him" (370). But such a feeling depends—as similar feelings have all along—on "seemed" and "as if." And now there is no further opportunity for them to be tested. They seem simply a way of extending the narrative past what it can establish, of going past all that has really happened, on past the story itself.

The narrative structure of *The Car Thief* is more nearly a matter of mere chronology than any other novel I know. In the passages I've quoted, the prose continually falls away from adding itself up, or condensing itself, or attending to itself in any way; and what it falls back on is, simply, what happened next. The transitions are almost always only matters of time. There may be a gap in the text, some white space, and then, just, "Another morning, when his alarm went off . . ." (335). Or a chapter break, with the next beginning, "One evening . . ." (278). And because this narrative does not seem to be subject to any rules but pure time, it continues new and unrepetitive, even by definition: whatever happens in such a sequence—where we are prevented from all other sorts of connection—must be new as it happens. In such temporal sequence, furthermore, anything can happen. When the dominant grammar of a fiction is temporal, then all events or acts are possible within it.

One can imagine the strain of writing this, of remaining so devotedly with time, of resisting always the possibility of stronger formal patterns within the story and denying the attractions of a more distinctive grammar. Such an effort amounts to a continuing argument for the newness and specialness of what is happening, to a constant insistence that the narrative is moving and interesting. What these efforts yield, in *The Car Thief*, are moments like the following:

> Once, after one of the football games, a man of fifty or so had managed to climb up one of the goal posts to the crossbar so only his feet were held in the grabbing hands below. Then someone caught his pants cuffs, and his pants broke loose at the waist and began, as he struggled with his legs to hold them, to slide down his legs. The full stadium, those waiting to file out, roared with laughter, for the man was wearing red long johns, the kind with a flap in the seat. Then the long johns were caught by the cuffs and pulled down, as he tried to hold the crossbar with one hand and tried to hold up his red underwear with the other. Then he lost the long johns and they were pulled immediately to his ankles, and he hung there for a moment with bare ass, white and hairy, before all the hands pulling at his ankles and at the pants and underwear around his ankles broke his grip, and it might still have been funny, but as he fell he was already being hit, and before he even reached the ground a fist rapped his face and blood rushed from his nose. (135-136)

This is a fine sequence. The occasion for it, and thus the narrative sense it achieves, is, as usual, almost no occasion at all. Alex is simply thinking about the city, and football games, and fights, and so, "Once. . . ." And the wonderful movement of the passage is made possible just because Weesner is so ready to say *then, then, then*, because the fictional line is absolutely devoted to what happens next. This absence of any stronger arrangement than the temporal is reciprocal in the narrative with the smallest possible rhetorical elements—nouns and short noun phrases, the briefest verbs, and the like—which seem present to us because they seem unformed, because they appear to invite or even to require the same imaginative processing that is invited by much of our everyday experience. Because the narrative seems to us, in its time, so basically unformed, we are encouraged to combine and reduce and solidify it, or to attempt to do so, just as we would if it were random experience. This, I believe, is the source of its realism: the most inclusive and precise definition of realistic process must mark not the "contents" of that process—what kind of furniture or animals the imagined world includes—but the action of it, what a reader does with it. We call fiction "realistic" when we seem to be acting on or in relation to it as we would in relation to nonfictional life, when we are acting to give it form, to make it a story, to understand it.

So far I have considered the narrative dynamics of realistic or visual narratives mainly in the positive. Continuous variation among relatively short rhetorical increments or sequences that are almost purely temporal seem, after all, to be actual features of narrative that we can point to as they occur. When a fiction fills itself with disparate and sharply distinguished images, it seems obvious that it is full, and its accomplished novelty seems substantial. In these ways and in others, the visual or realistic dynamic may be felt to be something achieved on the page.

But in our experience of reading, this dynamic is more accurately a perceived demand for a reader to act than a felt action of the prose. Continuous imagistic variation and insistence on sequence in a narrative, however substantial it may seem, is apprehended by a reader as a kind of vacancy that must be filled. Its very "substance," in fact, is the result of a reader's action upon its evident need for consistency, in which the continuity of its sequence is taken as the absence of imaginative symmetry and settlement. The realistic or visual form, in short, is perceived as the absence of form, and a reader's response to that perception is to begin and to extend a process by which form can be given. The elements of realistic fiction are therefore present in the way that all fragmentary experience is present, the way life may be present. But such presence is in no way satisfying; it is, rather, a negative presence that requires our action to achieve the kind of presence that only form can give. I shall say more about the imaginative presence of form later: what is more immediately important is the ramifications of our action upon the more negative condition of visual narratives. It may now become clearer how such narratives invite the individual agency of the reader, even demand his efforts to inform them, and why, therefore, it is appropriate to term them—in the negative—unvoiced.[2]

Unvoiced narrative is remarkable for its self-effacement. For all of its insistence upon its regular time and sequence, it demands that we take it over and re-form it. And for all its literal verbal proliferation, it strikes us as empty. That these paradoxes must hold may be more evident if we consider the process of this sort of narrative more closely and examine its own characteristic attitude toward what might be but are not the elements of voice—its own words. For the relation of unvoiced narrative to the words that compose it is one of strange disregard. Here is the opening, for example, of Lessing's *The Four-Gated City*:

In front of Martha was grimed glass, its lower part covered with grimed muslin. The open door showed an oblong of browny-grey air swimming with globules of wet. The shop fronts opposite were no particular colour. The lettering on the shops, once black, brown, gold, white, was now shades of dull brown. The lettering on the upper part of the glass of this room said *Joe's Fish and Chips* in reverse, and was flaking like stale chocolate. She sat by a rectangle of pinkish oilcloth where sugar had spilled, and onto it, orange tea, making a gritty smear in which someone had doodled part of a name: Daisy Flet . . . Her cup was thick whitey-grey, cracked. The teaspoon was a whitish plastic, so much used that the elastic brittleness natural to it had gone into an erosion of hair lines, so that it was like a kind of sponge. When she had drunk half the tea, a smear of grease appeared halfway down the inside of the cup: a thumb mark. How hard had some hand—attached to Iris, to Jimmy?—gripped the cup to leave a smear which even after immersion in strong orange tea had left a thumbprint good enough for the police. Across the room, by another pinkish rectangle, sat

Joe's mother, Iris, a small fattish smeared woman. She was half asleep, cat-napping. She wore an overall washed so often it had gone a greyish yellow. A tired soured smell came from her. The small fattish pale man behind the counter where the tea urn dominated was not Joe, who had gone off to the war and had never returned home, having married a woman and her cafe in Birmingham. He was Jimmy, Joe's mother's partner.[3]

Most readers will be struck with the ugliness of this prose. Phrases like "browny-grey" and "whitey-grey" and the rest are positively evil sounding. The imaginative contortedness of "*Joe's Fish and Chips* in reverse," too, is obviously unpleasant, but it is only part of a general unpleasantness that seems to proceed from determined and a-rhythmic visual density. Everything here, apparently, must have its insistent color and shape and texture: we are inundated with cracks and smears and rectangles, with the presumed data of the senses. The visual determination here, in short, seems to amount to a neglect for verbal harmony, to a carelessness about the words themselves. Seeing—and believing—is apparently so much at issue that the words that lead to seeing do not matter: "What if 'browny-grey' is an awful phrase," one might say. "That is the color it was."

It seems, in fact, that our awareness that seeing is the issue here is reciprocal with our awareness that sound and rhythm—and all other niceties of words as such—are not. It seems that we are not supposed to be aware of the words at all. Their justification lies in their imagined referentialness; they are not to be seen, but seen through, to something else. They are not pretty because they do not have to be, since they do not count as words but as pointers. We may suppose that they point to Martha's world; or we may infer that they point to some world that we understand as both the heroine's and our own. But that is not clear, for their essential aspect is active; it is not what they point to so much as the fact that they do, continually, point. The words of this narrative are like a treadmill slipping away beneath us, and we have to keep moving on them and away from each of them as they occur. In this way they are not a presence but an action; their substance consists of the motion of self-neglect, of leading beyond themselves.

The force of this visual process is so obvious here that even repetitions of phrasing—which are, after all, lapses in variation and so ought to slow or halt the movement—only serve to accelerate it. "Small fattish smeared woman" and "small fattish pale man" do not draw our attention to their repeated aspect; they do not seem even to begin a rhythm. On the contrary, the similarity of phrasing seems evidence that there are two different people in question. And when repetitions of phrasing are not felt as such, but as indications of more visual variation, then we may be sure that we are moving from the words themselves almost instantaneously toward what they signify, moving so quickly that we cannot remember the words as they pass.

This use even of repetition—normally the means of declaring the presence of verbal form as such—to give the illusion of unverbal, various experience is not so obvious, but is much more effective in Weesner. In the passage I have already quoted, where the goalpost hanger gets a bloody nose, the man's pants began "as he struggled with his legs to hold them, to slide down his legs," and "then the long johns . . . then he lost the long johns," and "all the hands pulling at his ankles and at the pants and underwear around his ankles." This is almost Hemingway; but Hemingway might have gone on repeating, bringing the words farther out to us, establishing them as words in a rhythm, and thus transforming a visual experience into its opposite. Weesner's repetition, on the contrary, seems founded upon a disregard for words, for the prose itself, as if the repetition were the function of looking not at words but at something else, the result of a gaze so fixed upon what in fact was happening that one could not pay attention to what one said. Unvoiced narrative in this way is always devoted not to its words but to some experience beyond the words, whose presence we feel just because the narrative seems to say, again and again, that the words do not count.

For in relation to the narrative itself, there is no experience here at all, nothing happening but the happening of a reader's own imaginative process, his own motion onto and past each new phrase or image or moment. And by discounting the presence of the language of the narrative as such, by transforming words into signs—not signs of experience or substance so much as signs of the necessity of moving toward, pointing toward, looking toward that substance—the presence of the fictional world is established.

It is characteristic of unvoiced narratives that they seem to extend to or into our own experience, or at least to experience beyond their beginnings and endings. They are relevant to worlds outside them. They even seem to refer to such worlds and to be about them. But their feeling of being extendable and referential springs not from any perceived substance within them—nor even so much from the recognized substance of imaginative contexts outside them—but from our perception of their own incompleteness and our resultant movement to complete and connect them with something. A narrative becomes realistic by placing itself upon the visual-intelligible grid and asking, What am I about? What can you see and know here?—and by our answering such questions. The eventual answers that we make are not nearly so important as the stimulation to make them, the felt process of seeing through and moving beyond what is given.

In realistic narrative, the words of the narrative are never sufficient to themselves. They are no sooner perceived than they become invisible as words, which is the same as inviting us to see through them. Their realism resides in the action we take with them, action we do not take when we feel the presence of words in a narrative. And thus for the feeling of realism to continue—for the illusion of visual experience to persist—the invitation that the words make to our capacity for understanding them must be sustained. This brings us back to another aspect of the negative energy of unvoiced narrative, for such a sustained invitation must take the form of resistance.

Stevens' line that a "poem must resist the intelligence/Almost successfully" is appropriate for realistic or visual narrative, but short of the mark. For because the realistic energy of a narrative depends upon the persistent novelty of its imaginative variation—and upon the invitation to follow and understand that such variation constitutes for a reader—that energy continues only so long as variation and invitation are sustained, so long as our efforts are sustained. And for these efforts to be sustained, they must be resisted. This energy of resistance in unvoiced narratives is always perceptible: the verbal insufficiency that we see as allowing our individual imaginative agency is also, obviously, a resistance to that agency. But this becomes all the more apparent as the insufficiency is extended. The farther we proceed with narrative variety itself, the more likely we are to feel that variety as the negative condition it always, really, was.

This matter of the visual resistance of unvoiced narratives—in its connection with their negative aspects of immediate insufficiency and uncommittedness—is not merely evident in the fact and theory of our reading. It is an active force in the practical business of composing such fiction. It means that the writer of visual or realistic narrative is always thinking of what he must not do and what he cannot say, that the controls experienced by the writer of unvoiced fiction are themselves for the most part negative.

We find, for instance, that the self-effacement characteristic of the language of realistic fiction extends, forcibly, to the narrative source of that language, to the narrator "himself." I place that last word in quotation marks because the idea of a personal narrator is in the case of unvoiced narrative a fictitious idea. We are accustomed to speaking, in literature classes and even in literary criticism, indiscriminately of the "tone" and "voice" of a narrative, but that—at least in the case of unvoiced or visual fiction—is merely a convention, and perhaps a misleading one. For as we experience it, realistic narrative has no voice: the narrators of such fiction pretend not to be speaking; indeed, they pretend not to be there at all.[4]

One of the particular methods of this general pretence—and perhaps the most common—we have already seen in *The Car Thief*. It aligns the narrative view—not the voice—closely with the central but uncommitted and wandering character. In this way, that view is severely limited in its own felt presence; it is for most purposes dominated by the perspective and movement of the character, and it offers little authority beyond that character. But at the same time, it is at least as unlimited as the character himself, as flexible and multiple and various as his indecisive course allows. And that course and view thus becomes the basic means of multiplying the story itself, of creating its variety. Lessing's heroine, Martha Quest, does not know who she is; her identity—even to the names that she calls herself or that others call her by—is radically undecided. She thus insists on her nondescript freedom. The course of her character is normally away from things rather than toward them; and she tends to rehearse possibilities even when these would seem excluded by what has already happened. The attachment of the narrative perspective to such a character generates an apparent imaginative variousness and density not possible with a steadier perspective or clearer character, and the situation is further multiplied when we discover that, although the narrative source is for much of the time connected to Martha's experience, it can also close in on other characters and their visions. It is, in short, multiple and various in that it is erratic and inconsistent in its possible attachments. But it is always attached. It is nothing in itself. It never stands alone and visible—or more to the point, audible—to us, and its freedom, along with that of the story it both originates and disappears into, is the freedom of absence and uncommittedness.

We may now see more clearly the connections among certain aspects of unvoiced narratives: the impulse to move beyond or to see through the words is the same as our recognition of their self-effacement as words, which is the same as the narrator's voicelessness, or invisibility, partial or total. But as negative as these aspects seem to be in relation to voice, we may see also that they are in fact claims to another sort of power, a power beyond the verbal. It is the color within or through "browny-grey" that counts. The imitated or represented world is supposed to be summoned up by the incompleteness of what refers to it, by the insufficiency of the language in which it is expressed. The sense or intelligibility of the narrative—the very validation of its process—is somewhere behind or beyond it and what it says. And the absence of a narrator becomes, by the same token, the claim of an authorial power beyond the text, beyond the words in which the narrative is not expressed.

Such "form" is seductive. It suggests that as we have pursued—as if on our own individual course—the narrative, we have pursued the narrator and that we may find him or her out and share his knowledge. And a story's realistic drive, its manner of resisting our intelligence, may escalate from a narrator's mere uncommittedness and invisibility to his obtrusive and declared elusiveness and to an imaginative resistance in the fiction that becomes absolutely the nonproductive subject of the story itself.

We may consider, for example, the narrator of John Barth's *The Floating Opera*. Todd Andrews is a narrator altogether too "visible": he is always there to claim that we do not really know him:

> And this *does*, in a small way, reflect a philosophical position of mine, or at least a general practice, to wit: being just a little bit less consistent in practically everything, so that any quick characterization of me, or general statement about me, will probably be untrue, or at least inadequate.[5]

> I caution you against inferring anything of a philosophical flavor from my practice. There is in my daily routine a great deal that legitimately implies my ideas about things, but you mustn't work from the wrong things or you'll go astray. (80)

> Disorderly? Think before you say so—it's too easy a judgment. It seems to me that any arrangement of things at all is an order. If you agree, and I don't see why you shouldn't, then it follows that my room was as orderly as any room can be, even though the order was perhaps an unusual one. If you're interested in accuracy, you mustn't jump at easy judgments while reading this book. (16)

Whether we are or not, this narrator is "interested in accuracy"; his narrative seems devoted to narrow—if not, as in the last quoted passage, downright silly—logic, and it is spotted with phrases, like "legitimately implies" and "it follows" and "it doesn't follow." But the most curious thing about this logic, and this allegiance to accuracy, is that it always functions as a block to intelligibility.

The book begins with a "logical" worry: "Good heavens! How

does one write a novel? I mean, how can anybody possibly stick to the story, if he's at all sensitive to the significances of things?" (8) Readers may be used to that sort of early disclaimer, of course, as the preparation for more productive narrative activity and may not be discouraged yet. But in fact, this "sensitivity to significances" never becomes a means of invention but continues the reverse, a way of continually refusing to imagine. In the chapter called "An instructive, if sophisticated observation," Andrews tells us why:

> So, reader, should you ever find yourself writing about the world, take care not to nibble at the many tempting symbols she sets squarely in your path, or you'll be baited into saying things you don't really mean, and offending the people you want most to entertain. Develop, if you can, the technique of the pallbearers and myself: smile, to be sure, but walk on and say nothing, as though you hadn't noticed. (117–118)

Such "tempting symbols" must be resisted in the interests of good taste, and out of concern for a reader and his attentions, one must not tell obvious stories. But it turns out that in relation to such anxiety, for one as worried as Todd Andrews about our awareness of what he is doing, all stories become obvious, and no committed utterance is possible:

> I'll have to end this chapter by mentioning, reluctantly, that one can see one's reflection sharply in the tile front of a jewelry store on Poplar St., across from the poolroom, and that as a matter of historical fact I paused for a moment there to adjust the knot in my necktie, which I'd loosened a bit during my morning's work. What is embarrassing about this mirror—for the tile reflects like a dark mirror—is its convenience, not only on the street but in my narrative: the next story I have to tell you is a mirror-story, the story of what happened in my bedroom on my seventeenth birthday, and it's unfortunate, considering what I said a few pages ago about life's naive symbolisms, that I must employ such a too-perfect, Hollywoodish bridge to reach that story, but there's no help for it.
> And I lose even by so explaining my discomfiture concerning these juxtaposed mirrors—the one on the street and the one in my

bedroom—because the explanation itself is arch, painfully so, and my pointing out its archness archer still, until, like any image caught between facing mirrors, this conclusion loses itself, like a surrealist colonnade, in an infinite regress of archness. I apologize. (122–123)

The curious thing here is that Andrews cannot refrain from establishing the "naive" significance in the first place, that he must first do something obvious, even cute, and then apologize for its obviousness, declare it beneath him and the reader, and then do the same thing to the apology, and so on.

The motive for this activity may be evident: both the narrator and his speech are trying continually, like "this conclusion," to "lose themselves," to disappear inside their confused possibilities, inside their infinite reflections, so as to contend that there is, indeed, an image there somewhere, a reality to reflect upon. But for me this effect is itself dominated—rendered unrealizable—by its presumable means, by the very unsubstantialness of the narrator's confusions themselves. For Andrews' anxiety as to what story and self to offer is itself flimsy; it thus depends for its force upon remaining, like everything else here, elusive. And its elusiveness is most often simply and flatly declared.

But Barth apparently wants to escape even the responsibility of such a declaration. There is the scene on the showboat, for example, where the actor recites "To be or not to be" and gets pelted for his efforts: this may be a self-conscious and ironic image of *The Floating Opera*'s action, implying that the author allows that the performance is execrable but that it is dramatized also, that he is not committed to it. If we are so committed, and are so taken in or aback by it as to throw old vegetables or small coins, then maybe the joke is on us. But this sort of irony, like his apology for his image of the mirrors, is an infinite regress, a series of concentric spheres where the author always occupies the next one out from the reader, dominating and energizing the imaginative situation by running farther and farther away from it. In this way, a commitment to realistic motives, and to the power of visual processes, has resulted in such a total and obviously deliberate resistance to a reader's pursuit that nothing can ever be unequivocally said, and the narrator himself can only attempt to maintain the illusion of his knowledge and power beyond the text by refusing to take any position, by always scurrying off one page to appear on the next and say, like the Gingerbread Man in the nursery story, "Run run run as fast as you can, you can't catch me . . ."

The imaginative life of *The Floating Opera* thus depends on an action of visibly refusing to commit its energies within the context of the narrative and insisting upon an authorial "presence" that at any given moment is by definition outside the fiction, outside the limits of his very expression and which validates itself by invalidating that expression. Something like this action is typical of realistic narrative more generally, where the world presented on the page is both undercut and justified by its pressure out toward some experience or knowledge imagined beyond it, whose imaginary substance is the consequence of the negative energy of the fictional world, of its pressure away from itself.

But what we see in Barth is what happens when the motive of intelligibility—the essential motive of realistic process—becomes so avowedly problematic and resistant to a reader's efforts as to be embodied completely in this anxiously declared imaginary life beyond the text. The actual substance of the fiction itself, in this case, and even its negative energy, becomes weaker and weaker as the assertion of it becomes more and more familiar, as the insistence upon the author in the wings repeats, until at last it may become merely a haggling drone about what or how to write:

> To what conclusion will he come? He'd been about to append to his own tale inasmuch as the old analogy between Author and God, novel and world, can no longer be employed unless deliberately as a false analogy, certain things follow: 1) fiction must acknowledge its fictitiousness and metaphoric invalidity or 2) choose to ignore the question or deny its relevance or 3) establish some other, acceptable relation between itself, its author, its reader. Just as he finished doing so however his real wife and imaginary mistresses entered his study; "It's a little past midnight" she announced with a smile; "do you know what that means?"[6]

What it means is that it is now the author's birthday, and cel-
ebrating that is the occasion for ending this story. Or rather for
stopping it, since it must not be ended, since the process of pursuing it ever further is designed to be spurred by the sign that the
author is after all a man outside all of this, and thus the real
substance and presence of these stories in *Lost in the Funhouse*,
their real life is always outside them, beyond them, just around the
corner or through the next door or on the other side of this page.

The narrative action that I have described in Barth, in which the
attempt to see and know a fictional world is—at least in design—
energized by total resistance, and in which the narrative power is
held inseparable from authorial uncommitment and elusiveness,
is extreme in him. We may consider it to mark one end of a scale.
But it is near there that all unvoiced fiction must operate. Barth
shifts away from internal narrative means of visual resistance—the
imaginative variety of the story itself—to authorial means—where
the imagined exterior person of the author is declared the only and
opaque source of narrative sense—very quickly, and in his doing so,
the gesture is enervated. Other writers preserve a better balance in
purveying the realistic mystery of a world beyond the text. That is,
in other writers we are held to the fictional surface longer; the
sense of its own mystery, and of the possibility of understanding it,
is maintained longer. But sooner or later all fiction that depends
for its life upon surprising and puzzling us—namely, all realistic or
unvoiced fiction—must force us past its cover, no longer to the
world to which the fiction seems to refer or extend, but to the
person of the author, as the only source of the knowledge that has
eluded us in the fiction itself. We will then want to talk about
him and to know who he is and where he is. And there is a current
writer who has proved so appetizing in this way as to become
material for the most teasing journalism. The title of a piece from
Playboy asks, "Who is Thomas Pynchon . . . ?" and declares that
Pynchon is "the most famous invisible writer since J. D. Salinger."[7]
This would not be worth mentioning if I had not heard this

question—"Who is Thomas Pynchon?"—asked so often in one way or another by critics and colleagues and students. That suggests that the question is an important one, that though gossipy in effect, it is not only so in motive; for it appears to be the inevitable result of our encounter with the riddles and mysteries of Pynchon's fiction. The act of reading that fiction extends to that of reading the author, for the difficulties of the fiction, the dazzling and multiple incompleteness of its substance, sends us on toward the source of the power, on to a more final intelligibility, to the fuller knowledge of it that we suppose its author must have. And our difficulty in finding that author—his own personal elusiveness—is a perfect match for the visual resistance of his fiction: it suggests a harmony, or perhaps a singleness, of individual motives that is both remarkable and disquieting.

Pynchon is the most visual, and so the most realistic, novelist we have. "Now I go back over some of these *sequences*," he is reported to have said of a draft of *Gravity's Rainbow*, "and I can't figure out what I could have meant" (my emphasis).[8] I have emphasized sequences here because it seems so perfectly revealing of his technique. Sequence is the heart of realistic fiction, and no one has ever written purer or better sequences than Pynchon:

> The corridor runs by the curtained entrances to four boxes, located to audience right at the top level of the summer theatre in the Ezbekiyeh Garden.
> A man wearing blue spectacles hurries into the second box from the stage end of the corridor. The red curtains, heavy velvet, swing to and fro, unsynchronized, after his passage. The oscillation soon damps out because of the weight. They hang still. Ten minutes pass.
> Two men turn the corner by the allegorical statue of Tragedy. Their feet crush unicorns and peacocks that repeat diamond-fashion the entire length of the carpet. The face of one is hardly to be distinguished beneath masses of white tissue which have obscured the features, and changed slightly the outlines of the face. The other is fat. They enter the box next to the one the man with the blue spectacles is in. Light from outside, late summer light now falls through a single window, turning the statue and the figured

carpet to a monochrome orange. Shadows become more opaque. The air between seems to thicken with an indeterminate color, though it is probably orange. Then a girl in a flowered dress comes down the hall and enters the box occupied by the two men. Minutes later she emerges, tears in her eyes and on her face. The fat man follows. They pass out of the field of vision.

The silence is total. So there's no warning when the red-and-white-faced man comes through his curtains holding a drawn pistol. The pistol smokes. He enters the next box. Soon he and the man with the blue spectacles, struggling, pitch through the curtains and fall to the carpet. Their lower halves are still hidden by the curtains. The man with the white-blotched face removes the blue spectacles; snaps them in two and drops them to the floor. The other shuts his eyes tightly, tries to turn his head away from the light.

Another has been standing at the end of the corridor. From this vantage he appears only as a shadow; the window is behind him. The man who removed the spectacles now crouches, forcing the prostrate one's head toward the light. The man at the end of the corridor makes a small gesture with his right hand. The crouching man looks that way and half rises. A flame appears in the area of the other's right hand; another flame; another. The flames are colored a brighter orange than the sun.

Vision must be the last to go. There must also be a nearly imperceptible line between an eye that reflects and a eye that receives.

The half-crouched body collapses. The face and its masses of white skin loom ever closer. At rest the body is assumed exactly into the space of this vantage.[9]

This sequence is pure, in both motive and effect, for many reasons. In the first place, it is both detailed and anonymous. All of the characters in it we have seen and known before—Porpentine, Goodfellow, Lepsius, Bongo-Shaftsbury, and Victoria—and yet here in this movement, Pynchon refuses to name them, and this results in a excess of descriptive detail that remains oddly empty by its resistance to any more conclusive identification. And the same is true of the fictional place itself: Pynchon is the great geographer and geometer of fiction. No writer has ever mapped out his scenes so precisely, yet once again the effect of this precision is to increase rather than abate a reader's hunger for intelligibility. The details of his scenic charts seem the very stuff of visual fullness, and they are, but that is to say that they repeatedly constitute a problem in seeing: "The railway from Alexandria to Cairo describes a rough arc whose chord points southeast" (78).

The more the scene I have quoted at length fills the eye, the more problematic it becomes; the more that the narrative attends to its detailed features, the more it resists and draws us: "Two men turn the corner by the allegorical statue of Tragedy. Their feet crush unicorns and peacocks that repeat diamond-fashion the entire length of the carpet. . . . Light from outside, late summer light now falls through a single window, turning the statue and the figured carpet to a monochrome orange. Shadows become more opaque. The air between seems to thicken with an indeterminate color, though it is probably orange." Here we may feel the sequence's amazing temporal determination and energy. Time seems crucial and dramatic here, so much so that Pynchon can effectively use a sentence that any other novelist would have to avoid: "Ten minutes pass." In this way, too, in its insistence on its own chronology, the sequence is pure.

These aspects of visual imaginative sequence are of course not separate. The scene's anonymity, its descriptive fullness that is at the same time an absence of form, the precision of its spatial coordinates and its time—these are all aspects of one motive and one imaginative gesture; for this movement is, above all, as the narrative tells us, a "field of vision"; and its sequence is felt as pure because "the silence is total." It is hard to imagine another writer's having the audacity and power to do that, simply to declare the sound out of his narrative by fiat. There is a violent struggle here, and first one shooting—"the pistol smokes"—and then another: "A flame appears in the area of the other's right hand; another flame; another. The flames are colored a brighter orange than the sun." And yet there is no sound, and the energy of the scene—even the horror of it—is generated by the determined visual sequence— "another flame; another"—in combination with its frightening incompleteness, by a reader's inability to make it "sound."[10] The intensities of both vision and soundlessness are two sides of the same coin here, functions of each other; and—as Pynchon insists on them right to the end—it becomes evident to us that the need for sound here is the need for feeling, that the relentless anonymity of this eye is terrifying. We know the man who is dying, as I have said, and he has not been unlikable, but this is how he dies:

> Vision must be the last to go. There must also be a nearly imperceptible line between an eye that reflects and an eye that receives.
> The half-crouched body collapses. The face and its masses of white skin loom ever closer. At rest the body is assumed exactly into the space of this vantage.

This last sentence is remarkable, remarkable as writing, remarkable in the way it sustains the narrative's soundless refusal to account for itself, to take a sounded form, which is its resistance to our intelligence. This is all the more striking because it is not careless. It is not a turning away, but an intensification, a magnification of the narrative focus. "This vantage" earlier meant a certain visual perspective—"from this vantage he appears"—and it continues to mean that: the narrative eye is therefore at the last filled with the body, with the fact of the death, and the absence that we feel is not for lack of visual concentration. But that concentration is a narrowing, a narrowing of the aperture through which we have seen, down to nothing. The body fills the space exactly; nothing can be seen beyond or around it, and so it too, finally, vanishes. The force of "assumed" here bespeaks the final imaginative resistance, not the usual resistance of extreme visual concentration, but the lapsing of that into a condition even more excited and deprived: "this vantage" is at the end no longer an angle of sight, but only a sentence, or perhaps just a phrase, holding and resisting all the scene's various life and what we want to make of that life. It is where the life has gone, disappeared into a phrase that now signifies not a narrative perspective but an author's words, a blank wall that we must imagine beyond. It is an explosive condensation, through which all the life of the narrative has drained away to somewhere else and lies on the other side of the words. It is perfect realism.

My feeling that Pynchon may be the finest realist of our time springs not only from his dominantly visual narrative processes but also from his dedication to plausibility, which is also his dedication to mystery: he is committed to the grid of knowing–not knowing and is fascinated with that sort of power. Indeed the very title of his first—and in my view his best—novel is an enactment of this power. V. is a model of how language works in the realistic mode. It is a mere initial, blank and trivial, and yet it is the title of a long book; it is the abbreviation that stands for the multiple life of the main character, the life that supplies the motive for most of the story. "V." is a perfect realistic word; reduced and bare, incompletely sounded, the narrowest possible aperture, again, but beyond which the fictional world—the world beyond the words—expands explosively and as if unverbally.

But the act of seeing through this aperture—like the signifying action of realistic fiction more generally—is problematic. "V." is a question—Who is V? What is V?—that a reader attempts to answer by looking through and beyond its word. In just this way, the substance of realistic fiction at large is simply the question of what its substance is. And the continuance of the realism, of the fiction's novel energy, is the continuance of that question unanswered. And no one, so far as I know, has ever "continued the question" better than Pynchon does in V.

The narrative fluctuates among various fictional contexts, one set of which is dominated by Benny Profane and his friends, the other by "V." and her connections. Herbert Stencil travels in both companies and enacts their dramatic connection. But his essential motive concerns V:

> STEN: Stencil reached his majority three years after old Stencil died. Part of the estate that came to him then was a number of manuscript books, bound in half-calf and warped by the humid air of many European cities. His journals, his unofficial log of an agent's career. Under "Florence, April, 1899" is a sentence, young Stencil has memorized it: "There is more behind and inside V. than any of us had suspected. Not who, but what: what is she. God grant that I may never be called upon to write the answer, either here or in any official report."[11]

MARG: A woman.
STEN: Another woman.
MARG: It is she you are pursuing? Seeking?
STEN: You'll ask next if he believes her to be his mother. The
question is ridiculous. (53–54)

"The question is ridiculous," I take it, in part because Stencil insists
that his quest for V. remain undifferentiated and undesigned. What
identifies the effort is its intensity, and that intensity precludes any
predispositions of the case. Everything, for Stencil, is connected
with V., and given such fixation, any precise expectations are superfluous. V. must mean, and that necessity is so great that what she
means cannot be considered before the fact. Though the question
is also "ridiculous" because it is not only predispositions of the
matter that Stencil avoids, but any dispositions whatever.

Stencil's predecessor in American fiction was not so open-minded.
Ahab was more biased as to what he would find when he "struck
through the mask" of the white whale; but he is nonetheless the
mold from which Stencil has been struck, just as *Moby-Dick*, more
generally, is the source book for V. On one side of it, a correlation
of the two novels seems to yield parody: Ishmael has been transformed into Benny Profane, Ahab into Stencil, Peter Coffin's Inn
to the Sailor's Grave, the cannibal crew of the Pequod into the
"whole sick crew," and, of course, the multiple and elusive image
of the whale itself to that of V. herself. Except for the last, these
transformations seem antiheroic; but this effect does not really
imply that Pynchon is parodying Melville. For the influence is too
dominating to allow that sort of irony. It seems rather that unheroic
transformations of heroic models—what goes on in the Sailor's
Grave, for instance—are self-directed ironies: merely Pynchon's
implicit declarations that he recognizes what he is doing and so,
perhaps, may be said to be free of his source, or at least beyond it.
And this, as I see it, turns out to be so.

But there is much more to the matter than even that most useful
sort of parody. For Herbert Stencil is not merely an unheroic
descendant of Ahab, but in some ways a new and improved design.
As his name suggests, he is a dramatized and ironized Ahab, whose

fixation upon the ultimate answer to it all is both muted and civ-
ilized by his diffident awareness that his quest is not open. And
more generally, V. enacts this sort of extension on its source: it is
Moby-Dick aware of itself, and it dramatizes and avoids what happens when the imaginative and fictional process entailed by the
earlier novel is pursued.

Like Ishmael, Benny Profane is a wanderer, a chameleon character who takes his color from his immediate surroundings, a
survivor. With Ishmael this is most apparent in the profusion and
multiplicity of his narrative voices, a variousness that contradicts
the feeling that he has any real, personal identity, that there is
anything to his saying "I." And in this way Ishmael is the most
energetic prototype in American fiction for the more obviously
anonymous central character of international realism—for the Alex
Housmans and Martha Quests and all the other personless persons
whose movement is the vehicle for their narratives' own open
motion. But Profane is truer to the role, for he is not a narrator,
and he is a very muddled character: his most characteristic utterance is "Wha?" and he is a schlemiel, a victim of the inanimate.

It is in this relation to the inanimate that Profane's extended
presence in the novel is perhaps justified. I have always felt that V.
might have been a shorter book and that what could have been
excluded was a whole lot of Benny Profane; so much of him—or
at least of the activity and even the prose that surrounds him—is
right out of a college humor magazine. But in his fear of and
resistance to the inanimate, he operates on the book's main frequency, which is a fascination with the process of following and
knowing and a fear of the inevitable results. Profane, of course,
does not follow; he just goes along. And he does not want to know
anything. But then, for all his pursuing, neither does Stencil himself. When all indications are that V. died during the siege on
Malta, Stencil insists instead that she was merely "passing through":

"A shipfitter named Aquilina has intelligence of one Mme. Viola,
oneiromancer and hypnotist, who passed through Valletta in 1944.
The glass eye went with her. Cassar's girl lied. V. used it for an
hypnotic aid. Her destination, Stockholm. As is Stencil's. It will

do for the frayed end of another clue. Dispose as you will of Profane. Stencil has no further need for any of you. Sahha." (451–452)

Thus he keeps V., and his quest, alive, at the expense that we stop taking him seriously. But that was inevitable. For the only way that he could continue seriously would be—like Ahab—to die in the midst of a final vision, and Stencil, because again he is a diminishment of Ahab, is in some ways an improvement: he survives, and so he keeps his search alive for himself. Most important, he allows Pynchon to shift away from him to his father, in the "Epilogue," and so to reanimate the mystery of V. A reader has seen the children on Malta picking the "bad priest" to pieces, and the pieces are all signs of V. that he has seen before: inanimate fragments that she wears—the ivory comb—or fixed on herself—the golden feet—or even incorporated into herself—the tattooed scalp, the artificial eye that is a clock, the jewel fixed in her navel. For V. herself, the drive to make herself inanimate is linked most frequently to a fetishism both sexual and religious, but it is important to realize that her "inanimatenesses" are the means by which we know her. Indeed, it is almost as if they are a reflection and a result of our knowing her, and a dramatization of the knowing process, by which a living mystery is fixed and frozen and deadened by its solving.

Melville never really approached the deanimation of his story's center the way that Pynchon—working with the same motives— does. Ahab dies, the whale swims away off the page, and the fictional world is as real as ever with Ishmael drifting on its surface. And V. has its diminished parallels, as Stencil chases away to Stockholm, and Profane and a new girlfriend run happily and aimlessly "through the abruptly absolute night, momentum alone carrying them toward the edge of Malta, and the Mediterranean beyond" (455). But Pynchon's fiction, as I have suggested, both knows its sources and passes them. He is able to dramatize the imaginative pursuit and end of realistic fiction, to cause it to reveal itself self-consciously at last as a disassembled mechanism beneath a fallen beam. But at the same time—even though we have pursued it, discovered it, and ended it—it survives our knowing. The mechanism weeps, still more than the sum of its fixed and recognizable parts, and at last the scene shifts to 1919, when V. and the mystery were still very much alive, and Stencil's father died with what he knew:

> Draw a line from Malta to Lampedusa. Call it a radius. Somewhere in that circle, on the evening of the tenth, a waterspout appeared and lasted for fifteen minutes. Long enough to lift the xebec fifty feet, whirling and creaking, Astarte's throat naked to the cloudless weather, and slam it down again into a piece of the Mediterranean whose subsequent surface phenomena—whitecaps, kelp islands, any of a million flatnesses which should catch thereafter part of the brute sun's spectrum—showed nothing at all of what came to lie beneath, that quiet June day. (492)

> Now small fowls flew screaming over the yet yawning gulf; a sullen white surf beat against its steep sides; then all collapsed, and the great shroud of the sea rolled on as it rolled five thousand years ago.[12]

I quote these passages together not merely to insist upon the similarity of their motives nor to declare again that Pynchon owes much to Melville, but to suggest that the debt goes both ways. For what is most remarkable here is that these passages are similarly effective. Both insist, successfully, that the real meaning of the fiction is permanently present and permanently elusive. Both persuade us of the reality of a life beneath and beyond their surfaces, a life that is or was real exactly because we shall never know it. But Pynchon achieves the effect while at the same time dramatizing it, while writing about it. The self-consciousness that allows him to write out of *Moby-Dick*, the self-criticism to which he subjects its realistic form, not only does not ultimately compromise that form's vitality within his fictional world but also regenerates and extends that vitality.[13] Which is how literary influence ought to occur.

Of course it is not all roses. V. resembles *Moby-Dick* also in that it is an immensely irritating book. In Melville's novel, for instance, the narrative range and variation that embellish Ahab's linear course may feel at times like Ishmael-Melville's self-indulgent clutter. Pynchon's novel, again, displays a similar penchant for narrative delay and deviation in relation to Benny Profane and company and to even more obvious sorts of fictional cuteness, but that is not its greatest liability. For V. may seem most irritating just when Pynchon is at his best in it, and the reasons for this have much to do with the very nature of visual-realistic fiction.

The range of Pynchon's narrative is not confined to the limits of a whaling voyage. The story of V. drifts from Alexandria to Venice to South Africa to Malta to Paris and back to Malta, and in most of these locales, a reader does not know where he is. But Pynchon always seems to know, right down to the names of little alleys, the directions of railway lines, the precise layouts of marketplaces and barrooms and museums. A reader is at once dazzled and convinced by this knowledge, just as he may be by how knowing Pynchon is in other contexts, like the history and politics of his settings, or the psychology of his characters, or the complex psychosexual implications of V's own career. In all of these contexts, in short, the story's energy is generated—and the realism is founded— upon an imbalance of knowledge between reader and writer. It is not that we know or even recognize the information we are given. Our belief in the narrative detail of V. stems rather from our awareness that even if we knew these places and people well, we would not know nearly so much as the author knows. Both places and people are real because they are strange, they are what we don't know; and our relation to the author is one of his dominance and our fascination and intimidation. The tricky question here is the same for all realistic fiction: when does our charmed ignorance become irritation at always being at least one down to Pynchon? When does the dazzling travelogue become so strenuous that we want to go home? This is the dangerous side, I should add, only for the great realists. Lesser operators in that mode cannot sustain their knowledge beyond ours, cannot continue to produce the new and various detail that leads us on, and their stories settle down before we need to. But that is never Pynchon's weakness, who never knows too little but sometimes, and for some readers, too much.

Besides our more emotional reactions to it, however, this issue of knowledge in Pynchon can tell us more about the dynamics of fictional realism. How is it, for instance, that Pynchon seems so right—about African geography, about Fausto Maijistral's mind, about the foreign service, about Esther's nose job? It almost goes without saying that his rightness, our feeling that he is realistic, cannot spring from any correspondence between his fictional detail and models in our minds. That is, the idea that fiction is realistic when it matches what we already know, that realism arises from mimetic correspondence, is obviously and simply inaccurate here. We probably do not know Alexandria, have a bare notion of what the "Fashoda Crisis" was, have no idea what Malta was like during the siege, and have never seen a nose job in progress. Yet in all these instances, Pynchon seems unerringly right and persuasive, and —at the end of any given sequence—we may feel that we know or at least are beginning to find out what really goes on in such cases.

Esther's nose job is perhaps the most striking example, grizzly and gratuitous as it is. All that puncturing and snipping of flesh, that chiseling and crunching of bone, I am told by friends who know, is quite accurate. But it was "accurate" for me, in my ignorance, already: it was perfectly real. And obviously this feeling of accuracy is not generated by relating the fictional sequence to that of an actual operation. It must, therefore, be a matter of the sequence's own internal variation and consistency and of what a reader does with it. Narrative movement through that operation— like narrative movement through the back alleys of Alexandria or through the convolutions of V's mind—is fundamentally a sequential positing of discrete and various images, and the real movement is enacted by the reader in following this line, in shifting from one image to another, in much the same way that the imagination may shift in nonfictional situations. What is accurate here, then, what corresponds to reality, is the imaginative action that the reader takes with the fictional sequence, the action that the sequence persuades him to take.

It is difficult to say whether that action, and the fiction on which it is enacted, is persuasive just because it seems the same as the way we often imagine in life or if in fact it is persuasive just because it is our action. The plausibility of a fiction clearly depends upon our encouragement to follow its sequences, to transform a condition of novelty and ignorance to one of familiarity and knowledge, and to close the books. And this "encouragement" may be felt even as a pressure, or as a negative state that must be rectified. What is not clear is whether the action we take needs to bear some precise relation to some special class of imaginative action from life or whether any seemingly independent imaginative progress of our own will seem realistic and plausible to us, just because it is our own, and no matter what it operates on.

I incline to the latter view. And in its terms, the single most important task for the writer of realistic fiction is to create the illusion that his reader's action is free and independent, to present sequences that seem pure—unmodified by any logic or intelligence external to them—through and upon which a reader may operate. But this idea—this illusion of unmodified time—may at first seem at odds with Pynchon's particular practice, with the felt dominance of his knowledge as we follow his narrative. That dominance is only recognized, however, in afterthought, if for some reason we draw back from our narrative motion. In the process of that motion, it is expressed in the variational resistance of his sequences to our intelligence; it is the very force that challenges and motivates our imaginative action. The more rich and variegated his fictional surface, the more his narrative energy flows away from his authorial person and into the imagined properties of the fiction, and the more his world resists us, then the more we are challenged by it, fooled by its very resistance into believing that we are doing something with it that is both free and necessary.

With this notion of visual fiction's plausibility in mind, we may begin to appreciate more fully the pressures of realistic writing upon an author. What he or she must work for constantly is the generation in the reader of the following and knowing process and must deny his or her own energy all of its channels save the one that feeds into the story's visual and sequential texture and establishes its seemingly autonomous life for a reader's operation. Of course, its life is not autonomous at all: it has prearranged consistencies and continuities in it not established by a reader. But, in the first place, these must not be evident or easily discoverable, and, in the second place, it is easy to overestimate their force. For very often, such "continuity" is really little more than the evident need for continuity, which quickly becomes the expectation of continuity, both created by the author's devotion to the sustained resistance of visual variation.

Thus, the way that realistic fiction proves itself to us is by sustaining our action upon and through it, by continuing ahead of us in its imagistic change. The energy with which it does this may be felt as a kind of confidence, a feeling that the writer "knows what he is talking about" or "knows his way around a place." This is nearly always the feeling in Pynchon, and in fact, such confidence may stem from his having done things and been places. But not necessarily, for though expressed and perhaps at times even felt by a writer as confidence and knowledge, it is, fundamentally, simply the artistic strength of the realist, his own ability to endure and to submit to the pressures of proving his story by sustaining his narrative's autonomy and openness and, thus, his reader's independent motion.

The pressure of realism, of course, is to put that strength always in question. This is why the realistic novel may be often seen to pose, sometimes even self-consciously, the issue of its realism, when the writer seems to be saying to the reader, "Can I continue this sequence? Can I stay ahead of you with this?" Such questions may themselves be an additional way of creating narrative energy: the question of whether a story can be presented at all provides another sort of challenge and resistance to a reader and may come to take the place—as it does in Barth on a wholesale basis—at times, of any actual presentation. But at the same time, they may arise in concert with a story's own progressive sequence. One of Pynchon's most habitual gestures, for instance, is to begin with a character that is obviously fictional, whose name is obviously contrived, a perfect name—Rachel Owlglass, McClintic Sphere, Pig Bodine—or just a fragment from a schoolboy joke—Bloody Chiclitz—or, more important, like V's own names, constructed of anagrammatic code—Victoria Wren, Vera Meroving, Veronica Manganese—and then proceed to treat and establish that character as human, to give it the sustained variousness that its formulated name belies, to bring it to life. Pynchon's writing often becomes in this way a high wire act, as if he had continually to perform the unlikeliest feats far above us and show us that there is nothing and nobody that he cannot write about and no opening that he cannot follow. It is possible to consider this his particular egotism and mania—especially as one tires of it and he does not—but I see it rather as an expression, even a spilling over, of the realistic drive and pressure in his imagination, an imagination always in a condition of testing itself, of asking itself over and over whether it can deny all its energies save those that further sequential variousness, forego all its own potential fictional presence so as to encourage the reader's motion, and relinquish all the pleasures and powers of fictional voice for the purpose of making one's language invisible. And for this effort, when he holds his reader, Pynchon gains his reader's conviction that the imagining of the fictional world is his own independent affair, and—when he doesn't hold him—his reader's intimidation and resentment at the writer's very strength. That is the nature of visual imagining and realism, of composing unvoiced narrative; it is hard, for me, to see why writers do it.

Six

Mixed Motives

"MY TASK which I am trying to achieve," says Joseph Conrad in perhaps his most famous nonfictional remark, "is, by the power of the written word to make you hear, to make you feel—it is, before all, to make you see. That—and no more, and it is everything."[1] And many readers have found it hard not to credit this as a real revelation of motive. It is so much what one would expect an artist to say, and at the same time it is nonetheless so earnest. But one does not even have to know Conrad well enough to know that, outside of his fiction, he adopted this tone of desperate earnestness very frequently, in order to know that his view of his task was not nearly so unequivocal as he declares here.

Of course we could just dismiss this and other such remarks out of hand—one could do worse—understanding that what novelists say in prefaces and letters and interviews is both generated and governed by the temporary conditions of the occasion and is thus merely another sort of fiction, a sort different from that of their novels. More specifically, we might object that Conrad's insistence on seeing reflects his momentary feelings about The Nigger of the "Narcissus"—an unusually bright narrative for him—and should not be applied, for instance, to "Heart of Darkness." But as reasonable as such reservations may seem, it will be useful not to invoke them here. For Conrad's declared intentions may cast some light upon the action of his fiction—as well as upon fiction at large—just because they are so askew to it, because their tension with it is evidence of the mixture of his motives.

But the particular point to begin with is that Conrad—contrary to his avowed program in the Preface to The Nigger—is in fact famous for his obscurity, in both the simple sense, where seeing means visual perception, and the complex one, where seeing means understanding and implies ultimate intelligibility. Critics of pronounced visual bias, of course, have attacked him for this and ended up designating books like *The Secret Agent*—presumably a clearer and certainly a very funny book—as his great work. Others may lament the obscurity but forgive or indulge it. But I am interested for the moment in what else might be going on, for example, in "Heart of Darkness," perhaps his obscurest work, while it is being visually obscure and in what other motives may thus be said to be operating in Conrad's—and a reader's—imagination than the visual.

In visual terms, unquestionably, "Heart of Darkness" ends blankly enough: "The offing was barred by a black bank of clouds, and the tranquil waterway leading to the uttermost ends of the earth flowed sombre under an overcast sky—seemed to lead into the heart of an immense darkness."[2] Indeed, if anything is seen and known at the end of Conrad's story, it is perhaps that all the problems of understanding in the narrative that we may have assumed to be temporary are now both permanent and certified. What is known at the last is that the story we have tried to know cannot be known.

Yet there is nothing unfinished about the ending of "Heart of Darkness." A reader may feel assured there that he has got, for instance, all the information that he needs and that this is not his difficulty. He may even feel, in this ending's qualities of both finality and continuance, another kind of knowledge: as if he knew, in "Heart of Darkness," all about what he didn't know, knew not only that he did not understand but also, strangely, what he did not understand—as if he somehow knew what the story had failed to make clear. This paradox may be explained—or at least established—by considering that a reader's expectations throughout "Heart of Darkness" may be said to be double.

One of these expectations is that we shall find here a story of the simpler sort: things will happen in their sequence, and as we follow them, we shall be able to reduce them for our understanding. This is, of course, the usual expectation for visual fiction, the confidence that we have in it and ourselves. And we have seen, too, how this confidence can grow even against largely negative reinforcement, how visual energy increases with visual resistance.

This, on one side of it, is just what happens in "Heart of Dark-ness," where our expectation of some ultimate enlightenment con-tinues and grows against the evidence of its improbability. Even though, at the beginning of the story, we have been given warning:

> We looked on, waiting patiently—there was nothing else to do till the end of the flood; but it was only after a long silence, when he said, in a hesitating voice, "I suppose you fellows remember I did once turn fresh-water sailor for a bit," that we knew we were fated, before the ebb began to run, to hear about one of Marlow's inconclusive experiences. (7)

This narrator seems to embody, in the attitude of unhopefulness and even resignation with which he awaits Marlow's story, literary tastes more conventional than Marlow's. Perhaps, like ourselves as we begin the story, he would prefer to hear about an experience rather more conclusive. But unlike us, he knows what is coming:

> The yarns of seamen have a direct simplicity, the whole meaning of which lies within the shell of a cracked nut. But Marlow was not typical (if his propensity to spin yarns be excepted), and to him the meaning of an episode was not inside like a kernel but outside, enveloping the tale which brought it out only as a glow brings out a haze, in the likeness of one of these misty halos that sometimes are made visible by the spectral illumination of moon-shine. (5)

These warnings may not discourage us simply because they occur so early in the narrative. Almost everything is yet to come, after all, and so we may suppose that there will be plenty that we can work with. Even though they seem clear counters to our expectation of discoverable significance, we may take them as a challenge to which we know we can respond. Or—at the least—we may take them as a nonprejudicial circumstance, like losing the first hand in a poker game. The night, we would say, is young.

But the current continues to run against us. As we follow Mar-low, the images in his course do keep changing and mounting, and so this story does seem to involve a journey that is visual, inquiring and promising. But at the same time, the scenery is not various at all: it all seems to participate in a consistent and continual pattern of ineffectuality and insignificance. Marlow sees a gun boat firing what seems to be a pop gun aimlessly into the bush; nothing happens. Explosives are detonated on a cliff without apparent purpose and, again, without effect. And the treatment of the natives is similarly directionless and impotent. They are called "rebels" or they are called "criminals"; they are left to die pitiably in the "grove of death," or they extinguish life themselves carelessly, even accidentally.

But a reader may still take the trend of these images as a temporary aberration, just because that is the way Marlow appears to take them. Whatever the consistent figure they seem to make, they are like all the useless and broken tools that he stumbles over in the jungle, noticed to be beneath his notice. He is, after all, going to see Mr. Kurtz, who is supposed to be different, and who will make all the difference. One way or another, Kurtz is a "remarkable man," the object of admiration and envy, wonder and contempt. So that the promise of Marlow as a narrator becomes identical with the promise of Kurtz as a character. This connection, furthermore, is dramatically founded: from jealousy and fear, the other employees of the company lump Marlow and Kurtz together; they are both members, it is thought, of "the new gang of virtue." And Marlow's professed curiosity about Kurtz, to see how "this man, who had come out equipped with moral ideas of some sort," would turn out, goes deeper than that. For Marlow, as we soon see, has moral ideas of his own. Thus he and Kurtz become isolated together against the background, one "remarkable man" going after another. And the narrative expression of Marlow's remarkableness is, once more, a certain sort of visual promise, his way of continually raising his sights, of discounting what is in front of him, of looking always ahead to what will be larger, more significant, and more suitable for his attention—to Kurtz, the Inner Station, the center of things. With every step that Marlow takes, with every moment where he looks at something—a dying "criminal" at his feet, the rapacious and empty "pilgrims," a human skeleton in the tall grass, the blank wall of the jungle—and looks away from it, past it, the promise grows. It is as if these bypasses were the guarantee of some larger image to come, some image that will set all the others aside and yet explain them, define and dispense with them at the same time. And as the number and intensity of images passed increases, so does the potential size of what is to come, which is by definition so much more significant than any one and all of them.

What is involved here is an imaginative process in which momentary narrative ends—the images and stops of Marlow's journey—become transformed into the means to the real end. Marlow's experience therefore becomes a series of stages. Each image that he passes functions as a momentary focus, a new set of limits for his imagination. But then he rejects it or passes it, and the limits are broken and raised. And yet the general motive for this process is only negative, merely hopeful. Marlow does not know what is coming. It is just that everything he sees is so unsatisfactory that there must be an alternative. Around and before him is what is brutal, sordid, foolish, weak, absurd. Kurtz therefore becomes an imaginative necessity: he must be more than what lies along the way to him. Thus, in Marlow's perceptual and narrative process, what he sees becomes both the impediment to vision—as if to see were only to understand what lies beyond what one sees and to know that one is not seeing whatever that is—and then, because he knows that he must see more, the imperative to vision, even the means of vision.

This sort of imaginative sequence—the very figure of visual resistance—once tripped, is inexorably convincing. So much so for Marlow himself that, as he moves through these stages up the Congo, toward the Inner Station, he is increasingly less eager to go beyond what is right in front of him. His incidental and superficial perceptions and activities become a sort of imaginative sanctuary from some vision so large and so increasingly imminent that he does not want to leave them. Though the imaginative layout remains the same, Marlow's feelings about it begin to change. As his journey advances as a progress, he becomes less and less willing to go beyond its stages.

Such a development does not detract from the apparent potential of the narrative progress in "Heart of Darkness" at all. If anything, the promise of some intelligible climax becomes the greater the more Marlow balks at its prospect, as if his hesitation were even better evidence than his curiosity that there was something there, beyond his surface realities, that could not be passed, that would end the progress and illuminate it all. It would seem, then, that once this sort of action has begun—once the sequence is tripped—almost any momentary gesture, no matter its direction, adds to the momentum. Up to Marlow's confrontation with Kurtz, everything that happens in "Heart of Darkness" works to produce more forward visual energy, persuading a reader that the greater significance he is pursuing is really there.

By this sequence, then, we are persuaded of the existence of an alternative to the sequence. At the center of things, we and Marlow shall find something else and other, and if one asks, "Other than what?" the answer seems to be, "Other than everything before." The very proliferation—as "Heart of Darkness" proceeds—of images perceived and discounted creates the illusion that the progress is not toward some ultimate image of the same sort—last and largest and clarifying—but toward something else entirely. So wide a range of possibilities is rejected in favor of something unseen to come that it seems that whatever is to come will be of another sort of existence, different not merely in size or weight but in quality, because—as Marlow insists—it is beyond his ever-widening vision, even beyond the limits of his narrative.

This, again, is precisely the drive and direction of the most intense realism; but to see how complex and compelling is Marlow's way of looking beyond the moment-to-moment experience of his story, his way of discounting that experience, we may consider a more extended example. Here is Marlow, arrived at the Inner Station, looking through binoculars at the house where Kurtz lives and at what has appeared to be the remains of a fence beside it:

> "And then I made a brusque movement, and one of the remaining posts of that vanished fence leaped up in the field of my glass. You remember I told you I had been struck at the distance by certain attempts at ornamentation, rather remarkable in the ruinous aspect of the place. Now I had suddenly a nearer view, and its

first result was to make me throw my head back as if before a blow. Then I went carefully from post to post with my glass, and I saw my mistake. These round knobs were not ornamental but symbolic; they were expressive and puzzling, striking and disturbing —food for thought and also for vultures if there had been any looking down from the sky; but at all events for such ants as were industrious enough to ascend the pole. They would have been even more impressive, those heads on the stakes, if their faces had not been turned to the house. Only one, the first I had made out, was facing my way. I was not so shocked as you may think. The start back I had given was really nothing but a movement of surprise. I had expected to see a knob of wood there, you know. I returned deliberately to the first I had seen—and there it was, black, dried, sunken, with closed eyelids—a head that seemed to sleep at the top of that pole, and, with the shrunken dry lips showing a narrow white line of the teeth, was smiling too, smiling continuously at some endless and jocose dream of that eternal slumber.

"I am not disclosing any trade secrets. In fact, the manager said afterwards that Mr. Kurtz's methods had ruined the district. I have no opinion on that point, but I want you clearly to understand that there was nothing exactly profitable in these heads being there. They only showed that Mr. Kurtz lacked restraint in the gratification of his various lusts, that there was something wanting in him—some small matter which, when the pressing need arose, could not be found under his magnificent eloquence."
(58)

To begin with, Marlow's response is dislocated from a reader's; or rather, the dramatic response is dislocated from the narrative response. Marlow throws back his head immediately, "as if before a blow," but only many words later does a reader know why and just what those posts are topped with. So that Marlow is looking beyond or over the image even before a reader is sure what it is; and when the fact is communicated, furthermore, it is as an aside. The effects of this sort of narrative double rhythm are complicated, but it should be obvious that the verbal form here, as always, is working not for visual confrontation but for lag or delay, not for excitement but for musing. And we may see too that this is not accidental, not a mistake of sequence or cadence. The mused form of Marlow's sentences corresponds with his professed lack of immediate feeling at the time: "I was not so shocked as you may think . . . nothing but a movement of surprise." From that movement he almost instantaneously disengages himself, and what follows disclaims all excitement and almost all interest, in a kind of judicious weighing of the economic facts: "there was nothing exactly profitable . . ."

Of course, that is irony. But the force of the irony is not to suggest, as if by understatement, that the heads are important. Quite the reverse: and in case we have doubts about where the emphasis lies here, Marlow returns to it on the next page: "After all, that was *only a savage sight*, while I seemed at one bound to have been transported into some lightless region of subtle horrors, where pure, uncomplicated savagery was a positive relief . . ." (95, my emphasis). I am not so interested, for the moment, in that "subtle region" as I am in the "bound"—in the sort of movement by which Marlow is so consistently "transported" in his narrative beyond or over what in other narratives might be crucial and climactic.

To better understand the effect of this narrative discounting and musing of visual detail, we may imagine, hypothetically, the opposite case. Suppose that "Heart of Darkness" proceeded as it does right up to the moment where the heads on the posts leap into Marlow's field of vision, but that when that happened, the response to them was like a response in Poe or in a Victorian horror story: "Good God! (or Great Scott!) They were *human heads!*" That sort of action is ultimate. To give the image such immediate recognition establishes a climax and is a way of ending the movement; and it could even be a way of ending the entire narrative.

After enough questions have been asked in "Heart of Darkness," enough tension established, any one of many images, if starkly and directly seen, would be terminal. The story could stop, for instance, with the recognition that these were human heads, and then it would be a simple story of moral degeneracy, like "An Outpost of Progress." Or it might stop like this: "But I am of course aware that next day the pilgrims buried something in a muddy hole"; and we might then say that it was a story of victimization, of the corruption of the potential heights of Kurtz by the obvious depths of his colleagues. "Heart of Darkness" is full of images that could be climaxes, images that—if Marlow attended to them immediately—would become the terminal images of completed and intelligible stories. Marlow's continuance through image after image, his manner of saying "only" to the moments of his experience, of refusing to allow those moments immediate and final presence, creates in "Heart of Darkness" an imaginative condition in which there is no story that will satisfy the demand that his imagination makes. The resulting visual illusion is that, when we get to the end, "Heart of Darkness" will somehow have ceased to be fiction, that all the stories it passes are being discounted in favor of something beyond stories, that what we are approaching is indeed the alternative to all words and all fiction. And at this point we may suppose, visually, that that will be reality and the truth.

But when Marlow arrives at the Inner Station, when he makes his penetration and encounters Kurtz, when all the imaginative bypassing ought to yield to an ultimate vision, what he finds—both outside and within himself—is not an alternative at all: it is more of the same. Kurtz is not different from what Marlow has seen and said before, nor is he even some part or selection or arrangement of that range. He is, instead, all of it; he includes it all. He is as grasping and mean and envious, and more rapacious and unscrupulous and generally appetitive, than the worst of the company that Marlow has so quickly set aside; but he is also powerful, austere, lofty, full of the same high moral talk that Marlow himself likes so much. Kurtz covers these and, it seems, all other possibilities, just because he is, more than anything else, a "voice."

Still, this too is as Marlow has expected: he has most consistently imagined Kurtz as a voice. But his feelings about voices are divided:

> "There was a sense of extreme disappointment, as though I had found out I had been striving after something altogether without a substance. I couldn't have been more disgusted if I had travelled all this way for the sole purpose of talking with Mr. Kurtz. Talk-

ing with . . . I flung one shoe overboard, and became aware that that was exactly what I had been looking forward to—a talk with Kurtz. I made the strange discovery that I had never imagined him as doing, you know, but as discoursing. I didn't say to myself, 'Now I will never see him,' or 'Now I will never shake him by the hand,' but, 'Now I will never hear him.' The man presented himself as a voice. Not of course that I did not connect him with some sort of action. Hadn't I been told in all the tones of jealousy and admiration that he had collected, bartered, swindled, or stolen more ivory than all the other agents together? That was not the point. The point was in his being a gifted creature, and that of all his gifts the one that stood out pre-eminently, that carried with it a sense of real presence, was his ability to talk, his words—the gift of expression, the bewildering, the illuminating, the most exalted and the most contemptible, the pulsating stream of light, or the deceitful flow from the heart of an impenetrable darkness." (47–48)

In this way, Marlow's ambivalence about Kurtz's power of speech appears to trace to a more fundamental one—his sharply, even agonizingly divided feelings toward language itself: "the gift of expression, the bewildering, the illuminating, the most exalted and the most contemptible . . ." On the one hand, language is either so contemptible as mere talk or so problematic that all one's hopes of discovery shift to its source. There must be something behind or beneath the words—a man at the end of the story. And when that something dies, or is just not there, the experience loses its substance. But on the other hand, Marlow's regard for Kurtz's voice and his disregard for any substance beyond it enacts an allegiance to language, as if words were the "real presence" not only of Kurtz but of himself and of all men and experience, and their source or target or whatever beside the point of that presence: "The voice was gone. What else had been there? But I am of course aware that next day the pilgrims buried something in a muddy hole" (71).

But before we pursue this split in Marlow's imagination, the dividedness of his own response to voice, we should see that more than Kurtz, or Marlow's relation to Kurtz, is involved here. For the image of Kurtz is general in "Heart of Darkness." It is not only he who is figured as a voice, whose reality is only the reality of words. As far as Marlow is concerned, this image will serve for everyone:

> "A voice. He was very little more than a voice. And I heard—him—it—this voice—other voices—all of them were so little more than voices—and the memory of that time itself lingers around me, impalpable, like a dying vibration of one immense jabber, silly, atrocious, sordid, savage, or simply mean, without any kind of sense. Voices, voices—even the girl herself—now—"
> He was silent for a long time. (49)

The mention of "the girl" here may remind us that this assessment may also serve for Marlow himself, that he, like everyone else in "Heart of Darkness," has gravitated to only words; for he compounds the idea of a merely verbal reality by lying—though he has told us that he hates a lie—to Kurtz's "Intended" in the dialogue that is so resonant with the sound of words. There the pervasiveness of "voices" seems to Marlow both horrifying and tragic, and in the passage quoted above, as senseless and threatening as an "immense jabber," and this, at least dramatically, is his response to the possibility that everything is nothing but words. Things lose their sense and substance: Kurtz, Marlow himself, the universe itself, and this story, are all hollow. There is no reality alternative to words, no source for the voices. The promise of some terminal truth that Marlow has seemed to make to us and to himself appears finally revoked. Kurtz himself—as the greatest liar of all—is not the narrative's alternative but its epitome. There is nothing in "Heart of Darkness" but fictions, and the imagination has been thrown back upon the images and stories that it had thought to pass. This is why, perhaps, Marlow has to be carried out of there in a collapse that is not merely physical; this is why—as he tells us near the end—it was his "imagination that wanted soothing."

If there is a moral to this story, that is it. It may even be the sense that we give to Kurtz's "final burst of sincerity." We cannot be sure what that death-bed cry—"the horror! the horror!"—means, but if we credit Marlow's insistence that it is the farthest point of the story and of his journey, that it covers everything, then we may infer that Kurtz has made the discovery that the entire narrative points to—that there is nothing, nothing in the world, to words but words, nothing beyond fiction but more of the same.

But here we are approaching the point where Marlow's imagination divides, for Kurtz's discovery is one that he refuses, explicitly, to make. He refuses—and his motives involve a paradox—both because he does not need to make such a discovery, since the idea that reality may be only words has been present all along, and because he needs not to make the discovery: because he declines to recognize it unequivocally, he refuses to make it final. And it is interesting to see that his very refusal here—his declining of the vision—is itself a corroboration and an enactment of it, of its idea that the world is perceivable only as words and fictions: the very inconclusiveness of attitude that prevents his movement beyond words may amount to declaring his allegiance to their primacy and at the same time relieves him from openly defining that primacy, as Kurtz does, in the negative and as a "horror."

Marlow does not take that "last stride," then. "I had been permitted," he tells us, "to draw back my hesitating foot" (72). As for why he is so permitted, it is but one more instance of Marlow refusing to recognize something immediately and directly, of his remaining with avowedly fictional surfaces, of his refusal to end a movement of his mind. This is central to Marlow's character, a character given him by the opening narrator:

> But Marlow was not typical . . . and to him the meaning of an episode was not inside like a kernel but outside, enveloping the tale which brought it out only as a glow brings out a haze, in the likeness of one of these misty halos that sometimes are made visible by the spectral illumination of moonshine. (5)

Every time that Marlow fails to penetrate a surface, every time he refuses to pursue a line, every time he circles, or discounts a pattern that he has also suggested, he is acting out a consistency of attitude discovered in him right at the beginning. His refusals and his hesitations and silences are therefore not to be figured as a failure before anything beyond them and not even as evidence of his visual expectation; for on this side of his mind, it does not appear that they were going anywhere: they have nothing to do with an ultimate or alternative reality—with whether it is there or not there—and so their inability to reach it is not a failure; it is a declining of the entire issue. And this way of imagining persists in Marlow, despite the aspect of inconclusiveness and even of failure that it has on the other side of his mind.

A reader understands this; there is no strain in accepting it. For we see that Marlow must continue as a storyteller. It is what we have expected both of him and of "Heart of Darkness" itself: it is our other, aural, expectation for this story, that as an imaginative journey it is not progressing and that its images are not merely discounted for the sake of ultimate visual force but, again, mused for the sake of musing. The figure of meaning as a halo around the moon, apprehended initially as a challenge to be met or disregarded as a temporary visual snag, no longer seems a passing resistance to some sense at the center of things, some inside reality. The farther Marlow goes, the more this figure comes to dominate the imaginative situation and to secure the expectations that it initially suggested: that Marlow as a storyteller will go on and on; that regardless of his sufferings as an actor in the story and of his judgment there that his experience is a failure, his chief reality is to sit cross-legged on the deck and talk. In this relation to him, we know that neither of us are following from image to image in the narrative in order to get beyond those images or that narrative, but that those images are what we have. We know that we are not following words to get beyond them either, but to another purpose and in another way. We are following a voice, and our purposes are musical. And—still in this relation—we know that it is all we want. In following words in this way, we are reassured that there will never be any cause or need to do anything more, or to go anywhere else, or to stop. Just as sure as Marlow must continue to talk, as sure as the "Nellie" is anchored over a river.

These are the double expectations, then, and the double action, of "Heart of Darkness," and we may see how they both depend on a more general, metaphysical doubleness. On the one hand, we are encouraged to move through an imagined visual series and to discount each subsequent image in that series in favor of some end that will not only dominate them all but will be of a different order of reality, as if beyond imagining itself; this is the visual expectation. On the other hand, we know that this sequence is not progressive at all and that, therefore, each image must not be put behind but held, regarded for itself, there being nothing else; and this is the aural expectation. Both of these attitudes, it may now be clear, have a polarized metaphysical foundation, where language and imagination are opposed to something beyond them. The difference between them, in "Heart of Darkness," is a difference of motive, in that one hopes to get there and the other does not, that one discounts language as fiction in the expectation of truth, and one both accepts and disregards the fictionalness of imagining because the unimaginable truth is just that—ultimately unimaginable.

The very staticness, hesitancy, and involutedness of Marlow's rhetoric—and of Conrad's language more generally—is thus itself a double signal to us: it is both a sign of the imagination refusing to confront some ineffable reality—a kind of productive visual resistance—and a sign that for the imagination there is no such thing, that all we shall ever have is the self-generating voice, musing over and over not some core of reality but of itself.

But now we may begin to see that the expectations and actions that have seemed fundamentally opposed in "Heart of Darkness" are in fact reciprocal with each other and energize each other. We may remember again the dominating image of the halo of meanings around the moon, where the source of illumination is not a source at all and imagining but the reflection of a reflection.[3] This is a pretty, and even a satisfying, illustration that what moves us always is just our continual reflective action. What could be truer? And yet there may be no accepting it. We may be as temperamentally incapable of seeing it as final as Marlow himself is. We must participate in his inconclusiveness and except from the range of such a figure ourselves and our futures. The idea that our light is a matter of continual reflection cannot become our position, for we cannot settle for it. Instead, it functions dynamically to set us going again, after the alternative, the source of the light and of our words. Marlow—looking like a Buddha—says we have only our minds, and we know that, and yet it remains the signal for further action. Conrad's image of the halo around the moon only makes us think again of the sun in its absence.

We may now realize, perhaps, just how settled and assured a narrative "Heart of Darkness" is, for the self-proclaimed fictional-ness of its process is both an end and an openness, a self-enclosure and a self-extension. Its repeating image of language's reflexive energy, of its self-consistency and self-fertilization, is unassailable as a metaphysic and aesthetically enabling, since it tells us that the imagination is all that the imagination ever needs. And yet at the same time, the conception of the imagination feeding like the worm on its own tail functions also as a signal for further inquiry and action, encouraging us to imagine, by opposition, some extra-verbal or unverbal truth beyond the imagination's circling.

So that the appropriate metaphor for this fiction's process is not that of a conflict between opposed attitudes nor even of an alter-nation between them so much as a flow from one to the other. This, perhaps, is why as "Heart of Darkness" approaches its actual end, its narrative is dominated more and more by the image of continuity upon which it is initially founded—as a story told not only both on and about a river but right over a swing of the tide that, of course, is missed: "We have lost the first of the ebb" (79). No first and no last either: only the imagination's continuous motion.

But this continuity has its price. Much earlier I suggested that an aural imaginative attitude takes for granted that what it perceives is fiction, and we may now see that aural perception is fictional perception, which attributes to images a substantialness that they have only because they are not subject to visual-realistic pressure and extension. But whereas this is an unquestionable aesthetic bonus that proceeds from a discounting of the visual and realistic for the aural and fictional, in "Heart of Darkness," it is dramatized as a process that involves an agonizing conversion for Marlow, and perhaps for Conrad himself. And there was nothing permanent about it: Marlow would go on, like Conrad, first discounting words in favor of reality, and then reality in favor of words, from eye to ear and back, from a love of truth to a love of fiction; and frequently these conversions would comprise the dramatic matter of his narratives. Marlow's ultimate presence in this story is as a voice and a storyteller—and a more general consideration of Conrad's rhetorical processes would indicate that the same was true of the author himself throughout his stories—and thus we may remark the settlement of story and narrator and author. But the image of Marlow sitting cross-legged and sallow on the deck is not an altogether happy one, especially when one considers what he had to do to get there.

In Conrad's friend Stephen Crane, however, we may observe a mixture of motives even more strained and balanced. Crane may be technically the most interesting of American fiction writers; certainly he is the most problematic. His sentences tend to be—surely in contrast with Conrad's—relatively short. More important, his characteristic rhetorical units—his grammatical clusters—are short as well. And at the same time, the sense of his prose is to a high degree perceptual: it treats explicitly of sights, sounds, and feelings or of the circumstances that might yield such perceptions. Even without this last characteristic, this rhetorical pattern is visual. The shorter verbal clusters are both associated with the general language of sensuous fact and encourage, or necessitate, a reader's moving over them rapidly and treating them as progressive sequences of perceived images. They create the commonest rhythm of realism.

But within that rhythm there can be decidedly unvisual and unrealistic effects. The most frequent one occurs when the actual language that fills the rhythm or occurs in the visual sequence is not realistic at all, but stiff, abstract, formulaic, and literary—language that calls attention both to its wordiness and to the narrator who is using it:

As it occurred to him, he roared menacing *information.*

The only sounds were his terrible *invitations.*

The man called to the sky. *There were no attractions.*

Instances like this, where the deviation from the visual depends upon the abstractness of a single word or a small group of words, may simply create through resistance a stronger visual effect—that is, a reader will meet the words that I have emphasized here as challenges to his translative power and will immediately work them into their respective sequences. The effect is of a realism heightened by a perverseness, by a stiff and impersonal humor; but there is no real change in the fiction's apparent motives.

But there are also situations in Crane where the visual reality of the story is more actively discounted:

> A singular disadvantage of the sea lies in the fact that after successfully surmounting one wave you discover that there is another behind it just as important and just as nervously anxious to do something effective in the way of swamping boats. In a ten-foot dingey one can get an idea of the resources of the sea in the line of waves that is not probable to the average experience, which is never at sea in a dingey.[4]

Though this language makes a claim for realism, it is not, itself, Crane's realistic rhythm; it is hard to say what it is. Its rhetorical effects are complex and shifting, from mock-academic stiffness ("a singular disadvantage") to waggish delicacy ("nervously anxious to do something effective") to a strung out and apparently simple-minded repetitiveness whose core is tough contempt and which was one of the tones that Hemingway might have taken from Crane. But whatever more or other one could say about these effects, one thing is clear: they all depend upon the language's being recognized as language, as one way or another of talking. All depend upon the story's being treated, for the moment, as fiction.

A few sentences later, the narrator says, "Viewed from a balcony, the whole thing would doubtlessly have been weirdly picturesque. But the men in the boat had no time to see it . . ." No, but the narrator does; and that is exactly what he does, part of the time; he views it all "from a balcony." He knows, to be sure, where the men in the boat are, and he can see their experience as they do, but, too, he is always adopting the balcony view.

One might characterize this narrative fluctuation in Crane in terms of spatial metaphor and perspective. Sometimes, then, he would be close to the men, sometimes distant. Or, and this is somewhat less awkward, one might put it in terms of how narrative energy is directed—either channeled toward and disappearing into the story's surface to establish that surface, or directed elsewhere, anywhere but at the men and boat and waves. The simplest way to define the difference in these narrative attitudes, however, is to consider that the "balcony" here is a balcony at a theater, and the "view" from it one that treats the experience of the story as fiction and that allows, therefore, for the "picturesque."

It is typical of Crane, however, that after adopting and then acknowledging—though hypothetically—this balcony view, he immediately, urgently, and gruffly shifts rhetorical gears: "But the men in the boat had no time to see it . . ." And this is not merely a return to a more visual and sequential mode, but a return that makes the previous, aural-fictional attitude appear as a betrayal of trust, so that the return to realistic verbal process is made to seem an act of fidelity to the men, to life, and so on.

It is no wonder that Crane and Conrad hit it off, and it is hard to say how interestingly their relation would have developed if Crane had stayed home more and lived longer. For the double mindedness of Crane is the same as we have observed in Conrad. What is most remarkable about both is not their complex of commitments to narrative as both realistic sequence and fictional arrangement, but the fact that in both of them this doubleness is felt as conflicting moral allegiances. It is not simply that they entertain or acknowledge two sets of technical possibilities or even two opposed artistic motives: but, from one side or the other, either words are bad and action good or vice-versa, and it should go without saying here that "action" entails the adoption of the verbal processes I have associated with the visual motive.

Conrad is the more explicit about the dichotomy in question, so much so that it becomes through his fiction a matter of stock phrases and oppositions: "words" as the "great foes of reality"; "land-life" (civilization, politics, complications, words) versus "sea-life" (primitiveness, obedience to a code, simplicity, unspoken feelings, fidelities, and actions); and, of course, the pervasive notion that action and imagination are radically and tragically opposed in men's lives. This, as I have suggested, is what much of Conrad's fiction is dramatically about, so it is quite clear that the choice between fictional techniques was at times much more than that. But ultimately Conrad is a writer, or a writer's writer. Ultimately, this choice has been dramatized and utilized in his work and imagination so long that it becomes fiction itself. And ultimately he discovers that he has always liked the imaginative conditions of words and fiction better than that of their opposites.[5]

With Stephen Crane this does not seem to be so. Indeed, the exaggeratedness of the difference between the rhetoric of realism and the rhetoric of fiction in his work suggests that he preferred a more tensed and embattled imaginative situation. When he is literary and aural, when his narrative and narrator demand our attention, he is frequently so almost in a burlesque way. And by the same token, the return to visual sequences is often so decided and vivid as to be melodramatic: "The sun swung steadily up the sky, and they knew it was broad day because the colour of the sea changed from slate to emerald green streaked with amber lights, and the foam was like tumbling snow" (70). The difference between visual and aural motives in him, in other words, often seems especially, even artificially heightened, and as we might suppose, this produces effects in our reading of him that are quite special.

Given that both writers are in some way aural, the experience of listening to Crane is very different from that of listening to Conrad. Conrad's rhythms are longer and softer, and much more harmonious, whereas the sound of Crane's prose is staccato, brittle, and telegraphic. His is a rhythm geared, once more, much more to the visual motive than is Conrad's. As a result, the aural aspect of Crane's fiction is less melodic, often talky rather than musical. Or if one prefers, it is a very different sort of music from Conrad's, and more readers than those who find Conrad monotonal and soporific will find Crane jumpy and irritating.

Thus, many readers will find him discontinuous. One's situation for reading Crane needs to be as undistracting as possible, just because one is continually looking up from the page. The density and energy of his prose often makes one want release from it. And the very shortness of his cadences, the tendency of the prose to break up into the isolated rhetorical units that generate this energy, especially when punctuated by stiff abstractions and wooden usage, makes this release possible. For Crane's relative a-rhythmicness, which inclines us to treat his language as realistic, something to be "seen through" as quickly as possible, becomes much more problematic when the sense of the language does not seem to fit this realistic rhythm:

> The cold passed reluctantly from the earth and the retiring fogs revealed an army stretched out on the hills, resting. As the landscape changed from brown to green the army awakened and began to tremble with eagerness at the noise of rumors. It cast its eyes upon the roads which were growing from long troughs of liquid mud to proper thoroughfares. A river, amber-tinted in the shadow of its banks, purled at the army's feet and at night when the stream had become of a sorrowful blackness one could see, across, the red eye-like gleam of hostile camp-fires set in the low brows of distant hills.
>
> Once, a certain tall soldier developed virtues and went resolutely to wash a shirt. He came flying back from a brook waving his garment, banner-like. He was swelled with a tale he had heard from a reliable friend who had heard it from a truthful cavalryman who had heard it from his trust-worthy brother, one of the orderlies at division headquarters. He adopted the important air of a herald in red and gold. (*The Red Badge of Courage*, 3)

The passage is full of words and phrases that appear to be "sense data," the labels of apparent perceptions arranged—listed—as such: the cold, the fogs, the army, a landscape changing from brown to green, troughs of liquid mud becoming roads, a river, hostile camp-fires, distant hills, and so on. "I can almost see it," one might say. But there is much here that one cannot see and that militates against any more general seeing throughout the passage. The prose is full of metaphors, but not metaphors that reinforce visual energy. They are weak, offhand; indeed, in terms of a strictly visual bias, they are "dead metaphors." But in a more balanced view, perhaps, they are literary conventions or formulas. The army is an animal, stretched out and resting. As day realistically breaks, the army extends its literary life and wakens and trembles. As the troughs of mud, realistically, dry out, they become not roads but more formulas: "proper thoroughfares." The river is seeable too, amber-tinted, a real stream, until at night it becomes a river in an old poem, "of a sorrowful blackness."

This fictional action has the highest frequency that I have seen anywhere of the sort of rhetorical transformation that I call visual-aural oscillation. A reader's action with its visual aspect may be by now more or less obvious, but what aural means in relation to these dead metaphors or formulae should be described briefly. First, rather than moving rapidly off and through the words, and regarding them as transparencies, we stop to notice and regard them as words used as such, words to be recognized from other occasions of words. The visual language here has the real legitimacy of words used to signify, whereas aural language has the literary legitimacy of convention, of special indulgence and circumstance, of fiction. One of our impulses with the latter is to treat it not in relation to imaginary life, but in relation to other literary phrasing. And this is especially true in Crane's prose, because when his language is so regarded, it seems not musically inventive: it seems to want only to repeat, rather stiffly, previous conventions, and thus it is formulaic in the most fundamental sense.

A reader's own oscillation here is thus the more problematic. He may feel that the real energy is feeding into the visual and realistic aspect of the fiction and that the aural formulae are just window dressing. Some students in a literature class—the same ones who drew my attention to Crane's discontinuousness by complaining about how hard it was to hold their eyes to his pages—once told me that he was "poetic." When I pursued the idea, it turned out they meant he was "fake," that the conventional aspect of his language was evidence both of unseriousness or insincerity and of a rather careless attempt to ornament the realistic line. But rather than suppose that Crane is interested in the visual aspect of his fiction and careless about the aural, I would put it that his aural interest—which is evidently not careless just because it is so continual—is in formulas, and his impulse often to stock literary properties as such. This seems to be so not merely from speculation about his motives, but from the consistency with which he gravitates to those literary figures that will surely be recognized, those metaphors that are conventional, even dead.

It should be noted here, however, that the fakeness or deadness of Crane's aural effects, the obviousness of their formulaic aspect, is so striking in part because these effects occur on what is otherwise so visual a ground. Within the drive and color of the fiction's visual impulse, they often seem just visual negatives, impediments to seeing, and so the dominance of the visual brings us to regard them pejoratively. Aural energies always have their inception in visual lapse. What facilitates and extends the conversion, however, what causes us to recognize that we are not just reading failed visual prose but should be attending to aural effects, is the consistency and the energy that we discover from the aural attention. But Crane's own aural consistency is often stock, mechanical, and as if institutionalized, and in contrast with his visual force. If we suppose, because he is so consistent in this, that it is what he wants to do, the effect is then often one of a strange and indeterminate irony in which he sometimes seems to be making fun of his characters, or of his story, or of himself as a writer and sometimes to be deliberately muting and damping his own visual energy or insisting on a faded and archaic literary legitimacy for fictional movements that are in fact strong and novel.

But the essence of the mixture of Crane's motives can be caught precisely in the opening phrase of the second paragraph of *The Red Badge of Courage*: "Once, a certain tall soldier . . ." As Bowers' account of Crane's manuscript alteration suggests,[6] the author's original impulse was to write "Jim Conklin" after "once"— that is, to specify realistically and visually. This he deleted and wrote, above the line, "a certain soldier." That is an aural substitution. "Once, a certain soldier" is manifestly formulaic and fictional; it may sound to us like a tale even if we are not aware that "a certain man" is a stock device of tale telling that goes all the way back to Anglo-Saxon poetry. But then Crane inserted, above "a certain soldier," "tall," as if in an effort to specify again.

It is an interesting sequence of revision in its attempt to deal with an aural-visual or literary-realistic fluctuation. Of course, considering the phrase as a series of changes makes it seem indecisive, though we may feel the indecision natural for a young writer at the beginning of his second novel, which is always a more difficult beginning than that of the first. But some readers may feel such indecision throughout this novel. The pitch or tilt of "once, a certain tall soldier" is aural rather than visual, and so its effect is relatively smooth, especially since it is a beginning formula occurring right where we would expect it. Later, however, we discover that Crane continues to gravitate consistently to such formulas though in the midst of dense visual variation and specification. Though we may come to see and know Henry Fleming very well, for instance, he remains, to the narrator, "the youth," as Conklin, no matter how present to us, remains "the tall soldier," and another "the tattered soldier," and "the loud soldier," and so on. At the very least, this sets up a visual resistance or distancing, and often the result is ironic, for irony is a form of visual resistance, and this irony is most often directed at the hero:

> A little panic-fear grew in his mind. As his imagination went forward to a fight, he saw hideous possibilities. He contemplated the lurking menaces of the future and failed in an effort to see himself standing stoutly in the midst of them. He re-called his visions of broken-bladed glory but, in the shadow of the impending tumult, he suspected them to be impossible pictures.
>
> He sprang from the bunk and began to pace nervously to and fro. "Good Lord, what's the matter with me," he said aloud.
>
> He felt that in this crisis his laws of life were useless. Whatever he had learned of himself was here of no avail. He was an unknown quantity. He saw that he would again be obliged to experiment as he had in early youth. He must accumulate information of himself and, meanwhile, he resolved to remain close upon his guard lest those qualities of which he knew nothing should everlastingly disgrace him. "Good Lord," he repeated in dismay. (10)

"Hideous possibilities," "lurking menaces," "standing stoutly," "broken-bladed glory," and many other phrases are obviously conventional and fictitious, but they are connected to Henry's naive imagination and so are opposed to the impending realities of war and fear and heroism that the narrative will develop. As images, they are similar to Lord Jim's heroic derivations from "light literature," and they function in the narrative in the same way: it is their dramatic and ironic disintegration that drives the story. Crane, like Conrad, employs this tension between fiction and reality, between heroic phrasing and unheroic facts, as the definition of his main character's consciousness and the subject of his story. But as every reader of *Lord Jim* knows, there are times when Marlow sounds just like Jim; and so too the narrator of *Red Badge* at times employs conventional and formulaic language that is not dramatically restricted to his character's imagination, but comes apparently straight from the narrative source—even as he does here with language perhaps less melodramatic than that we might associate with Henry, but nonetheless conventional enough: "impending tumult," "impossible pictures," "laws of life," "obliged to experiment," and so on. At such moments, we may also feel irony, but it will be an irony much less pointed. It will not say to us, "Hear how Henry talks about this; soon he will know better," but, "Listen to how the story sounds." The obvious fictional quality of the narrative at these points is not dramatically—that is, visually—functional, and the effect of this obvious tale telling in the midst of the action is most curious.

For most of the narrative of *Red Badge*, however, the narrative perspective is so close to the "youth," to Fleming's own imagination, that exploded and grandiloquent phrasing resonates ironically with his altering character, and we shall be inclined to feel it explained and justified dramatically. But such an attitude places great emphasis on where the story goes and how the youth ends up. And that is somewhat difficult to say:

> For a time, this pursuing recollection of the tattered man took all elation from the youth's veins. He saw his vivid error and he was afraid that it would stand before him all of his life. He took no share in the chatter of his comrades, nor did he look at them or know them, save when he felt sudden suspicion that they were seeing his thoughts and scrutinizing each detail of the scene with the tattered soldier.

Yet gradually he mustered force to put the sin at a distance. And at last his eyes seemed to open to some new ways. He found that he could look back upon the brass and bombast of his earlier gospels and see them truly. He was gleeful when he discovered that he now despised them.

With this conviction came a store of assurance. He felt a quiet man-hood, non-assertive but of sturdy and strong blood. He knew that he would no more quail before his guides wherever they should point. He had been to touch the great death and found that, after all, it was but the great death. He was a man.

So it came to pass that as he trudged from the place of blood and wrath, his soul changed. He came from hot-ploughshares to prospects of clover tranquility and it was as if hot-ploughshares were not. Scars faded as flowers.

It rained. The procession of weary soldiers became a bedraggled train, despondent and muttering, marching with churning effort, in a trough of liquid brown mud under a low, wretched sky. Yet the youth smiled, for he saw that the world was a world for him though many discovered it to be made of oaths and walking-sticks. He had rid himself of the red sickness of battle. The sultry night-mare was in the past. He had been an animal blistered and sweating in the heat and pain of war. He turned now with a lover's thirst, to images of tranquil skies, fresh meadows, cool brooks; an existence of soft and eternal peace.

Over the river a golden ray of sun came through the hosts of leaden rain clouds. (135)

When Henry manages to "put the sin at a distance," and open his eyes "to some new ways," we may disregard the fact that he has had this sort of conversion before and credit this last one. Even though his history suggests the possibility of further fluctuations, we may suppose that this last change is decisive and gives the dramatic irony of the narrative its point and leverage. But even if Henry really does now "despise," the "brass and bombast of his earlier gospels," they continue in the narrative. Those most closely associated with him seem now perhaps less assertive—as the nar-rator declares—but they nonetheless remain conventional heroic formulas: "sturdy and strong blood," "the great death," "he was a man."

Even supposing that Fleming's last conversion has been more substantial to us than I really think it can be, what do we make of the recitation of formulas that follows? The closing lines of the narrative are so dense with literary conventions that Crane seemingly cannot include enough of them to satisfy himself. But what is most interesting is that while all of them sound like time-honored stock phrases, many of them are unrecognizable, as the shift from "hot-ploughshares"—which is familiar enough—to "clover tranquility"—which is not—manifests. What we have here is the rhythm of convention embedded in unconventional images. "Scars faded as flowers" sounds like something storytellers have known and said time and again, but it is not. It has the tone and density of a well-known aphorism, but its meaning is not merely not assumable but indecipherable. And this should indicate that throughout the narrative of *Red Badge* we may have been mistaking the form of stock phrases for the fact, that at least part of the time what sounded like familiar literary convention—which "red sickness of battle," "sultry night-mare," "tranquil skies," and so on are—were strange expressions like "made of oaths and walking-sticks."[7]

What this suggests is that Crane is pressing for this rhythm continually, whether he has an actual formula to fit or not, and plugging fresh and various images into the aphoristic cadence. It is not so remarkable that he is striving for a "sound" of some sort; most fiction writers do, though usually not side by side with such strenuous visual commitment. But it is remarkable that in *The Red Badge of Courage* he tries so consistently for this same sound, this archaic, worn, overfamiliar sound that makes the story sound old even when it is so new and various as to be unintelligible.

No writer is quite so frustrating as Crane, therefore, when one is looking, as he may be at the end of this narrative, for the ultimate sense of it all. For what is the visual sense of the last line? Is that a "partly sunny" or a "partly cloudy" image? The doubleness of its meaning is belied and smoothed by its formulaic glibness. One may say, of course, that it is just a conventional tag, just a standard way of ending a story; so long as one remembers that Crane has been doing this all along, reaching for this sort of rhythm all along, often in the midst of rapid and problematic sequence, in the midst of realistic variation where the pressure of intelligibility was very nearly as great as it is here at the end. There has never been a writer whose motives seemed more divided.

But to say that we are frustrated in reading Crane does not begin to cover the range of potential response to his fiction, especially his later, shorter fiction. There the visual energy of his prose is, if anything, even more pronounced. It depends less upon simple vividness and rapid sequence than it does in *Red Badge*, though Crane is still at times strikingly, even melodramatically, imagistic. But his later stories are not so regularly paced. The overall rhythm of his fiction becomes less even and capable of creating extraordinary tension and momentum, extraordinary visual pressure. His essential imaginative process becomes, even more emphatically, that of realism; something seems always *happening* in Crane's best stories, no matter what the narrator is saying.

What that narrator characteristically does say, furthermore, has also developed away from *The Red Badge of Courage*. The habitual gravitation to particular stock phrases and aphoristic formulas in the book later flexes. But Crane continues to use abstract and formal and even polite language as if it had the obvious weight of familiar convention. He drops such phrases into his story like stones. To cover a dramatic moment in "The Blue Hotel," for instance, when the relation between Johnny and the cowboy and the Easterner on the one hand and the Swede on the other is soured and brittle and full of tension, the narrator says, "Men by this time had begun to look at him askance, as if they wished to inquire what ailed him" (*Works*, V, 145). The anonymous "men," where the drama demands more specification, is oddly general and removed. And the entire middle section of the sentence is impossibly, stiffly polite and talky, given the situation, and in contrast to the harshly colloquial "what ailed him." But we may feel that we know what is going on here in spite of language that is blatantly inappropriate to those goings on. This, again, is a visual insistence founded upon visual resistance: the very blankness of the language in relation to the dramatic situation is felt as a challenge and transforms a dead end into an access. Such an effect can be seen more simply at another moment, when the story erupts around the card table, and Johnny and the drunken Swede will now have to fight: "Then suddenly there was a great cessation" (157). A reader may very well read right through "cessation," just as if it were a more active and appropriate word. But its inappropriateness may create a vacancy in the sequence: we know that something—some sort of pause or silence—has suddenly occurred, but what, exactly? The visual energy created by such resistance seems greater than what would be generated through more obviously visual specification: something mysterious and awful may be happening in "cessation"; we cannot be sure.

Similarly, when Crane takes his more formulaic tone and says of the Swede, "In his eyes was the dying swan look," the visual effect is out of all proportion to the flat, worn sentimentality of the phrase. The Swede's look, because described so unacceptably, seems something beyond description, past description, and real. This effect is one in which visual energy is increased by visual lapses, by shifts to language whose motive is in some way aural. It arises from treating the aural language as visual. And this happens just because the visual force of Crane's narratives is elsewhere so pronounced, not only in his consistently realistic rhythm but in moments that are themselves amazing in their purely visual effects. In other words, if one were to argue the issue, and ask how we know something is going on at aural moments—at moments when the language, whatever else it is doing, is not appropriate to the drama and sequence—we might say that we know because just a moment or a page before something did go on, something like this:

> The dog of the bar-keeper of the Weary Gentleman saloon had not appreciated the advance of events. He yet lay dozing in front of his master's door. At sight of the dog, the man paused and raised his revolver humorously. At sight of the man, the dog sprang up and walked diagonally away, with a sullen head and growling. The man yelled, and the dog broke into a gallop. As it was about to enter an alley, there was a lound noise, a whistling, and something spat the ground directly before it. The dog screamed, and, wheeling

in terror, galloped headlong in a new direction. Again there was a noise, a whistling, and sand was kicked viciously before it. Fear-stricken, the dog turned and flurried like an animal in a pen. The man stood laughing, his weapons at his hips. (117)

This is a fine example of pure visual sequence, with Crane using balanced constructions and repetitions to increase, gradually and wonderfully, the feeling of variation and movement until, at its climax, all the rhetorical symmetry breaks down into a phrase absolutely brilliant in its freshness and density: "the dog flurried like an animal in a pen."

Another such moment, no more intensely vivid but even more dramatic, occurs in "The Blue Hotel," when Scully, who is almost hysterical with his hotelkeeper's fear and pity, cajoles and then forces the Swede to drink with him, and the Swede—who is hysterically afraid for his life and convinced that he is about to be poisoned—terrifiedly accepts: "The Swede laughed wildly. He grabbed the bottle, put it to his mouth, and as his lips curled absurdly around the opening and his throat worked, he kept his glance burning with hatred upon the old man's face" (151). Prose as electric as this belittles one's account of it: it seems a poor thing to say that sequential variation makes the effect here, but that is what happens. First the discrepancy between the Swede's fear and his laugh, then the repulsive and greedy masochism of his image as he drinks, then the violence of his "glance burning with hatred" against the softer, pathetic "old man's face"—the sequence is disparate and terrifically fast, and so it seems complex almost to absurdity and yet inexorably unified and convincing. It is as if we see right through a sequence of words to an image too faceted and simultaneous for words.

Crane's visual capacity is always, sooner or later, evident, and it is this capacity that creates a permanent field of energy with which his unvisual language resonates, to generate realism by resistance. But this describes only his visual aspect, for while his odd and inappropriate narrative rhetoric may be functioning in concert with visual momentum, it has also an action of its own:

But still there was no offer of fight. The name of Jack Potter, his ancient antagonist, entered his mind, and he concluded that it would be a glad thing if he should go to Potter's house and by bombardment induce him to come out and fight. He moved in the direction of his desire, chanting Apache scalp-music. (118)

Scratchy Wilson, in a drunken fit both of absurd rage and of sinister playfulness, is moving toward the town marshal's house, and the narrative is tending toward its climax. But against the single-mindedness of this action, the narrative rhetoric is at constant variance while varying also within itself. "Ancient antagonist" is heroic formula; "concluded" far too rational an image; "a glad thing" is that peculiarly, carelessly "poetic" phrasing that seems original to Crane; "by bombardment induce" a grotesque mix of inflated, storybook brutality and delicacy; and "chanting Apache scalp-music" probably a melodramatic joke but (is there such as thing as "scalp-music" among the Apaches?) possibly quite accurate and realistic.

Wilson's motion, on the visual side, thus becomes something erratic and mysterious, submerged and hidden beneath the narrative. But the very separateness of the phrasing from the dramatic sequence, its obvious aspect as language, demands attention apart from our visual attention to the story's movement. This is Crane's aural aspect as such, and our response to it is to consider his phrasing not as inappropriate to something else but in terms of its own, interior, word-to-word relation, to hear its quality as a voice. From that consideration, however, comes no consistency.

Like the voice of *Red Badge*, this one is formulaic, but it is also inflationary, abstract, and burlesque. And such a mix is general in Crane's most successful fiction. The diction of his narratives is multiple, with no sense that any single way of talking is more committed or acceptable than any other. This effect is insured, not only by the constant variation of his voice, but also by the fact that there is usually something wrong with the individual, discrete vocabularies that it shifts into. These vocabularies continue to be as stock as possible; their abstractions are stiff and unwieldy; their specific ironies crude; and their more elaborate metaphors strained and conceited. Against the linear visual energy of his stories, and against the obvious and flexible aural energy that ranges through these vocabularies, the vocabularies themselves are remarkably flat and unattractive. Crane's narrators thus seem both dutiful and careless. Their insistence on their aural range is strong and even automatic. But both the fixed pace of that insistence and the quality of what they range through suggests carelessness or, more accurately, a curious neutrality. In visual terms, this neutrality seems often not even to recognize the story, not to know who or what is going on there: "He resembled a badly frightened man" (144). In that way it makes for provocative visual effects. But its aural effect is to suggest a narrative presence immediate and committed in its attention but remote and neutral in the specific realizations of that attention. In Crane one thus hears a "voice" that is voiceless, whose only constant is its continual and almost random motion. That motion bespeaks its engagement, both with the ongoing narrative sequence and with the reader to whom its variegated phrases are addressed. But in its flighty, whimsical neutrality, in its range so unpredictable as to seem careless, it seems not there at all, not an authorial presence but an invisible writing machine.

The assurance that one feels in aural fiction generally, in other words, is only half-felt in Crane. All that is assured is his energy, while the erratic variations of phrase that it produces only rarely knit together in any music that we might recognize. He is there, using words at us, and in the aural aspect calling attention to the fact that he is doing so, but the sound he makes is hard to hear. Crane's rhetoric is aural, then, only because so much of his imaginative action seems separate from the visual sequence and so makes us feel his authorial presence apart from his narrative. And we may take pleasure in the very thing that makes that presence so difficult to characterize: its various life, its mechanical insistence upon its own range and freedom. At the same time, however, this freedom issues back into standard verbal mechanisms, and so its variation—both within itself and in general relation to narrative sequence—will be felt as ironic. Crane's neutrality may then seem cold and bitter, a chancy and undifferentiated irony that, whatever its occasional effects, cannot be pleasing for long—just because it is demonstrably endless—and a reader may be quickly saturated with it and begin not to care whom the joke is on. This, in combination with Crane's terrific realistic energies and tensions, make it hard, once more, to read him at any length. Perhaps it is why we have so much ignored him.

It is, at any rate, where he and Conrad diverge, permanently. For despite the doubleness of his own imagination and the difficulty of choice within it, Conrad seems to settle—even as Marlow is carried out of the Congo on his back—for being a writer, for the self-generative action and assured commitment of voice associated with the aural motive. But in Crane we feel an imagination perhaps as great as Conrad's that for all its intensity and presence will not settle for or into a voice, that in its perpetual variety yields a flatness. Crane writes like a man of wonderful imaginative power who hates words. But let it be said also that many writers have done that, and among them, he is the best.

From what one hears about him, Hemingway—in another case of mixed fictional motives—would seem to have even less love for words than Stephen Crane. Surely he is thought to be more of a realist. But side-by-side consideration of these two writers suggests otherwise. Hemingway's rhetoric is apparently more economical than Crane's, and from that it is often inferred that it is realistic. And though—contrary to their reputation—Hemingway's sentences are not usually short, not nearly so much so as Crane's, his grammar looks like the grammar of realism because it is so simple. It is composed of relatively short and discrete rhetorical units linked by coordinating conjunctions, and thus it approaches the list arrangement that is realistic fiction's simplest and most fundamental pattern.

But we have seen that Hemingway does not always use that sort of grammar for purposes of sequential variation, but for its opposite—repetition. We have also seen that his characteristic prose rhythms tend not to be short and brittle, as Crane's are, but long and continuous, even overextended. And these aspects of his fiction do not contribute to his realism at all. The trouble here with Hemingway and with all fiction writers of mixed motives, however, is that they require readers whose motives are also not only mixed but also more or less balanced. A reader with a strong visual bias, for instance—and these are the readers that we most often hear from—will lament Hemingway's chanting repetitions and rhythms as visual lapses, as a failure and even a parody of his realistic powers.

Still, it should be admitted that some of the pressure to consider Hemingway a realist, dominantly interested in composing sequences that can be seen through, has seemed to come from the writer himself:

> Some days it went so well that you could make the country so that you could walk into it through the timber to come out into the clearing and work up onto the high ground and see the hills beyond the arm of the lake. A pencil-lead might break off in the conical nose of the pencil sharpener and you would use the small blade of the pen knife to clear it or else sharpen the pencil carefully with the sharp blade and then slip your arm through the sweat-salted leather of your pack strap to lift the pack again, get the other arm through and feel the weight settle on your back and feel the pine needles under your moccasins as you started down for the lake.[8]

This passage, with others like it, could easily be taken as evidence at least of Hemingway's full intention to make his fiction transparent, a window through which we might see into other worlds. But there are problems with such a reading. For one, he is describing here the experience of the writer and insisting that, for a writer, composing an experience can be indistinguishable from having it. The claim could be made for a reader as well, of course, but there is a self-centered and exclusive tone here that reduces that possibility. There is no doubt that the "you" of the passage means "I" and that the experience that Hemingway is having here is a remembered one of his own. This works in at least two ways: it lessens any relevance this image might have to the interrelation of fiction and life and reader, and it increases the hopeful nostalgia, the fairy-tale quality of the entire imaginative movement. So the act of imagination described here seems both exclusive and magically easy: Hemingway himself moves from writing something to having the experience of it just like that and no means are necessary, except that "it" "go well." Both aspects of the situation leave the reader's imagination out, and though this moment is charming, a good deal of its charm springs from the fact that, in terms of our own experience, we don't believe it for a minute.

Put another way, Hemingway in this passage expects more than seems reasonable for our reading. If we want to take such a passage as evidence of his interest in or production of realistic fiction, we have to ignore the insistent and perhaps isolated ambitiousness of it and take its nostalgic excess as a forgivable figure for what is in fact a more balanced attitude. But Hemingway's attitude at other moments is not balanced either. When he talks about the process and product of his writing, the situation sounds not so much like any two-way relation between words and reality, or a three-way relation in which a reader might somehow see through the Hemingway glass to an experience, but like magic, like a peremptory and exclusive act of transformation: "From things that have happened and from things as they exist and from all the things that you know and all those that you cannot know, you make something through your invention that is not a representation but a whole new thing truer than any thing true and alive."[9]

"Not a representation but a whole new thing": that does not sound like a writer interested in the clearest image of the way things are. But it is simply the declaration of an intention, and so we may turn to the fiction itself: "Nick looked down into the clear, brown water, colored from the pebbly bottom, and watched the trout keeping themselves steady in the current with wavering fins. As he watched them they changed their positions by quick angles, only to hold steady in the fast water again. Nick watched them a long time."[10] As we try to account for the effect or to describe the action of this movement, it may be that the familiar lines about Hemingway will reappear: the sentences—at least some of them—are shorter than they might be, and the language most surely is plainer, monosyllabic—as if undecorated and even unformed in any literary way. These rhetorical characteristics may persuade us that what we are reading is not rhetoric at all. There is so little in this language of what we normally consider literary feature and convention that we may suppose that it is, indeed, ordinary language, language that works as efficiently as possible to signal things and action. And for a while, the process of this passage seems to correspond to such an assessment. The writing keeps tendering new and different items: the brown water, the bottom, the trout, their wavering fins. This variation among images keeps us busy both in trying to read through noun clusters so discrete that they are taken as signs and in trying to accumulate them as we move on, if not to some composite meaning then at least to a composite image, as of the scene itself. The continuance and energy of this visual action depends upon what we don't know, upon the continuing novelty of the sequence. Our feeling that the movement of this passage is realistic depends upon its extending its variousness even as it accumulates, upon its "quick angles." But such variousness is not all there is to Nick and the trout:

> Nick watched them a long time.
> He watched them holding themselves with their noses into the current, many trout in deep, fast moving water, slightly distorted as he watched far down through the glassy convex surface of the pool, its surface pushing and swelling smooth against the resistance of the log-driven piles of the bridge. At the bottom of the pool were the big trout. Nick did not see them at first. Then he saw them at the bottom of the pool, big trout looking to hold themselves on the gravel bottom in a varying mist of gravel and sand, raised in spurts by the current.

For it is only at the beginning that the prose maintains its "quick angles." With the next paragraph it begins to repeat: "he watched" again; and then "many trout," and "many" does not keep it from being "trout" again; nor does "deep, fast moving water" refigure "fast water." Then, after another "he watched," there is a change: "down through the glassy convex surface of the pool." But what follows—"its surface pushing and swelling smooth against the resistance of the log-driven piles of the bridge"—seems a way of saying that over again. And next is the last new item: "At the bottom of the pool were the big trout." That is the end of the progress and sequence. We can see how it has gradually diminished, and now it recycles insistently: "Nick did not *see them* at first. Then he *saw them* at the *bottom of the pool, big trout* looking to *hold themselves* on the *gravel bottom* in a varying mist of *gravel* and *sand*, raised in spurts by the *current*." I have italicized the repeating parts here to show that as they begin to dominate rhythmically, whatever lies between them seems to fall away. The tendency of these sentences is to elide. We find ourselves reading not the prose as written but "at the bottom of the pool were the big trout Nick did not see them . . . saw them . . . bottom of the pool, big trout . . . hold themselves . . . gravel bottom . . . gravel . . . current." This is a very different sort of fullness from that with which we began here. Before, the scene seemed visually full because of quick changes and onward motion, but by the end its progress has ceased, and it is full in its self-restriction to its preestablished properties, full in its self-unification. This amounts to an imaginative change of state. We begin by encountering different images in a various line; we end by muttering over images that have somehow become all one: "Trout trout trout trout trout."

Such a feeling of chanting, hypnotic unification is frequent in Hemingway, and it invariably results when insistent variation diminishes, just as insistently, into forms, both imagistic and rhythmic, of repetition, when linear sequence returns on itself. A reader's sense that the images of the fictional world are thus reducing arises from this felt reduction of the fiction's range or, to put it more accurately, from a fictional change of shape.

For the dominating illusion of visual sequences is that we can follow them right off the page and into a new reality. As we both move over and accumulate the disparate images of such sequences, seeing through them as we go, we expect also to do the same with the final, composite image, and what we shall see through that, we may suppose, is not merely the dim shapes of trout and stream and man but some figure that comprehends them all—one large image, a covering idea even, even an entire world. The crucial, expected value of linear visual sequence resides in its presumed extendableness, past the last word of any narrative, right on into life.

The effect of such a line's turning back on itself is a denial of such extendability and a reforming of fictional shape toward self-enclosure and self-referentialness, and the sort of meaning and signification and relevance that depends upon imaginative lineation lapses. For readers of pronounced visual bias, this will amount to literary failure. It would seem, furthermore, that for any reader one sort of imaginative expectation has failed, since the promise of realism has been revoked. But most, I think, will not be disappointed by this change of fictional form that is the visual-aural conversion: quite the contrary. For though the realistic tendencies and extensions are lost in the process, a reader may not feel that he has had to give anything up.

For when a sequence begins to repeat and circle, though the fictional line has been lost, it is not so obvious that the elements composing it have been lost. The images are still there, after all; indeed, they are all the more there because they are repeated and affirmed. Our perception of them is no longer strained by onward motion, but more dwelling and assured. Their relation is no longer to anything beyond or outside them, but only to each other; we are not going anywhere with them now, and that absence of inclination makes for a perceptual freedom, within the fiction's self-constructed enclosure, that increases rather than diminishes the apparent clarity of the images.

We have seen this perceptual effect most strikingly in Stevens' poetry. It is what I mean by "aural perception," and I shall consider it more generally in the next chapter. But at this point we may make a connection between our noticing this change in fictional shape—from extension to enclosure—and the more obviously aural phenomenon of feeling a narrator's presence and hearing his voice. For to perceive linear sequence in fiction, or to treat fiction as such sequence, requires that we feel our own imaginative action to be crucial and central as we read. The only voice we hear in such action is our own. In the effects of repetition, however, we begin to hear some other voice and feel another's action. Images in their repeating reveal themselves as artifice, implying their artificer beyond us: and rhythms in their self-insistence and establishment begin to be heard as something we ourselves are not generating. At that point, we may be said to be listening rather than seeing, to be passive rather than active. But what "passive" means here is not that we are no longer doing anything, not that we do not see and know, but that such perception takes place only within the range of the fiction's restraining form and is not extended elsewhere. Aural perception, then, occurs within a self-encircling range; it is restricted by that range, but it is also intensified and secured by it. And this recognition of imaginative enclosure is what we mean when we say or feel in reading fiction that we are hearing a voice, when we therefore relinquish our imaginative powers to an operation only within the range of that voice, as we so often do in music.

Perception of all kinds continues with the fictional conversion to the aural. It is no longer realistic or even intelligible in that it has given up connecting the world of the fiction with other worlds or extending it into them, but it may therefore seem more substantial and more clear than realistic vision. For this reason, we generally do not resist visual-aural conversion or oscillation. For the same reason, we sometimes even confuse one condition with the other. A fictional world may seem—because of its aural process— so dense, so assured and there, that its very substance seems, as we have seen in "Heart of Darkness," forcing, seems to demand that it be taken somewhere, used somehow. And we may want to take this sort of action even though such use or relation appears otherwise at least inappropriate and perhaps impossible, so strongly do we mistake the power of aural effects for realism. This is precisely the kind of mistake that criticism has tended to make with Hemingway, attributing what are predominately aural effects to exclusively visual causes and sources. In Hemingway, this mistake occurs, usually, when "voice" is confused with "character."

Frederick Henry sees a friend die:

> I had liked him as well as any one I ever knew. I had his papers in my pocket and would write to his family. Ahead across the fields was a farmhouse. There were trees around it and the farm buildings were built against the house. There was a balcony along the second floor held up by columns.[11]

There is only one sentence here that seems a response to Aymo's death, and then the narrator's vision forces away, on "across the fields," and absorbs itself in the detail of the farmhouse. A reader may know what this is about—anything to look at, or talk about, will do, so long as it is not Aymo lying there in the mud. Whatever will best restrict or deflect his vision is what Henry wants. The dead man must not be seen. As the narrator narrows his range or distracts his sight, however, he widens and directs ours. We know that those phrases about the farmhouse are really a response to Aymo's death, an unbearably strong response, though what they say is not clear.

The adjustment that we make here, and that Hemingway at such times encourages us to make, is so easy and reasonable that we may come, as we read him, to think of it as the main thing, something that we shall always have and something our experience of his writing requires. The stylized action of his fiction may then seem to depend always on a particular dramatized psychology—the character or character-narrator, under pressure, reducing his ground in self-protection, ritualizing his experience and so inversely marking all that lies beyond it. This is obviously a perfect example of the visual energy that arises from visual resistance. The energy with which we see through a character and what he does or says, at such moments, is proportional to the evident impediments to vision that his action and speech create. The more stiffly and narrowly he moves, the more brusquely and woodenly he speaks, the more we seem to see and hear through and beyond him. This dynamic is probably the source of the notion that Hemingway's prose is always "understated."

But the model of his prose as visually resistant is not adequate to all of its action, and the basic distinction here is characteristic of visual-aural differences. Visual resistance requires that we discount the character's immediate speech or action so as to look through it. So, for example, when we are moved by the action of Jake Barnes' packing trout religiously row on row in ferns,[12] we can be thinking back to that moment at night alone in his room when he looked in the mirror at his naked body: we can remember that in order to certify our feeling that something is still going on inside Jake later, something that explains the rigidity and narrowness of his action.

An aural response to the same moment would not be conscious of "seeing through"; it would not specify any moment beyond the moment itself, as if just Jake and the trout and the ferns were moving enough. And they are, or they can be. So much so that it is possible to say that our emotion in encountering such passages is ready and direct and that thinking back to Jake's earlier troubles is not so much a way of feeling something as it is of justifying and explaining our feeling to ourselves or to others. One might say that it is an attempt to visualize a musical dynamic in order to trace its power.

Some might argue that such tracing is necessary, that any musical effect in prose is visually resistant and—sooner or later—must be translated to the visual. But I think that aural action in fiction may be so resistant as to prevent visual response—save for a very special sort of such response that I shall consider in the next chapter—and to declare a release from that response. For to treat Nick Adams' or Jake Barnes' cases as psychological, and to see through or around them, is to treat them as cases of "character," whose actions are dominated by some authority—whether of the text as a whole or the reader's action with that text; it is the same thing—beyond them. But suppose one so feels Barnes' presence, for instance, that nothing he does needs to be explained or justified. Suppose that his narrative becomes, as any first person narrative may, autonomous, drawing all our imaginative energy to itself and its moment: "The train started with a jerk, and then ran smoothly, going down grade around the edge of the plateau and out into the fields of grain that blew in the wind on the plain on the way to Tafalla."[13] There is a decided visual effect here; we remember at first that there is a dead man, killed in the festive running of the bulls, in this train, with his widow and his two children, all going home to Tafalla. But that knowledge is not so much the source of the energy of this sentence as its point of departure. What moves us here is not what we are reminded of, as I see it, but what the sentence in its working causes us to forget. For even as this moment is developing it is overextending: "in the wind on the plain on the way." The repeating grammar and rhythm of these phrases generates a feeling of repetitive sense. Each phrase serves the one before it so closely, the sequence from "train" to "Tafalla" is so unbroken, that all of them seem to be included in a unified motion. And thus the sentence breaks its connection with the narrative line; its sequence is transformed into a rhetorical unit and circle into which we may be absorbed.

This is a standard instance of visual-aural conversion. What is important about it for my present purposes is its obvious autonomy: it is unlikely that here we shall be hearing Jake Barnes as a character whose language must be translated or referred to something somewhere else. Our response to the words' circling and unifying here—to their intensified presence as words—amounts not to seeing a character but to hearing a voice. And the voice we hear is not that of a character but that of an author; it is not a voice that we can take action with or upon, but a voice that dominates our imaginations and holds them enclosed in its range. It has ceased to be a first person voice in the sense that we have to or want to translate it: it has become simply the voice of the fiction itself.

But this is a delicate matter, and depending upon our occasional visual-aural bias, we may read the same passage of prose differently. Opposing character to voice is simply a way of establishing the figures of visual and aural processes in critical theory. At times these figures function as isolated and pure models, but more often they mark the ends of a scale along which the prose and its readers slide.

Therefore my concentration on Hemingway's aural aspect more generally may not reflect a balanced view, but a counteremphasis against his visual-realistic reputation. There can be no question of his commitment to sequence as such, to realistic variation in his prose, nor of the frequency with which his fiction works by visual resistance. And, just as evidently, his motives are not merely mixed but—as in Conrad's case—symbiotic. For his simple grammar is the most natural means of sequential variation yet at the same time the weakest grammar, given its liability to visual fault, to obvious repetition and dominating rhythms, and so it is the grammar that most facilitates visual-aural conversion.

Hemingway may be seen, however, to resemble Conrad much more than he does, for instance, Stephen Crane. Like Conrad, his tilt seems always to fiction's musical aspect, though he begins over and over, like Conrad, with the visual. And in comparison to Crane's telegraphic, high frequency, rhetorical oscillations that occur even within single short phrases, Hemingway's seem usually much longer, and his orchestrated units a paragraph or even a page. In this way, his conversions seem far more single-minded and deliberate, and his aural action dominates.

The question that arises most pointedly in Hemingway's fiction, however, of the visual effects of character as opposed to the aural effects of voice, is an interesting one and may be pursued. In the fiction of Faulkner, it is often even harder to tell the difference or to make a choice than in Hemingway, and in certain works this suggests a visual-aural mixing nearer to equilibrium than any we have encountered thus far.

As I Lay Dying, though it does not ultimately produce this equilibrium, dramatizes clearly the poles of visual and aural:

> And so when Cora Tull would tell me I was not a true mother, I would think how words go straight up in a thin line, quick and harmless, and how terribly doing goes along the earth, clinging to it, so that after a while the two lines are too far apart for the same person to straddle from one to the other; and that sin and love and fear are just sounds that people who never sinned nor loved nor feared have for what they never had and cannot have until they forget the words. Like Cora, who could never even cook.[14]

The lines that Addie Bundren lays out here, with words going "straight up" and "doing" "along the earth," have obvious—if for the moment hypothetical—affinity with the dichotomy of aural and visual motives in fiction. We may associate the vertical line of words with the aural dynamic, with a self-insistent verbalness that may suspend narrative movement in favor of more stable and resonant energies and the horizontal line of "doing" with visual sequence and progress. But for Addie the line of words is much the lesser of the two: a "thin line, quick and harmless," as compared to "how terribly doing goes along the earth." This does not merely derive from her antagonism and contempt for Cora Tull's talking. The bias toward doing, or toward visual progress and extension, is nearly general among the character-narrators of *As I Lay Dying*, and in their fictional courses, their words ultimately become their doing, and their independent narrative voices come to be dominated by a narrative momentum that reduces them to characters.

But to begin, we may compare Addie's metaphysics with those of her husband, Anse:

> A-laying there, right up to my door, where every bad luck that comes and goes is bound to find it. I told Addie it want any luck living on a road when it come by here, and she said, for the world like a woman, "Get up and move, then." But I told her it want no luck in it, because the Lord put roads for travelling: why He laid them down flat on the earth. When He aims for something to be always a-moving, He makes it long ways, like a road or a horse or a wagon, but when He aims for something to stay put, He makes it up-and-down ways, like a tree or a man. And so He never aimed for folks to live on a road, because which gets there first, I says, the road or the house? Did you ever know Him to set a road down by a house? I says. No you never, I says, because it's always men cant rest till they gets the house set where everybody that passes in a wagon can spit in the doorway, keeping the folks restless and wanting to get up and go somewheres else when He aimed for them to stay put like a tree or a stand of corn. Because if He'd a aimed for man to be always a-moving and going somewheres else, wouldn't He a put him longways on his belly, like a snake? It stands to reason He would. (34–35)

Anse's road may be taken as a model—though in part a parodic one —for all the roads of *As I Lay Dying*, for the journey to Jefferson, the "terrible doing" of the story itself. But perhaps more interest-

ing is that he imagines the stationary vertical—trees, corn, houses—
as essentially the human province. The general force of his image
is diluted by his own hypochondriac inclination to motionlessness,
but the combination of his conception with Addie's is suggestive,
for it implies that the vertical action of words is, above all, a
personal action, a matter of human presence. But in *As I Lay
Dying*, even as Anse's insistence on his "bad luck" acknowledges,
this presence is anything but stable. Each character's narrative fragments here, his "thin line of words," goes up against the story's
run, and a reader's run with it; and each is bent to the narrative
momentum and carried along on the journey to bury Addie.

Addie's son Jewel is both the primary instrument and the victim
of the story's visual motion. More than any other character, he
presses on to fulfill his mother's wish and to get her rotting corpse
into the ground, sacrificing to that effort even what may be the only
clear sign of his originality and of his special relation to her, his
horse. In this way, he is the most single-minded inheritor of her
realism, her allegiance to doing. But if Jewel is the character who
most extravagantly impels and surrenders to the story, his predica-
ment, ultimately, is general. Each character at last loses freedom,
imaginative and otherwise, to just the degree that he is capable of
it and ambitious for it. All of the Bundrens then, save perhaps Darl,
are tilted by the horizontal stresses of road and river. Cash—the
eldest son, whose leg is broken on the journey—has a practical
solution, at least for his dead mother: he makes her coffin "on the
bevel," to resist the vertical-horizontal stress. But whatever this does
for Addie, it does not help the others. By the end, all of them have
yielded to these stresses and surrendered to appetites and needs, to
realistic progress: Anse goes on to a new set of teeth and a new
wife, Cash to his gramophone, Dewey Dell and Vardaman to a
treat of bananas and the pursuit, respectively, of alleviated preg-
nancy and a toy train—and all of them collaborate in getting Darl
into the madhouse.

That, of course, is the only place for Darl in this fictional world.
Given his continuing insistence on his isolated visionary power, on
his ability to know and to say, that is where the other characters
have to put him. In a world finally so committed to doing, to

sequence and its extension, one either goes along and becomes a character in it, or one becomes—or is ruled—insane. Darl is first and last the true voice and narrator of *As I Lay Dying*. Though ultimately the story's movement dominates him, by force, along with the rest, from time to time he stills the savage forward energy of the narrative and turns its continuity into something else:

> "Come here, sir," Jewel says. He moves. Moving that quick his coat, bunching, tongues swirling like so many flames. With tossing mane and tail and rolling eye the horse makes another short curvetting rush and stops again, feet bunched, watching Jewel. Jewel walks steadily toward him, his hands at his sides. Save for Jewel's legs they are like two figures carved for a tableau savage in the sun.
>
> When Jewel can almost touch him, the horse stands on his hind legs and slashes down at Jewel. Then Jewel is enclosed by a glittering maze of hooves as by an illusion of wings; among them, beneath the upreared chest, he moves with the flashing limberness of a snake. For an instant before the jerk comes onto his arms he sees his whole body earth-free, horizontal, whipping snake-limber, until he finds the horse's nostrils and touches earth again. Then they are rigid, motionless, terrific, the horse back-thrust on stiffened, quivering legs, with lowered head; Jewel with dug heels, shutting off the horse's wind with one hand, with the other patting the horse's neck in short strokes myriad and caressing, cursing the horse with obscene ferocity.
>
> They stand in rigid terrific hiatus, the horse trembling and groaning. Then Jewel is on the horse's back . . . (12)

I do not mean to suggest that the story does not move here, or that Darl as he tells it is not engaged with that movement, but only that he is much more engaged in another way: his dominant motive here is to perceive a "tableau"—and a beautiful one—to fix a moment in "rigid terrific hiatus," to make imaginative space against the narrative's urgent and powerful movement in time. And this is especially emphatic here in its tension with Anse's favorite images of motion; the horse and the snake are suspended. In such a way this narrative continually links, in its course, moments of charged stillness.

It is Darl's effort to accomplish this space that is the most obvious and the most considerable, but each character can, at moments, talk like Darl and thus except himself from the story's progress and establish for it and himself a more independent and stable presence. This imaginative dynamic is a consistent one in Faulkner: his readers are familiar with the efforts of characters and narrators to disengage from the run of the fiction and so achieve permanent clarity and rest. Familiar, too, is the sort of image that results from this effort: suspended within and from the narrative, charged both with its own internal energy and by its resistance to the story's visual drive. But the commonness of this effect in Faulkner's work should not blur our vision to its special quality in As I Lay Dying. For in this novel, the imagination's effort to remain in place, or the efforts of the narrators to take themselves and the story out of progressive sequence, is more embattled than it is elsewhere. It is a matter of obvious and dramatized conflict, and finally—and this is certainly not always the case in Faulkner—it issues in a surrender to the visual and to realism.

That surrender is ultimately figured in Darl's incarceration and madness, but the continuing sign of the struggle that precedes it, which Faulkner returns to, as if gleefully, again and again, is the cross. This is the image made by Addie's upended coffin as Jewel saves it from the fire; it is the image made by the log that overturns their wagon, rising up perpendicular to the river's flow; and at last it makes the repeating figure in the interwoven wires of Darl's cage, "where, his grimed hands lying light in the quiet interstices, looking out he foams" (244).

The image that As I Lay Dying finally makes, however, is not that of the cross, or of any lasting tension, for at last all attempts to stand up against onward sequence have been relinquished or expunged. It is symptomatic that, for Addie, Jewel himself is the cross: "He is my cross and he will be my salvation" (160). Because for a reader, Jewel comes to enact only the line of doing; more than any other, it is he who insists that the journey and the story go on. Out of love for his mother, perhaps, but ultimately the effect is to put her, and perhaps himself, utterly behind in favor of this progress, in favor of something new: " 'It's Cash and Jewel and

Vardaman and Dewey Dell,' pa says, kind of hangdog and proud too, with his teeth and all, even if he wouldn't look at us. 'Meet Mrs. Bundren,' he says" (250).

As I Lay Dying is thus an extravagant model of mixed fictional motives. Within the fiction itself, these motives are displayed as a struggle in which aural energies are overcome by the continuous sequential pressure of the story; and it should be added that the individual voices here are strong, so strong that the narrative line must become violently melodramatic to convert them. From this we may draw at least two inferences that make *As I Lay Dying* remarkable: first, that in it Faulkner is so explicitly conscious of and so engaged with the tension that I have termed *aural-visual* that its image is dramatized, almost as if he were plotting for us the alternatives of his fictional strategy as he wrote the story.

But the second inference is more interesting and has to do with the choice that Faulkner both makes and shows us he is making here. For like Jewel and all the other characters save Darl, Faulkner consistently and finally settles in this narrative for something new. If it is apparent to us that in the story's course, two opposed kinds of imaginative power are in tension, it must be clear at the end that this tension has been resolved—and that it was to be resolved—in favor of the new, of the future, of visual and realistic extension of the story's sequence. All these potential voices are reduced to characters; this is Faulkner's evident option, and he—like Jewel and the rest—has chosen the kind of power that resides in realistic novelty.

This is why *As I Lay Dying* is so special and at the same time so unsatisfactory as a novel, why it is a kind of brilliant potboiler. There is nothing inherently wrong, perhaps, with the taking of the visual option, even though it may not be to one's taste. But that strategy depends here upon melodrama, upon fictional sequences so extravagant and violent that they will balance and overturn the energies of voice. This suggests that the real power of *As I Lay Dying* resides in its voices, that the inclination of this multiple narrative is toward the aural and can only be redressed by moments like the one where Vardaman drills through his mother's coffin into her rotting face.

For before the ultimate lapsing of the story into realism, before the voices surrender to their characters, Faulkner has committed his energy to their aural aspect. Each has one moment or more, before the visual progress dominates him, when he pointedly and obviously exceeds that progress. This is true, in the most obvious way, for Addie's own narrative, which is perhaps the most compelling and moving in the novel, though when it occurs, Addie has been dead for some time. But it is also true for Vardaman,[15] for Dewey Dell,[16] for all of them. Any character here, evidently, can speak far beyond the limits of his character. Each one at some time can do what Darl does, can be the source of a voice that seems dominating and autonomous. That these voices reflect authorial or narrative presence, rather than the presence of mere characters embedded in the story, is evident both in the way they dramatically exceed their circumstantial limits and in the way they counter the sequential energy of those limits with effects so obviously aural that they need not be catalogued.

The aural impulse is established as general throughout As I Lay Dying, then, and thus when its most extravagant embodiment is thrown into jail, just as all the other voices are jailed in their appetites for ongoing sequence and the future, most readers may be dissatisfied. For the power that has been felt in them is too great to be so narrowed and focused at the last. Perhaps this too is merely a matter of personal taste, but it would seem from As I Lay Dying that in cases where visual-aural conversion occurs dramatically, it may occur appropriately, as it does in "Heart of Darkness," only in one direction—that an obvious change of fictional shape from aural potential to visual specification will be felt as a diminishment and too much regretted. This is so much the case in As I Lay Dying that Faulkner's choice seems as arbitrary and cheap as Anse's choice of a new wife and new teeth, for the obvious sake of self-extension and continuance. But at the same time, that gesture seems forgivable, even redeemed, because in this narrative it is so well known, because in this work Faulkner diagrams and declares the choice for us even as he makes it, as if he were making a statement about his artistic process and, more important, because in other works such a choice is not so easy for him. For As I Lay Dying dramatizes, and even burlesques, a tension that in other novels so dominates and compels Faulkner's imagination that he both cannot decide between visual and aural motives and seems not to know why he cannot. Nor does he seem to know that, perhaps more than any novelist ever has, he is therefore insisting on having it both ways.

The least important but most obvious evidence that Faulkner was of two minds about the motives of his fiction comes from what he said about it, in interviews and the like. As we have seen in Conrad's case—and might have seen in many others—the remarks that a fiction writer makes about his work on nonfictional occasions are often at considerable variance with what can be experienced and observed from the work itself. But with Faulkner, the disparity between what the fiction is doing and what the author says it is doing seems nonetheless striking.

There is, for one example, the powerful closing passage in "The Bear," where Ike encounters Boon in what is left of the "big woods," sitting at the foot of the gum tree:

> the whole tree had become one green maelstrom of mad leaves, while from time to time, singly or in twos and threes, squirrels would dart down the trunk then whirl without stopping and rush back again as though sucked violently back by the vacuum of their fellows' frenzied vortex. Then he saw Boon, sitting, his back against the trunk, his head bent, hammering furiously at something on his lap. What he hammered with was the barrel of his dismembered gun, what he hammered at was the breech of it. The rest of his gun lay scattered about him in a half-dozen pieces while he bent over the piece on his lap his scarlet and streaming walnut face, hammering the disjointed barrel against the gun-breech with the frantic abandon of a madman. He didn't even look up to see who it was. Still hammering, he merely shouted back at the boy in a hoarse strangled voice:
>
> "Get out of here! Dont touch them! Dont touch a one of them! They're mine!"[17]

I have considered elsewhere[18] both this passage and the story from which it comes, and so I shall try to be brief about them here.

Boon appears to be mad. It may be that—as the killer of the bear—
he has been touched by the wilderness and has become one with it
somehow: his passion may be that of ownership, or it may be that
of stewardship—a distinction crucial in "The Bear" and to Ike
McCaslin himself. Either sense of his motives could arise from the
image of his apparently destructive action upon his gun. But according to Faulkner, in an interview at the University of Virginia,
Boon is merely trying to repair his gun, to free a jammed shell so
that he can shoot the squirrels, and he is telling Ike to wait because
he saw them first and so has first rights. In this way, the passion of
Boon and perhaps of the entire story is reduced to a hunter's greed,
and we have to assume that the man who killed Old Ben with a
knife is nonetheless covetous of squirrels, and that Ike may be also,
and that one who knows the woods as well as Ike or Boon would
treat the squirrels' isolation in the gum tree as a great find, and
so on.

But the insufficiency of Faulkner's account is perhaps not so
important here as the direction of it—toward a simple, mundane,
easily explained sort of clarity in which the motives of a fiction are
glibly described in terms of usual expectations from ordinary life.
It is a denial not only of the specialness and mystery of the fiction
but also of the complexity of Faulkner's own agency in terms of it;
and so it may arise from, among other things, an affected country
simplicity, a kind of cracker-barrel modesty. But the form it takes
is to assert for the fiction an intelligibility that the fiction in its
working neither has nor attempts.

Cases like this one of what I consider authorial misreading pro-
liferate through Faulkner's nonfictional remarks before audiences.
When he was asked how the novel *The Sound and the Fury* was
conceived in relation to his own "impression of a little girl up in a
tree," the image of Caddy's "muddy drawers," he said, "And that's
what the book—it took the rest of the four hundred pages to
explain why she was brave enough to climb the tree to look in the
window."[19] Just so: the novel as four-hundred-page explanation. But
this insistence on the motive of intelligibility, we must remember
again, is occasional; it may have been, or Faulkner may have thought

it was, just what his audience wanted to hear, and—as most writers would have—he obliged them. The significance of this visual motive for Faulkner himself, however, becomes clearer as he continues:

> It was, I thought, a short story, something that could be done in about two pages, a thousand words, I found out it couldn't. I finished it the first time, and it wasn't right, so I wrote it again, and that was Quentin, that wasn't right. I wrote it again, that was Jason, that wasn't right, then I tried to let Faulkner do it, that still was wrong.[20]

Here "right" may imply the sufficiency of the explanation, in which case the visual bias that he expressed before is sustained—as if Faulkner conceived both his writing progress and the narrative progress of the novel, at least hopefully, as a progress toward intelligibility, a progress that was ultimately frustrated. But the tone of his account of the frustration seems oddly settled and satisfied, as it is when he is later reminded of *The Sound and the Fury*'s "failure": "The one that failed the most tragically and the most splendidly. That was *The Sound and the Fury*—the one that I worked at the longest, the hardest, that was to me the most passionate and moving idea, and made the most splendid failure."[21] This fondness for the "failure" of *The Sound and the Fury* is not simple nostalgia for hard times that one has got through, for Faulkner returns to the idea of failure again and again throughout these interviews and in relation to many different novels, his own and other writers'. In this way, his visual or intelligible bias, though constantly proclaimed to this sort of audience, is, strangely, almost never a claim of visual efficiency. When he speaks of his attempts at clarity and explanation in his fiction, it is nearly always of attempts that have failed. Walter Slatoff has established Faulkner's interest in failure, suggesting that "if it is the act of trying which gives man his immortality and which even . . . makes life matter and gives it meaning—then one cannot really risk success and failure becomes a kind of success."[22] But I am not sure that the "failed success" of "trying" is all that Faulkner is after; I am not sure that he gravitates to the failed intelligible only because it is the way to

keep his visual pursuit alive. There is no doubt that this motive
is in him: he is always speaking—concerning both himself and
other writers—in Southern knightly terms of the "gallantry of
failure." But that image is too pat; its energy does not really meet
the frequency and insistence with which Faulkner returns to the
idea of failure, an idea with which he seems so regularly satisfied
and secure that the word itself is on the way to becoming a kind
of magical refrain. I suspect that this is because there was magic
in the idea for him and not merely that of gloriously failed trying.
For Faulkner may at times depend too much upon failure, to paraphrase Slatoff, to risk trying itself, even the sort of juiceless trying
that is expected to fail. It may be that visual or intelligible lapse
in his fiction is not so much directed to continue the visual trying
but to provide—as we have seen it may do in other writers—a
different kind of imaginative access. But this may be overbalancing
in the other direction; and it may be better to say that Faulkner's
repeated trying for and failing with the intelligible enabled him
at the same time to go on telling.

This distinction itself may perhaps seem oversubtle; but I think
it may be justified by considering, first, the "Appendix" that Faulkner composed for *The Sound and the Fury* more than a decade
after the novel had been finished. One would expect such a thing
to be, as appendixes usually are, intelligibly motivated, designed to
support and to clarify the fiction; and to some extent this appendix
does that. It contains, for instance, psychological glosses on the
novel's characters, like this one of Quentin:

> QUENTIN III. Who loved not his sister's body but some concept
> of Compson honor precariously and (he knew well) only tem-
> porarily supported by the minute fragile membrane of her maiden-
> head as a miniature replica of all the whole vast globy earth may
> be poised on the nose of a trained seal. Who loved not the idea
> of the incest which he would not commit, but some presbyterian
> concept of its eternal punishment: he, not God, could by that
> means cast himself and his sister both into hell, where he could
> guard her forever and keep her forevermore intact amid the eternal
> fires. But who loved death above all, who loved only death, loved
> and lived in a deliberate and almost perverted anticipation of death

as a lover loves and deliberately refrains from the waiting willing friendly tender incredible body of his beloved, until he can no longer bear not the refraining but the restraint and so flings, hurls himself, relinquishing, drowning. Committed suicide in Cambridge, Massachusetts, June 1910, two months after his sister's wedding, waiting first to complete the current academic year and so get the full value of his paid-in-advance tuition, not because he had his old Culloden and Carolina and Kentucky grandfathers in him but because the remaining piece of the old Compson mile which had been sold to pay for his sister's wedding and his year at Harvard had been the one thing, excepting that same sister and the sight of an open fire, which his youngest brother, born an idiot, had loved.[23]

The image of Quentin presented here is of explanatory value, precisely because even though it insists on its difficulty—mostly by means of the "not this but that" construction—it is in fact much simpler than the complex of motives that Quentin's own narrative in the novel expresses. Of course, this explanatory power may be rejected for exactly the same reason, as might the "clarifications" upon other characters here. But questioning the visual efficiency of these sections, once more, seems somehow off-target, as it usually does in Faulkner. For in their rhythm—as in the rhythm of the "Appendix" as a whole—they seem as much a capitalization on the novel's obscurity as an attempt to clarify it, as if the problematic nature of his fiction provides Faulkner with an excuse, many years later, to go on and on, as if the novel's intense and permanent tensions legitimize his inclination to indulge his favorite rhetorical mannerisms over it. Surely it does allow him, as he was wont, to write sentences without subjects—and without the attention that would be necessary in a novel to shifting cadences and relief, but one after the other—just as the presumed condensation of this appendix allows him other sorts of phrasing that seem even for him excessive: "the waiting willing friendly tender incredible body of his beloved." More generally, there can be no question that throughout this "Appendix" his prose, perhaps even more than usually, is expansive rather than reductive. At times this expansion does develop its own wonderful symmetry, as when Faulkner tells, in a parenthesis, of just what his plundering of and by his niece amounted to for Jason:

(it was not $2840.50 either, it was almost seven thousand dollars and this was Jason's rage, the red unbearable fury which on that night and at intervals recurring with little or no diminishment for the next five years, made him seriously believe would at some unwarned instant destroy him, kill him as instantaneously dead as a bullet or a lightningbolt: that although he had been robbed not of a mere petty three thousand dollars but of almost seven thousand he couldn't even tell anybody; because he had been robbed of seven thousand dollars instead of just three he could not only never receive justification—he did not want sympathy—from other men unlucky enough to have one bitch for a sister and another for a niece, he couldn't even go to the police; because he had lost four thousand dollars which did not belong to him he couldn't even recover the three thousand which did since those first four thousand dollars were not only the legal property of his niece as a part of the money supplied for her support and maintenance by her mother over the last sixteen years, they did not exist at all, having been officially recorded as expended and consumed in the annual reports he submitted to the district Chancellor, as required of him as guardian and trustee by his bondsmen: so that he had been robbed not only of his thievings but his savings too, and by his own victim; he had been robbed not only of the four thousand dollars which he had risked jail to acquire but of the three thousand which he had hoarded at the price of sacrifice and denial, almost a nickel and a dime at a time, over a period of almost twenty years: and this not only by his own victim but by a child who did it at one blow, without premeditation or plan, not even knowing or even caring how much she would find when she broke the drawer open; and now he couldn't even go to the police for help: he who had considered the police always, never given them any trouble, had paid the taxes for years which supported them in parasitic and sadistic idleness; not only that, he didn't dare pursue the girl himself because he might catch her and she would talk, so that his only recourse was a vain dream which kept him tossing and sweating on nights two and three and even four years

after the event, when he should have forgotten about it: of catching her without warning, springing on her out of the dark, before
she had spent all the money, and murder her before she had time
to open her mouth) (424-426)

But the symmetry of this passage is redundant, resonant, and
musical rather than explanatory: a reader knows immediately why
it is not nearly three but almost seven thousand dollars that she
has taken and what this means for Jason. Thus almost the entire
length of the passage, in terms of intelligibility, is superfluous.
Nonetheless it is delightful, both because its repetitions upon three
and four and seven thousand dollars and conflicting thieveries
reflects so beautifully the bitter and burlesque fixation that is so
familiar and engaging in Jason, and, of course, in close association,
because it resonates into Faulkner's musical celebration of Jason, a
voice that he did better than any other. So one might say that in
this case Faulkner simply wants to do Jason some more—so much
so that this account of him appears in the appended section describing his niece, Quentin—and in others that the novel's characters have persisted as energy sources for his imagination far past
their novel's completion. The motive for the "Appendix" in these
instances thus begins to seem repetitive and aural rather than progressive and visual.

Something similar might be said of the opportunity that Faulkner takes here to give a genealogical history of the Compsons and
thus to develop characters that—so far as I know—do not appear
anywhere else: Quentin Maclachan Compson, and Charles Stuart
Compson, and Jason Lycurgus Compson I and II. This history is
like the more important history of Jefferson, Mississippi, itself: it
suggests that the fictional world he gives us bears relation to a set
of facts, that—visually and realistically—we may see through it to
all that has actually happened. The dense articulation of the fictional world, the way all its pieces fit, seems evidence of its close
relation to historical truth. The neatness of the relation of these
pieces to each other creates the illusion that they relate just as neatly
to something beyond them. Thus, when we read that the town of
Jefferson was "laid out by the same architect who built the col-

umned porticoed house furnished by steamboat from France and New Orleans," we may guess that this was Thomas Sutpen's architect, and the thrill of our own active recognition may persuade us that it is a recognition from life. The correspondence of a detail from one fictional sequence with a detail from another—or perhaps our transition from one to another—seems proof of a life beyond both sequences. This is the realistic force of a story's "hanging together."

So, too, there may really seem to have been such a town, and the individual but dovetailed fictions become the fragments by which we can imagine its entirety. A somewhat different inference, however, may be taken from the map of Jefferson appended to *Absalom, Absalom!* Here it all is in geographic layout: all over it there are notes and arrows to show where incidents from the various novels and stories actually occurred: What could be more realistic? And yet at the bottom of the map he has noted: "William Faulkner, Sole Owner & Proprietor." To understand the effect of that signature, we may imagine how we would feel if those beautiful and detailed maps bound in with the volumes of *The Lord of the Rings* were tagged, "All invented by Me, J. R. R. Tolkien." Or, we may imagine what would happen if a densely charted scene in Pynchon ended with, "I don't know a thing about Cairo; I made it all up. (signed) Tom Pynchon." Whatever the force of such appropriation, it would be anything but realistic; it would declare the limits of the fiction as such and categorize its energy as an internal matter within it and between it and its author, in an aural manner: though, by contrast to the heavy visual tilt of these images themselves, it might do so inefficiently.

This example of Faulkner's map is a slight one, perhaps, but it does express a tension characteristic both of him and of his readers, between his fiction's aspect as problematic history and its aspect as music, between our feeling that *Absalom, Absalom!* extends historically to something beyond itself—at least to its own failure to compose history—and our feeling that its drama is self-enclosed, that its motive is both to establish and to isolate itself, discounting what it proves in favor of increased intensity and imaginative substance.

I have considered *Absalom, Absalom!* before,[24] and argued that the process of its narrative not only does not yield intelligibility—despite all the various narrators' efforts—but also that its resistance to the ordering imagination is both sanctioned and dramatized by Faulkner. Since then, I have not found reason to change my mind, and so I shall restrict much of my explication of the novel to summary statements. And my concern at this point in the present discussion, furthermore, is not to explicate novels so much as to show how the results of past or potential explications are themselves illuminated by the dichotomy of visual versus aural motives.

To anyone familiar with *Absalom, Absalom!*, it may be clear that it really is—at least in terms of the motives of its progressive narrators—what Faulkner said *The Sound and the Fury* was: an attempt to get the story "right." All of the narrators try vigorously, even desperately, to make a structure that explains and covers the details they know. The first two principal narrators, simply, do not know enough and, besides, have their own special interests in telling the story of Thomas Sutpen in particular ways. Quentin's father's basic metaphor that it was all a kind of Greek tragedy that shouldn't "explain," as well as Rosa Coldfield's image of Sutpen as a "demon"and challenger-seeker of "respectability," are both visions in service to their personal needs. Yet Quentin's own ostensibly more capable and balanced and meshed narrative—in his dialogue with Shreve—though surely more consistent and more intensely felt and established—is itself called explicitly into question: "the two of them creating between them, out of the rag-tag and bob-ends of old tales and talking, people who perhaps had never existed at all anywhere."[25] This is somewhat like saying, "William Faulkner, Sole Owner & Proprietor." Still it is not nearly so destructive to the narrative's claims to realistic intelligibility as are Quentin's own agonizingly divided motives toward the story he and Shreve make, which is at times a new and strange story that Quentin "sees" and even identifies with, but at times also an imaginative cage, an inexorably repetitive and circular exercise:

> *Am I going to have to have to hear it all again* he thought *I am going to have to hear it all over again I am already hearing it all*

*over again I am listening to it all over again I shall have to never
listen to anything else but this again forever so apparently not only
a man never outlives his father but not even his friends and
acquaintances do. . . .* (277)

Many inferences about Quentin's motives are possible here, but
one of the most obvious is that he wants to stop talking, to get out
of the story and its telling—that he wants to get it right to be quit of
it. This may be one of the motives of any realistic seeing and seeing
through: one's effort is to act upon images in a sequence both to
accumulate and to reduce them and ultimately to reestablish the
imaginative dominance of the seer, to resmooth the surface of his
mind. Quentin, like the other narrators of *Absalom, Absalom!*, is
unable to do this, unable to be quit of the process by getting through
it to a conclusion that satisfies, and so—rather than muse about it
over bourbon, or ask *"why why why"* for forty-three years—he
relinquishes all such attempts forever when a few months later he
kills himself.

But the interest in Thomas Sutpen, and in his father, and in the
South that he thus destroys is hardly less special and personal than
the interests taken by his father and by Rosa. Like theirs, it is an
attempt to locate the self in historical and imaginative sequence,
an attempt to assert one's independence and power over such a
sequence, over an accumulation of discrete images beyond the self.
And when we put it this way, we may see that this visual motive
is not only the source of the narrators' energy and efforts, but that
it also characterizes the novel's central character, Thomas Sutpen
himself, whose "design" is to challenge and infiltrate the social
system that excludes him and to repossess and reindentify himself
within it.[26]

When Sutpen fails, repeatedly, he declares that it is because of
"mistakes," that his design merely depends for its success upon the
consequent power of the right arrangement of details, among them
"land and niggers and a fine house" (238) and, of course, a son.
What is wrong, morally and otherwise, with this view has been
variously decided, but in the simplest terms what is wrong with it
is that it doesn't work, that Sutpen's imaginative force and sig-

nificance cannot be permanently established just because their motive and object is what by definition lies beyond them. Quentin's grandfather says that "Sutpen's trouble was innocence" (220), and this again has many readings. But the inference I draw, based upon Sutpen's course and vision and failure, is that it is the simplest innocence of all, a hope and a need that the self be established through independent action upon what is outside the self, that the self may be discovered in the other. And it should be evident that this innocence is shared by all the principal narrators of *Absalom, Absalom!*—by Quentin's father and Rosa and Quentin and Shreve —who in their various ways gamble their imagined identities upon their abilities to arrange the details of Sutpen's life, and lose. Thus, not only is the visual motive dramatized to fail throughout the entire range of this novel, but also it is assumed itself to be faulty as a motive—to pursue such a course reflects innocence, a fundamental lack of understanding as to what the imagination can do.

In this way the total imaginative bias of *Absalom, Absalom!* is opposite to that of *As I Lay Dying*. There are no winners here. In *As I Lay Dying*, the realistic and futuristic progress through and toward images outside the characters' imagining is successful: everyone—everyone but Darl—gets what he wants and gets on with it. But in *Absalom, Absalom!* there is no Anse Bundren to achieve his new teeth: there is no establishable power for Sutpen, no secured and extendable imagining for the narrators, no future. The failure of the visual imagination here is thorough and, as we may see in retrospect, assumed.

But then we may ask, What can the imagination do? What is Faulkner doing by this wholesale dramatization of the collapsed visual? He is, for one thing, "creating . . . out of the rag-tag and bob-ends of old tales and talking, people who perhaps never existed at all anywhere." As we have seen in "Heart of Darkness," with which *Absalom, Absalom!* has obvious affinities, the dramatized failure of the visual imagination, no matter how convincing or final it appears, cannot be accepted or incorporated into our moment-to-moment imaginative experience. It will always be regarded as a resistance, which we can see through and around. This, of course, is part of the motive for the visual failure in this novel, which is a way of energizing its fictional life. For Rosa Coldfield, the anonymous narrator tells us, it is "as though in inverse ratio to the vanishing voice, the invoked ghost of the man whom she could neither forgive nor revenge herself upon began to assume a quality almost of solidity, permanence" (13). And in the same "inverse ratio," the fictional world of *Absalom, Absalom!* gains its own solidity and power from our powerlessness to see it: the more we need and fail to understand the figures in it, the more convinced we are that they exist, that they are there to be understood—which, I suppose, is our own innocence.

But just as the failed visual is a constant source of regenerative visual power, it is also, on its other side, more directly a source of aural energy. This may be seen, most simply, at those moments in the narrative when the very impossibility of seeing is established by the transformation of narrative sequence almost explicitly into a kind of music:

> And you are—?
> Henry Sutpen.
> And you have been here—?
> Four years.
> And you came home—?
> To die. Yes.
> To die?
> Yes. To die.
> And you have been here—?
> Four years.
> And you are—?
> Henry Sutpen. (373)

This passage seems a brilliant invention. It forms an almost perfect rhetorical circle, but is at the same time infinitely extendable in urging its repetition. What moments like this mean for Quentin, of course, is that he will have to "hear it all again" and to say it all again and again, that as visual dead ends, they are also intensely unified and compelling imaginative circles that generate their own repeating, their own future, and create the need for going over and over again the "old tales and talking." It should by now be evident that this is a need that, unlike Quentin his character, Faulkner himself is well satisfied with, that he has no intention of resisting or escaping. For though moments like this are more obviously musical than the narrative of *Absalom, Absalom!* at large, it is nonetheless clear that to use a phrase like *narrative sequence* to describe this narrative's general shape is to misname it. For the form of it even more than that of any other narrative in Faulkner is recapitulative and resonant to the point of wholesale imaginative inflation. The images of the narrative are repeated and repeated until they become formulae, and what seem to be merely visual details thus become both the occasions for and the elements of a celebratory chanting that seems recurrent and endless: "sweet and oversweet with the twice-bloomed wistaria against the outer wall by the savage quiet September sun impacted distilled and hyperdistilled" (8). The wistaria of *Absalom, Absalom!* blooms not twice, but again and again and again, and in its multiple blooming is both the compelling source and the result of the fiction's life. The modifications in the detail of this narrative—the real sequence of it—are nearly weightless against its recurrency, and it is no wonder that Quentin, at last, is in despair.

But his despair is not Faulkner's. Even though the thrust of Faulkner's prose, perhaps more than for any other author, is constantly counter to visual efficiency, though it usually "fails," it is not only evident that he does not regret that failure, but it is also impossible to say exactly why he does not. Is it that the lapsing of the visual creates the need to redo the story again and again, in efforts to get it right that then by failing regenerate again; or is it rather that the very need to repeat is the primary motive, which seeks visual failure as its necessary occasion and justification? There may be no deciding this. From its beginning *Absalom, Absalom!* resonates, explicitly, with this symbiotic tension between visual resistance and voice; from its beginning it dramatizes visual failure as the energizing source of its visual life, just as it demonstrates that if voices are to have life, then sight must be relinquished. And this may clarify my earlier suggestion that Faulkner was not himself aware of the processes of his fiction, for in him there is no separating the inverse energies of visual resistance from the more direct musical effects of compelled recurrence and resonance, from the "old tales and talking." Faulkner's visual-aural oscillation is thus a matter of the total oscillation of his entire form. In their most extravagant dynamic, visual and aural come to reinforce each other and grow out of each other; and this is what happens in *Absalom, Absalom!*, where the dichotomous actions always implied in the fiction of mixed motives become so reciprocal as to appear processes whose power we cannot unequivocally trace, whose source we—and perhaps Faulkner as well—cannot exactly know.

Seven

The Theory of Music
and Fictional Form

M^{Y INITIAL CONSIDERATION} that certain fictional processes should be said to be musical arose, simply, from the judgment that in certain ways they approach the experience of music for a reader and generate aural motives. The force of these motives is to create a different order of imaginative perception from the realistic— where the imaginative senses still function, but to entirely different purposes and, thus, in entirely different ways. It has proved some-what easier, however, to say what musical process and perception— in the case of literary form—is not than what it is. In part, this is justifiable: for what such process is not is inextricably involved in its working. We have seen that musical imagining is, crucially, a re-lease from more visual or intelligible imagining, that it gains a good deal of its energy by its departure from and conversion of another sort of energy. More important, as I shall develop more fully in what follows, the change of fictional shape that I have called aural con-version, although it amounts to a wholesale imaginative change, operates on a single artistic "material"—language—and in this aural condition, the other, visual properties of this material may be felt even as a kind of "residue." So that musical narrative is always to some degree actively in touch with what it is not and plays against it.

But even while accepting these reasons for characterizing the aural experience of narrative by defining its more familiar opposite, one still may want to know more about what it is and does itself, especially if he is skeptical that our perceptual motives may be transformed so radically and efficiently. So in attempting both to describe more intensively and positively the musical motives and conditions of narrative fiction and to support the ways in which I have already described them, I want to consider now, more explicitly, the source of the analogy, musical experience itself.

We have seen that what in visual terms is imaginative passivity or stasis is within a strictly aural context an act of imaginative self-restriction, a limiting of one's response to the evident range of the given form; and if musical theorists agree upon anything, it is upon the necessity of this voluntary and energetic self-limitation in one who listens to music: "The ideal listener, above all else, possesses the ability to lend himself to the power of the music."[1] The "power of the music" may be understood variously here, for it implies among other things an ultimate willingness in the listener to be moved and affected, but just as surely it implies an initial willingness to be moved in the sense of controlled; it suggests that one's fundamental posture in relation to music entails the awareness that one is yielding to the music's terms and action. And initially, of course, this awareness of a control beyond the perceiver is really just an expectation: "It is not . . . the control actually exercised over a situation which distinguishes pleasant from unpleasant emotions," Leonard Meyer suggests. "It is the control which is believed to exist."[2]

In the context of aural fiction, as we have seen, this belief in control is traceable to the felt presence of an authorial imagination; the assuredness and, especially in fiction, the personalness of that presence seems most important to aural energies. We may relate this expectation of control that Meyer considers so important to what he later describes as the "preparatory set" of the listener, which is the predisposition to certain kinds of imagining:

The belief that we are dealing with an aesthetic object leads to what Henry Aiken has called the idea of "framing," that is, the belief that an aesthetic object is a special kind of stimulus to which we do not respond by overt action. The fact that the response to aesthetic experience is not overt has . . . very important consequences in conditioning our responses; for the repression of overt behavior is a vital factor in the development of affect.

The idea of framing does not, however, detract from the feeling of reality which is so important in the aesthetic experience. "The mechanism of denial can operate; a firm belief in the 'reality of play' can coexist with a certainty that it is play only. Here lie the roots of aesthetic illusion."[3]

Perhaps the most important distinction here is established in terms that are largely negative, for the "aesthetic" process is defined by what it is not: "a special kind of stimulus to which we do not respond by overt action." But in inquiring about what this process is, and what its specialness amounts to for our response, the idea of the perceptual frame is suggestive, for what the recognition of such limits points to, in aesthetic situations, is a special kind of process and of meaning that depends upon relations within the frame. This Meyer calls "embodied meaning," and though he does not remark upon its dynamic connection with the idea of the aesthetic frame, that connection is to my mind evident.[4]

"Embodied meaning" is opposed, in Meyer's terminology, to "designative meaning." While the former describes meaning that is interior to the form, the latter describes meaning that is generated by relating the music, in part or whole, to contexts outside it, in a process that I call visual or realistic extension. Wilson Coker, who is perhaps more philosophically thorough than Meyer, expresses a similar opposition with the terms "congeneric" and "extrageneric": "*Congeneric meaning* grows out of an iconic sign situation in which an observer interprets one element of a work . . . as referring to another such element in either that work or a different work in the same medium."[5] There is, as one might expect, an extended controversy among theorists as to which sort of meaning—embodied or designative, congeneric or extrageneric—is in music the more fundamental and ought to be held ascendant in theory, but that debate need not concern us here for two reasons.[6] In the first place, the musicologist in his concentration upon music alone may be aware often of more or less subtle distinctions within it between these two kinds of meaning, but when one is crossing aesthetic contexts, and comparing music and fiction, then musical meaning will seem, normally, decidedly more "embodied" than that of fiction. And so when fiction itself seems to approach that order of meaning, to describe it as musical is practically to describe it as congeneric. In the second place, we are not concerned here so much with theoretical exclusion as with theoretical possibility: "embodied" and "designative" may thus be said to mark the ends of a scale, a scale that obviously applies to music and that I contend applies also to fiction.

As far as fiction is concerned, we have little difficulty understanding its potential for designative, or for visual-intelligible meaning. It is easy to see that a novel's extrageneric process involves our action of relating its narrative to things outside it, but it is difficult to understand what we might be up to if we are not engaged in such an action, to understand what imaginative processes and effects an embodied or congeneric formal action might produce in fiction.

It will be useful here to bring together what occurs in Meyer's discussion as separate elements—the expected control and the aesthetic frame in their relation to embodied meaning. We have seen that in fiction the aural tendency toward formal self-enclosure occurs simultaneously with the recognition that we are dealing with fiction. This, I take it, is the way in narrative of framing the experience. It is the awareness of fictional quality that removes from our action all realistic pressure or anxiousness, and transparent and transitory visual images become—because they are no longer means but ends—paradoxically more substantial because they are obviously fictional.

Our awareness of this imaginative situation amounts, if the analogy continues to hold, to our awareness that we are doing something aesthetic. And if our action is to continue aesthetic, we must throughout the fiction be reminded and reassured of the frame, the expected control. Conversely, this action of framing in aesthetic situations implies that realistic, or visual, fiction is not aesthetic. Whether this is to say that such fiction is not art, I don't know; but it is to say that we do not treat it as such and that we are thus acting in accordance with its felt demands. For if the realism of fiction depends upon the illusion that our movement over and through its sequence extends beyond the first and the last image of that sequence, then we may now infer that that realism depends on what amounts to a denial of the aesthetic frame and that realistic fiction is therefore, at least by design, nonaesthetic. The generally realistic inclination of the novel as a form, furthermore, arises evidently from its simplest formal characteristics, for the action of prose fiction of any length is obviously to make us forget beginnings and endings, to suspend us in a long middle where the feeling that we are doing something special or aesthetic—that we are, after all, reading a fiction—is easily forgotten. But the matter is both more complex and less trivial than this. For the fact is that even if we kept our eyes as we read upon the front and back covers of the book, so long as the narrative continues its linear variation, it is not framed. The last image in its sequence, once again, is not the last: the narrative energy and progress continues by extension right through that and out into the world. And thus though at its end it is undeniably a book, a fictional form, that fact may be insignificant because thoroughly unrecognized. In this way, a realistic line or sequence cannot be said to be enclosed even though it ends, since its putative destination is some reality beyond a merely verbal finish, beyond its verbal limits.

This suggests that the circle or self-enclosure that more aural fiction makes must be both conspicuous and recurrent, just because the linear inclinations of the novel militate so energetically against it. For its action to be aural and its imaginative substance thus intensely self-contained, a novel must continually remind us that it is framed, that it is a special and self-limited utterance, a fiction. Susanne Langer is the only aesthetician I know who seems aware that this formal avowal of fictionality is necessary in literature at large:

> The second major concern of literature, therefore, correlative with having to give a work "the air of reality," is the problem of *keeping it fiction*. Many people recognize the devices whereby a writer attains life-likeness; but few are aware of the means that sustain the difference between art and life—the simplification and manipulation of life's image that makes it essentially different from its prototype.[7]

I have suggested that the novel's formal characteristics make "keeping it fiction" an especially sustained problem. But speaking very generally, this occurs in the repeated faulting of its own visual sequence in favor of more musical—for the moment, simply more repetitive and rhythmic—consistency.[8]

When sequence, and visual consistency, is thus faulted, a narrative is revealed as evident fictional utterance, and the presence of a fictionalizer, of someone telling the story, becomes obvious and undeniable. In this way, the circle that a narrative makes in its aural action is, even in the smallest incidence of that action, decided indeed. For it amounts to and is apprehended by a reader as an actual return by the words to their source; their quality as utterance directs us to their personal origin both within the form and defining the limits of the form.

Such an evident return, in visual situations, where realistic signification is expected, is at least a momentary failure and possibly a disaster. This is associated with the necessary invisibility of realistic narrators, their necessary self-negation. By the same token, this aural recognition of the artist's presence should not be mistaken for the mere curiosity about the artist that occurs in quasi- or even pseudoaesthetic situations. That sort of anxiousness is a realistic phenomenon, where the appetites of the perceiver extend unsatisfied past the work toward its maker in hope of greater intelligibility, even of solution. In such cases, the artist is imagined—like everything else—to be beyond the experience and not present in it. But in aesthetic contexts, the artist's presence is felt as unquestionable and evident, inseparable from the enclosure that his work makes—as we shall see in Nabokov.

The force of this apprehension of the imaginative presence of an author—and the responsive attitude that it signals and stimulates in a reader—can hardly be exaggerated. In relation to music, Meyer considers it as a kind of aesthetic predisposition: "Our belief in the creative power of the great artist has about it an aura of primitive magic. . . . Our willingness to become involved in aesthetic experience is partly a function of the relationship we feel with the artist's creative force."[9] But this felt relation with the artist, far more than a mere predisposition, is dynamically revealed and constantly reinforced by the self-enclosed process of the art itself. In an aural situation, we are continually reminded of our dominated relation with an author whose very presence establishes the aesthetic frame or expected control of the situation, defines it as fiction, and converts our realistic engagement into play. Meyer associates our belief in the artist's power—again, as a presupposition—with a "belief in the importance of the individual creator"; but the imaginative power that a reader feels in authorial presence when that presence is invoked by a narrative action is much greater than any such abstract belief in anybody's importance might generate.

From this we may draw the inference that there is an interdependence between literary form and the voice that we hear in that form. And even in aesthetic media where "voice" seems too audible a term to apply in the way that it does in literature, as perceivers we may feel the reciprocity of the art form with the mind of its maker even as we perceive it, and our very sense of its circumscribed presentation keeps returning it in our imaginations to its source. But this effect is the more powerful, I think, in aesthetic forms that may be heard, in which the self-generative and self-isolating energies that assert their own formal integrity and independence, and their dominance of our imaginations, are indistinguishable from the voice that we hear in them.

Again, this may be truer in literary form than anywhere else. So acute a theorist as Mrs. Langer, for instance, does not consider the crucial awareness, in the forms of art, of felt authorial presence, control, and—in literature—voice. Perhaps this is because she considers that any notion of authorial presence might imply that one looks outside a work for such control—an implication that I do not intend at all—and would thus deny rather than establish the evident autonomy of the work. This, too, may be the reason that she takes such exception to descriptions of the special attitudes involved in aesthetic perception, for to recognize such biases might seem again to postulate an authority beyond the work, to which we would have to refer in order to respond to the work. But the perceptual attitude that I have associated with aural imaginative processes—given a reader whose own attitudes are in some balance —is generated in the formal action of the work itself and is indistinguishable from that action, reciprocal with the felt presence of the author in the work.

This may be supported by asking again, What is this formal action of a work? What goes on within the limits of aesthetic form? What does it mean to relate inner part to inner part, without translating to exterior images and contexts? What are the processes and responses that, in relation to ordinary communicative discourse, I have termed noncognitive or unintelligible? Here it should be remarked that Leonard Meyer and most other theorists of music consider that even music, whose meaning is more embodied and interior, surely, than aural fiction, may be said to be in certain ways intelligible. The action of a reader as well, in both the visual and the aural processes of fiction, involves a kind of "following," but the contrasting motives of following in these cases are most important. Under aural conditions, whatever following that happens does so within the form: we do not follow anything out of the form, as we do in sequential imagining. Whatever intelligibility occurs in such cases is fundamentally different, in its discontinuity with other verbal contexts, from the meaning normally associated with language use.[10]

But the most congenial, though perhaps not the most clear, account of musical perception as a kind of intelligibility that I have found is one given by Gabriel Marcel. Marcel argues, very gently, that we not only "follow" music but also, in a special way, "dominate" it:

> But is not that act of domination—which is in no way a mode of conception or intellection—one by which what is, in fact, flowing becomes consciousness of that flowing, and, in some ways at least, the representation, the figuration—but non-spatial—of the becoming? When we speak of the beauty of a melodic line, the aesthetic qualification does not apply to the inner progression, but to a certain figure which is, I repeat, non-spatial. . . . As I go from note to note, a certain whole takes shape, a form builds up which can certainly not be reduced to a succession of organic states. . . . From this point of view, it is relatively easy to perceive what is generally meant by musical comprehension. Is it not in fact identical with the act by which the form builds up?[11]

But where this activity of "dominating figuration" takes Marcel, by means of some delicate lines, is to an ultimate attitude not dominating at all. In speaking of music's "profound idea," he says, "In this sense, the profound idea is the one which hits me just where I am still vulnerable, where the hardening acquired under the influence of repetition, that is to say, the mechanization of myself, still contains gaps. In a word: it builds me; it is *formative.*"[12] We shall continue to see—for both readers and especially narrators of fiction—how the domination over a fiction becomes a reverse force by which the dominator is himself formed. Marcel's argument, though rather lyrical than logical, is a fruitful one in this regard. But what is important for my simpler purposes here is that what begins as an apparently almost visual sort of imagining, in its independent movement over and through the music, is transformed —in the very act of listening as Marcel describes it—to an attitude that is not dominating at all, but a condition of receptiveness so extreme as to be a kind of vulnerability, in which one is hit, and then built and formed, by some force so active and dominating itself that one has no choice about it. Marcel's idea of the particular action of repetition is interesting here, for contrary to what I would think, he considers that in perceiving repetition one becomes less, rather than more, vulnerable to the processes of the form. But even so, he does not imply for a moment that we are exercising our free imaginative agency in such situations, but rather that we are so acted upon as even to be "mechanized."

The dynamics of our own perceptual processes in these aesthetic situations, therefore, are always the dynamics of response. They depend upon, and may even be said to be identical with, our recognition that the processes of the form that confronts us are not continuous with our more normal, aggressive modes of understanding or intelligibility. This recognition is stimulated by a radical alteration in that aspect of the fiction that realistically invites agressive action, its progressive and various sequence. And the particular means by which this alteration is most obviously accomplished is by sequence's opposite, repetition.

Even in the less verbal processes of music, repetition may be conceived as the principal action not merely of the form but of the "inwardness" of the form, as Basil De Selincourt suggests:

The value of repetition in music belongs of course to the peculiar inwardness of the art. A musical composition must be content to be itself. The reference and relations into which analysis resolves its life-current need point to no object, no event; they take the form of the creative impulse which is their unity and they repeat one another because iteration is the only outward sign of identity which is available to them.[13]

It is also by means of repetition that a fictional composition displays its "content to be itself." De Selincourt does not attempt here to describe how repetition both establishes and justifies the inwardness of musical form, as I am trying to do for the case of fiction. Rather, he considers it a fact of musical experience and then remarks the interior—and, in my terms, the evidently nonvisual and even nonintelligible—imagining that it necessitates. And in doing so, he allows what is for my purposes a crucial distinction. "Iteration," he says, "is the only outward sign of identity which is available" to musical terms or elements. But obviously this is not true for the musical processes of verbal narrative. Words have their significations apart from the formal process in which they are involved; and what repetition accomplishes, in the narrative action of words, is not to identify those significations but somehow to set them aside and to declare for the words an intelligibility not signifying but musical. At the same time, however, the fact that the elements of this musical process are words and not tones may make them, even in their musical action, all the more powerful. Susanne Langer gives an excellent account of how the recognition that words embedded in a musical process have meanings elsewhere—meanings now dominated by the musical context—may itself function toward musical shape and feeling:

Words may enter directly into musical structure even without being literally understood; the *semblance of speech* may be enough. The most striking illustration of this principle is found in plainsong. In such mediaeval chant the tonal material is reduced to the barest minimum: a single melodic line, small in compass, without polyphonic support, without accompaniment, without regular

179

recurrent accent or "beat." Play such a line on the piano or on any melody instrument, it sounds poor and trivial, and seems to have no particular motion. But as soon as the words are articulated it moves, its wandering rhythmic figures cease to wander as they incorporate intoned speech rhythms, and the great Latin words fill the melodic form exactly as chords and counterpoints would fill it. The fact that the syllables supporting the tones are concatenated by their non-musical, original character into words and sentences, causes the tones to follow each other in a more organic sequence than the mere succession which they exhibit in an instrumental paraphrase. It is not the sentiment expressed in the words that makes them all-important to Gregorian chant; it is the cohesion of the Latin line, the simplicity of statement, the greatness of certain words, which causes the composer to dwell on these and subordinate what is contextual to them. Even a person who has no inkling of Greek—perhaps does not recognize the incursion of Greek words into the Latin mass—feels the sacred import of the text:

> *Kyrie Eleison,*
> *Christe Eleison,*

because the exploitation of those four words is a full musical event. (*Feeling and Form*, 151)

What I am suggesting is that when words "enter . . . into musical structure," they in fact cease to be "literally understood," and they are converted to what Mrs. Langer calls here "the semblance of speech." And it is important to note that by that phrase neither Mrs. Langer nor I mean to suggest a diminishment in the words' power. "Semblance" here means "appearance," not in the sense of reduced "imitation," but in the sense of fundamental, evident quality.[14] When repetition converts the words of a narrative from a cognitive function to a musical presence, and so discounts their signifying action, it may at the same time be said to insist on their "quality." But this needs to be clarified.

The sense of language's quality here—as contrasted with the more active function of words in realistic or discursive situations—depends, once more, upon our recognition of language as utterance, a recognition that we do not come to when language is working— and we are working it—in more ordinary ways. The reason why the quality of words goes unrecognized when they are functioning visually should at this point be evident. I have frequently remarked that the motive of language used realistically is self-effacement, that such language functions ideally as a transparency. It tries, in this way, to be itself uninteresting:

> The more barren and indifferent the symbol, the greater is its semantic power. . . . little noises are ideal conveyors of concepts, for they give us nothing but their meaning. That is the source of the "transparency" of language, on which several scholars have remarked. Vocables in themselves are so worthless that we cease to be aware of their physical presence at all, and become conscious only of their connotations, denotations, or other meanings. Our conceptual activity seems to flow *through* them, rather than merely to accompany them, as it accompanies other experiences that we endow with significance. They fail to impress us as "experiences" in their own right, unless we have a difficulty in using them as words, as we do with a foreign language . . . until we have mastered it.[15]

What this suggests is that the visual functioning of language—for purposes of ordinarily communicated meaning—is not qualitative, that in this visual working, language has no consistency. Words are printed in order to vanish and spoken not to be heard: their heard aspect in ordinary communication is a matter of a-rhythmic and inconsequent little noises not identifiable as sound. As Craig La Drière suggests, "in general in the non-aesthetic use of language, sound is very distinctly subordinated in the service of meaning: it functions simply to achieve meaning, *and to be effaced in that achievement.*"[16] To the extent that language does have quality or consistency, then, that quality is a matter of its aural aspect. Thus, when words become more than little noises, when they become rhythmic and symmetrical utterances that is felt as utterance, their presence and quality is not so much generated as revealed. This seems important because it suggests the rootedness of aural processes and experience, not merely in our imaginations, but in the nature of language itself. The perception of words as such amounts not to a special and temporary transformation but to a return to an original condition, from which the visual function of language may be seen itself as a special reduction and even a denial of language's quality.

But at the same time, the words' aural return to their qualitative state cannot entirely divest them of the uses to which they have been put beyond that state. Thus to recognize their quality is also to recognize, in a certain way, their potential for signifying use and to see not only that they are not working at present but also that they have worked before, and how. This is a recognition of what I conceive to be language's residual significance in its qualitative state. To perceive words' quality is thus to be aware of a residue of past and potential uses for the words, uses not now active but nonetheless felt to be residing in the words themselves, in a much more intense and present way than would be possible if these uses were actually being exercised.[17]

This intensity and presence of imaginative potential in musical language derives primarily, I think, from our feeling that in the musical dynamic it is secured. For although in their musical condition words' quality seems to contain previous uses and associations and thus to indicate a potential for future uses, the dominant tendency of this condition is much more toward a past than toward a future, implying something already done and known much more than something yet to be accomplished. This seems true for two reasons: first, because the words' conversion to their qualitative state is felt as a return, because that state is felt as both prior to and more natural than their more actively signifying condition; and second, because the signifying potential of words in musical processes is restrained by those processes from any active inclination to a future, to new functions of meaning. For even as this potential is suggested, it is continuously rendered inactive by the immediacy of the musical process itself, which keeps redefining language as quality, as something prior even to potential, even to the potential of potential, as it were. This is why, perhaps, so many aestheticians have suggested that the meaning of language in aesthetic situations is a kind of potential, but this is also why that is the wrong emphasis. For even as that potential is generated, it is denied and is shown—by the very processes that generate it—to be inactive within those processes as they immediately occur, as they continuously insist upon the words' quality as greater than any expression, even a potential expression, of itself. In musical process, the experience of language's real quality as utterance is thus both felt as a kind of natural priority and as an immediate, moment-to-moment counteraction of the words' tendency toward meaning, by which that tendency is kept residual. One might say that therefore such tendency is caught, suppressed between a double perception of verbal quality that seems both prior and subsequent to it. Thus, the tendency toward meaning itself, the significant potential, is felt more than anything as an intense and multiple past of what the words have done before. In their evident aesthetic quality that past is kept alive—alive though it cannot be reborn so long as the musical process and form dominate—constantly regenerated and constantly suppressed.

Now it is becoming clearer, I think, just how much it means to speak of the interior processes of language in literary form, how much it means to say that in such form words are related only to each other. For this is not a narrow perspective, as it might once have appeared to be, at all. In their relation to themselves, words announce their felt original or natural condition, their quality as rhythmic utterance that both contains and denies their potential for signifying use and seems so much greater than such use, which as the invoked, prior source of meaning actively cancels meaning's tributary fuctions even as it implies them.

That there are at least two sorts of pasts felt in the aural, and aesthetic, processes of language—the past of the words' original, qualitative condition, and the presumably more recent past of multiple use and association now rendered inactive by the music—is important in another way and reemphasizes the force of the interior action of words in aesthetic form. For the most consistently felt but difficult to explicate property of aural experience is the feeling in it of a peculiar, unspecified nostalgia, the sense of a past that, evidently, never happened.

In listening to music itself, perhaps, one may feel very strongly this odd nostalgia, which seems unquestionably generated by the music but has no specific relation with it. I am not speaking here of particularly nostalgic music—like Schumann's *Kinderscenen*—in which musical images specifically childlike may seem evoked, but about music that has nothing so programmatically past about it, one of the Brandenburg concerti, for example. Even in such a case, the feeling of some past may be intense, though the music itself in the relentless immediacy of its assured progress would seem, moment to moment, to deny it; and a childlike relation to the music may be felt, although apparently the music has nothing of anybody's childhood—not even Bach's—in it.

This feeling of childlikeness in the perception of musical form may for one thing be a way of one's noting one's own receptiveness to the musical process, a receptiveness that this process creates in its domination of one's imagination, whose resulting openness resembles the imagination of childhood. The image of childhood itself may contain one's joint perception both of this receptiveness and of the compelling feeling that one is in the presence of a created but unspecified past, as if having a memory that was not a memory of one's own experience.

Again in particular relation to the experience of music, Gabriel Marcel remarks the possibility of something he calls "pure memory" and suggests that "any true musical creation consists first of all in conjuring up in us *a certain past,*" and by "certain" here he does not mean "specified," but quite the opposite:

> When I speak of the decomposition of the past, it is indeed difficult not to believe that I mean subdividing it into *historical sections.* Mozart would transport me to Vienna in the 18th century; Monteverdi to Mantua a century and a half or two centuries earlier, etc. Moreover that sort of evocation would be achieved by means of a play of association of ideas which are diversified *ad infinitum.* But actually there is no question here of any such thing. In this instance, the past is not any particular section of a historical becoming, more or less explicitly assimilated to a movement in space, such as a film sequence. It is rather the inner depths of oneself, inexplicable with respect to what the present not only

arranges, but—again and most particularly—qualifies. These multiple pasts are really sentimental perspectives according to which life can be relived, not as a series of events, but to the extent that it is an indivisible unity which can only be apprehended as such through art. . . .[18]

Marcel is not altogether clear on how this sense of a past is generated in music, nor does he mean to be. He is concerned more with marking it and declaring it as a feeling central to musical experience. We may suppose, however, that its generation has something to do with repetition. Repetition itself is so indigenous to musical experience that one does not speak of it generally in that context, but particularly, of all its varieties that are simply the total possible devices of musical composition. But I am concerned here with musical experience only as a general analogy for certain aspects of literary experience and aesthetic experience at large, and so what might be imagined as the general force of repetition is at least initially important. Kierkegaard—obliquely and waggishly, and untenaciously—draws a suggestive connection between repetition and recollection, maintaining that repetition is to the present and future as recollection is to the past,[19] and though there is not much more to what he says than that, there may be a clue in it to the dynamics of musical or aural illusion. We may speculate that the experience of repetition, the fact of an immediate repeating as we hear it in music or in musical prose, itself resonates or even corresponds with a feeling of earlier repeating, as if the fact of the repeated present blurred into the feeling of a repetition from a past more distant than just a moment ago and thus generated the illusion that one were not merely repeating the present but recollecting the past.

Such a general explanation may perhaps seem rather too speculative. But this feeling of unspecified recollection may be traced more precisely, in aural literary processes, to the dynamic of residual meanings within those processes. If repetition may be said to be the source of such feelings in generally musical situations, then we may see again that its force in literary contexts, in particular situations of word-music, is double. For the varieties of repetition in literary form have some of the more abstract nostalgic force common to certain kinds of purely musical repetition, but at the same time, literary repetition operates upon the more specific energies of the words' meanings, upon the past uses and associations of the words, rendering them inactive and residual. And thus the unspecified past of musical processes at large is multiplied in literary form by the residual force of the once meaningful words now enmeshed in a musical dynamic. A more specified past than music ever suggests is therefore both implied and undercut in word-music; and as it is more specifically potential, it seems all the more energized in its suppression. So one may feel, more sharply than in music, always on the verge of a memory one cannot have, in the presence of a past that is vital but that is only maintained, as Marcel says, as "inexplicable with respect to what the present not only arranges but . . . qualifies."

The special power of aural processes of language derives from continuous visual-intelligible expectations that are continuously denied. Specific visual energies are constantly redefined in these processes as mere and unextendable aspects of the original quality of language that the music invokes. And this suggests also that the feeling, in aural processes of language, or a return to an imaginative source—associated most particularly with the perception of an originating voice and author—has its roots in one's recognition of this quality that seems natural and original to language and of the unspecified past with which that quality seems imbued. Such a recognition, however, should not be supposed to counter the authorial figure, but rather to indicate how the perception of a personal authorial presence and source is reciprocal, in word-music, with the repetitive and reflexive word-to-word effects of aural process and the imaginative condition that these effects establish.

For all the formal devices by which fiction accomplishes its aural conversion and insists upon its self-enclosed fictionalness inevitably create the vital illusion of a voice issuing from a past and personal author. Susanne Langer refers to these devices as "the means that sustain the difference between art and life—the simplification and manipulation of life's image that makes it essentially different from its prototype" (*Feeling and Form*, 292). I am not sure of the relevance of "simplification" here, but I am sure that all such "means" are felt by the perceiver as evidences and forms of "manipulation." In the particular case of narrative fiction, the inclination of words—through repetitive dynamics—to reveal themselves as such, and of images to isolate as qualitative rather than to meld into the steps and stages of imaginative progress, and of the entire narrative to enclose itself in its own action: all these are felt as the function of a manipulative presence whose power is undeniable and to whose range a reader yields his imagination. This authorial presence is not merely something that one may postulate or not postulate theoretically, but is something intensely perceived in the experience of reading. By incorporating it into our model of fictional process more generally, we may see that the fictional worlds of certain novels are not, as we might have supposed, compromised by "authorial intrusion," that, on the contrary, such worlds may seem the more real just because of their evident aspect as manipulated fiction.[20] The example I want to consider for this purpose is Nabokov's *Bend Sinister*; no work I know of gives better evidence of the imaginative fertility of vocal manipulation and presence.

In its visual aspect, *Bend Sinister* is a melodrama, though at its later stages it becomes so effectively gripping and moving as to belie such a label. Its hero, Adam Krug, is ultimately taken prisoner by the fascist state and so separated from his young son, who is to be held hostage pending Krug's endorsement of the government. Frightened completely and for the first time in the story, Krug agrees at once to anything and everything, but through a series of the incompetences that are this government's rule, his son David is misplaced and then murdered so horribly and sadistically that one declines the full imagining of it. Then, to make the best of the situation, David is anxiously embalmed and cosmeticized and costumed for the new patriot Krug's approval. Soon afterward, Krug's mind snaps. At the end, he is chasing after the dictator, Paduk, as he did when they were schoolboys together, and one bullet takes his ear off, and "just a fraction of an instant before another and better bullet hit him, he shouted again: You, you—

and the wall vanished, like a rapidly withdrawn slide, and I stretched myself and got up from among the chaos of written and rewritten pages, to investigate the sudden twang that something had made in striking the wire netting of my window."[21]

This, although not quite the end of the novel, is all there is to Krug's story. With that dash after "You, you," we are wrenched finally away from him—as by the rapid withdrawal of the visual slide—and into the sole presence of the author "among the chaos of written and rewritten pages." This is authorial manipulation with a vengeance. All the moment-to-moment narrative techniques —all the visual faults and regular rhythms—that convert realistic sequence into the fictional patterns controlled by an artist are dwarfed by this sort of takeover. The wall that Krug is approaching simply vanishes along with the story's entire visual substance, and we are confronted with its absolute controller and possessor.

But this is surprising only in its extravagance, for, of course, Nabokov has been in possession throughout. From the beginning, he insists upon his despotic authorial rights, upon a power over fiction and reader so pronounced that it seems godlike. At the beginning, therefore, while there remains some question as to what sort of story we are reading, the narrative does not seem serious. Its imaginative play—so long as we harbor conventional visual-realistic expectations—makes its sequence seem inconsequent.[22] Krug initially introduces himself, for instance, in the first person, then is reintroduced in the third, and then, with melodramatic embellishment, introduced again: "Krug—for it was he—showed her the blurred paper. He was a huge tired man with a stoop" (6). A few pages later this gambit is both insisted on and, perhaps along with the reader who has accepted it, mocked: "Krug—for it was sitll he—walked on . . ." (13).

But the range of imaginative play in *Bend Sinister* is far greater even than such examples suggest. This narrative shifts so constantly and dizzyingly from one mode to another that at moments it seems that Krug becomes Nabokov, that this wholesale trickery is a mask for, among other things, absolute directness and honesty in the narrator. And the resultant multiple aspects of the hero, far from undercutting his realisticness as we might have expected, seem somehow to reinforce it: " 'Yes, of course—how stupid of me,' thought Krug, the circle in Krug, one Krug in another one" (39).

The story itself, by the same token, may be intensely visual just because its visual sequence is doubted. After a crucial meeting with the dictator, which is imagined devotedly in a single-minded straight line—offered, that is, as normal sequence—the narrator shifts:

> Which, of course, terminated the interview. Thus? Or perhaps in some other way? Did Krug really glance at the prepared speech? And if he did, was it really as silly as all that? He did; it was. The seedy tyrant or the president of the State, or the dictator, or who-ever he was—the man Paduk in a word, the Toad in another—did hand my favourite character a mysterious batch of neatly typed pages. The actor playing the recipient should be taught not to look at his hand while he takes the papers *very slowly* (keeping those lateral lower-jaw muscles in movement, please) but to stare straight at the giver: in short, look at the giver first, *then* lower your eyes to the gift. But both were clumsy and cross men, and the experts in the cardiarium exchanged solemn nods at a certain point (when the milk was upset), and they, too, were not acting. (151)

This is dazzling; but the most remarkable thing about it is that it does not appear to dazzle us out of the realism. The sequence is ostentatiously called into question, but then its very "silliness" is made to reinforce its occurrence: "He did; it was." Next Paduk is the more present because manipulative changes in his identity turn out to be merely nominal, and Krug's existence vibrates between the visual emphasis that he at least and especially is there—"did hand"—and the aural avowal that he is especially fictional—"my favourite character." Then all the false finickiness about acting the drama out is extended until, in a shift that is both offhand and startling, it becomes the very proof that the drama is true: "and they, too, were not acting."

This is only another single instance. I do not want to try to cover the range of Nabokov's play with his fiction, but just to show for a few occasions of it—while asserting this for others—that beneath or within the play, the story maintains its visual power. The effect here resembles to some extent the action of *As I Lay Dying*, where the visual sequence presses through the aural fixations of the individual narrators because it is melodramatic. A philosopher's son in the hands of murderous fools is as urgent as a mother cooking in her coffin, and no matter how involved and attracting and distracting the superstructure becomes, what runs under it will be attended. But the melodrama of *Bend Sinister* is not our dominant interest, for the relation between the narrative's independent, visual energy and the narrator's aural manipulation of it as fiction is much more complementary than such an interest would entail. Here is Krug entering prison:

> Krug was led through several yards to the main building. In yards Nos. 3 and 4, outlines of condemned men for target practice had been chalked on a brick wall. An old Russian legend says that the first thing a *rastrelianyĭ* [person executed by the firing squad] sees on entering the "other world" (no interruption please, this is premature, take your hands away) is not a gathering of ordinary "shades" or "spirits" or repulsive dear repulsive unutterably dear unutterably repulsive dear ones in antiquated clothes, as you might think, but a kind of silent slow ballet, a welcoming group of these chalked outlines moving wavily like transparent Infusoria; but away with those bleak superstitions. (210)

Whether the play with *rastrelianyĭ* is fake or not, it would seem to have the same mock-precious tone, indicating that the entire occasion for this movement in the narrative is, in the first place, whimsical. Nor can one get smoothly over the "interruption": is it Nabokov's own invitation to the "other world"? Or a less ultimate interruption of his writing? But the movement that follows it is a perfect example of the imaginative combination so frequent in him, where what begins as verbal whimsy is soon felt to be suffused with committed feeling, where the narrative act of fiddling with an image both becomes passionate itself and issues into further images that are thoroughly engaging as both play and realism—"moving wavily like transparent Infusoria"—which may then, as happens here, be redefined once more as digression and wiped off the board.

The next paragraph, where Krug enters his cell, is perhaps even more strikingly illustrative:

> So suddenly did his guards disappear that, had he been a character in fiction, he might well have wondered whether the strange doings and so on had not been some evil vision, and so forth. He had a throbbing headache: one of those headaches that seem to transcend on one side the limits of one's head, like the colours in cheap comics, and do not quite fill the head space on the other; and the dull throbs were saying: one, one, one, never reaching two, never. Of the four doors at the cardinal points of the circular room, only one, one, one was unlocked. Krug pushed it open. (210)

The first sentence here, in a lesser novelist, would very likely have held sway and been followed with others like it. But Nabokov is making fun of such an elementary gesture, and he not only shifts against it, but also turns the break in the story's visual surface to visual account. The image of Krug's headache in comic book colors is so isolatedly hilarious and ingenious that it ought to be distracting, and the change to auditory metaphor should have made an impossible mix; and yet the movement is extended so tenaciously that its aural resonance—"one, one, one, never reaching two, never"—carries right into and motivates its further visual sequence: "only one, one, one was unlocked."

But it may be felt that such an account of narrative alternations and conversions is making issues where there are none. Other writers may lead us to think in terms of divisions between a narrative's visual involvement and the play of its voice, but in Nabokov, any separation between his narrative's visual intensity and its manifest quality as fiction is not felt for long. Nor is there the feeling of strain or marked achievement in his conversions of one into the other. Nabokov's action is largely not that of the writer who seems deliberately to set himself unlikely exercises with the effect that his mastering them seems a deliberate display of visual power—as, for instance, one may see in Pynchon. Perhaps because of Nabokov's undoubtable and pervasive control of narrative and reader, there seems no worry about power here at all. His multiple relation to his story seems altogether fluid and single-minded:

> It was at that moment, just after Krug had fallen through the bottom of a confused dream and sat up on the straw with a gasp— and just before his reality, his remembered hideous misfortune could pounce upon him—it was then that I felt a pang of pity for Adam and slid towards him along an inclined beam of pale light— causing instantaneous madness, but at least saving him from the senseless agony of his logical fate. (233)

It is amusing and even absurd, that the author's presence becomes here godlike, and his interruption divine intervention; and yet the emergence of this "I"—with all its amazing self-regard and manipulativeness—once again does not dissolve the substance of the story, but solidifies it. It does so because this "I," as cognizant as it is of the realistic story in which Adam must have his "logical fate," is even more devoted to Adam as a kind of life for whom such logic would be a "senseless agony." This defines the imaginative attitude in Nabokov by which narrative manipulation and aural control of the fiction becomes the means of recognizing its dominating substance. For though this fiction is continually interrupted and ultimately thrown over, though repeatedly exposed and discounted as a fiction, the life in it always remains first, the main thing, the object of the narrator's continuing interest and even of his passion. Nabokov in this way enacts perfectly how dealing not with extendable reality but with enclosed fiction is imaginatively enabling for both writer and reader and makes possible an immediate commitment of energy and a devotion to the internal substance of the story that more visual motives, in their insistence upon narrative sense and a reader's own action with it, must restrict.

Here the discounting of the story's reality becomes a way of establishing its imaginative ascendancy, and the energy of Nabokoy's play all round and over it expresses not only his control over it but its control over him. Here, authorial manipulation reverses itself and reveals itself as inescapable imaginative engagement with the fiction. So in the aural process it is not simply that a reader and a world are controlled by an author, but that the author himself, and thus the reader as well, are manipulated by a force that proceeds from within that world. This reciprocal domination may remind us of something that Mrs. Langer calls, in connection with music, the "commanding form," which initially is "conceived" or "intuited" by the composer and which then dominates his every movement through the course of the work. The action of this form within the work might seem obvious enough; but its compelling power over the listener or reader seems greater than any interior action would, rationally, seem accountable for. And its power over the composer or author himself may seem magical, something given or visited upon him, perhaps, from the surrounding field—as Mrs. Langer's aesthetic might have it—of potential forms that are the "virtual reality" of the world.

But I prefer a slightly different and more personal image for this relation, in which, for instance, the author of *Bend Sinister*, just as he dominates us to his range and engenders in us what I have earlier characterized as a childlike receptiveness to a storyteller, is himself dominated by the storyteller that in his fiction he makes and hears, in an absorbed response to his own voice. And this voice, for its very power, may seem at times not even of his own making, as if it signaled the presence of not merely his own energy but that of some storyteller beyond him, in relation to whom the author himself is childlike. To put it somewhat more abstractly but more literally, the evident domination of the author by his voice may arise from the fact that that voice amounts to both the re-creation and the recognition of the musical quality of his language, a quality that his voice establishes, but that seems original, and prior to that voice—that seems even to be the magical source for his and for all voices.

This articulation of the vocal or aural figure is for me the most expressive image of the intense energies that I have associated with the interior processes of fiction and of the forms of art at large. Our difficulty, or hesitancy, in accounting for such energies—and at times even in feeling them—in narrative fiction may be seen to stem from the more obvious and appetizing currency of realistic or extensive fictional processes:

> The difficulty which many people encounter in judging prose fiction . . . lies largely in the medium—discursive language . . . it is hard not to be deceived into supposing the author intends, by his use of words, just what we intend by ours—to inform, comment, inquire, confess . . . (*Feeling and Form*, 288)

From Mrs. Langer's account of just what "discursive" means, furthermore, we may derive a better understanding of the obvious and persuasive power of realistic or visual narrative form:

> All language has a form which requires us to string out our ideas even though their objects rest one within another; as pieces of clothing that are actually worn one over the other have to be strung side by side on the clothesline. This property of verbal symbolism is known as *discursiveness*; by reason of it, only thoughts which can be arranged in this peculiar order can be spoken at all; any idea which does not lend itself to this "projection" is ineffable, incommunicable by means of words.[23]

One might stipulate here, however—as she herself does later for aesthetic forms more generally—that discursiveness is not language's only form, for we have been dealing throughout with certain verbal processes that counter the discursive arrangement. But the discursive is the only form for ordinary language, language used for purposes of realistic communication and meaning.

Here this discursiveness—with its capacity for imagining experience only in sequence—is figured as a limitation, a matter of the restricted pattern into which language that is realistically motivated must fall. That is to say that whether or not we would argue that such sequential imagining is true to the nature of some kinds of experience, it is obviously true to the nature and capacity of language itself. Our faith in sequence as the most accurate verbal form, and our feeling that it is the most normal verbal form, spring in part from the fact that sequence is the only form that language can take under realistic conditions. But that linguistic inclination itself may be seen to arise from our everyday needs, since movement through sequence is our readiest expression of our individual imaginative powers.

A comparison to the opposite sort of power that verbal repetition and rhythm—the aural imagining of words' quality—may express, then, is not necessary to suggest the artificialness of sequence as an imaginative conception. For "artificial" here means simply that sequential imagining arises evidently, first, from the possibilities of form in language itself—which are obviously successive—and, second, from our interests in and demands upon that successive form. Thus it is impossible to say how accurate discursive or sequential processes are, because we require that they be accurate and because they predetermine the shape of the very experiences that we suppose them, accurately, to describe.[24]

Even though it may seem philosophically simple-minded to insist that the sequential process of discursive verbal forms is as obviously fictional as any other sort of imaginative process, it is worth doing so just because we do not consider sequence as fiction. It is, again, our great realism. Because it seems to be all that language can do, and because it is ordinarily all that we want language to do—because we can perform so satisfactorily upon it—it becomes our way to the truth. This sort of prejudice, along with the apparent limitations of sequence as an imaginative and even a perceptual form, constitute the liabilities of discursiveness.[25]

But in the context of realistic fiction, those liabilities become assets. The mythical realism and normalness of sequential imagining—which has its roots not in the nature of real experience but in the nature of language itself and in our more aggressive motives for it—is the source of its narrative power. Narrative becomes even more normal than experience itself, for the successiveness indigenous to ordinary language is allowed freer play in fiction even than it is in our day-to-day lives. The sequential aspect of verbal form thus has both its farthest expression and its exemplar in the novel.

We should not be surprised, then, at past tendencies to mistake musical processes in the novel for realistic ones or at past reluctances to relinquish the pleasures and powers that sequential imagining offers in narrative fiction.[26] And this, essentially, is why I have used terms like *noncognitive* and *nonintelligible* to describe the imaginative motives and processes other than the sequential that are perhaps more vitally important to us, but whose dynamics and even effects may be buried under what is more normal and known and more obviously rewarding. Mrs. Langer's term for such motives is "nondiscursive," a more balanced phrasing that grants and provides that our imaginative life involves at least two sorts of intelligibility and not one. But her balance on this issue is not general; as she notes herself, perceived energies that do not lend themselves to sequential postulation are generally considered incommunicable, and this reflects the imaginative situation that I began by calling, in the first chapter, a tyranny. So I have used terms stronger than *nondiscursive* to draw attention to our prejudicial faith in discursive language itself and our resulting practical disregard of other, more aesthetic, imagining as special or artificial.

The stronger terms are also useful for establishing the radical difference between the interior intelligibility of musical or aural process, and perhaps of aesthetic process more generally, and the extensive intelligibility of ordinary language. For verbal energies are so transformed by their aesthetic enclosure and unification that, in comparison to our more practical imagining, they are indeed not intelligible at all. Their quality declares from moment to moment the inexpressibleness of the intelligence that resides in it.

This verbal quality is perhaps harder to recognize and to allow in narrative fiction than anywhere else, for there the discursive rule of ordinary imagining may seem to hold sway even more strongly than in our practical experience. Whereas in the case of a piece of music or even in that of a lyric poem we may be ready occasionally to relax our visual concern for moving through sequence to real meaning, the novel—just in the exaggerated and artificial successiveness of its usual arrangement—seems to invite us to proceed realistically with even more intensity and freedom than is possible anywhere else. And even a narrative structure that distorts or confuses such succession easily may maintain a-rhythmically its visual demands and challenges and so be effortfully but satisfactorily regularized as we read. In the absence of the fixed countersequential patterns and obvious rhythms that we perceive in other literary modes—in the absence of obvious form—fiction appears always to us as probable sequence, until it converts such sequence entirely.

When it does so, however, the counterforce is all the greater, and the opposed strengths of both of the motives of narrative fiction are all the more marked. The strength of the visual-realistic motive is felt in imaginative motion. It creates the illusion of extensiveness, endless novelty, and limitless imaginative range. Its corresponding weakness lies in the dependency of this motion upon narrative instability and insubstantialness, but in the grips of the illusion, such a price seems worth paying. For that illusion, as it arises from stimulated imaginative fluidity, from the necessary sequential progress from word to word and image to image, is that in this direction lies reality. This illusion reinforces and regenerates our confidence in our free imaginative agency, and that agency seems efficient: we are sure that we are going somewhere. At the same time, the very instability at the source of the motion and illusion, the absence of felt substance, transforms that confidence into a need for imaginative action, as if we felt—even as Thomas Sutpen felt—that it was only through such action that correspondence between the self and the world could be generated or through such action that both self and the world could be completed, even achieved. The confidence of the visual is that we can do something in order to recognize ourselves; its anxiety is that we must.

Against the active force of these motives and this dependency upon aggressive motion, it is no wonder that aural motives may seem, at first, passive and unintelligible. For in the aural process, fictional worlds are substantial precisely because, since they are fictions, we are not going anywhere with them. Their words and images are felt as qualities in themselves and of the dominating voice that expresses and enforces their formal nature and enclosure, their fictional quality. Our attitude in response to that voice is not free and acquisitive but yielding and receptive, and our will to move becomes a willingness to be moved. The consistency and composition of the self are here no longer at issue, for its immediate importance as the imagination upon whom and for whom the fictional play is committed is clear and secure. Within and because of these limits, the imagination's own play is more intense, more multiple and various, more devoted and more patient than it is felt to be in realistic processes. In this sense, aural and aesthetic attitudes are not passive at all; nor are they really unintelligible; they are indeed more active and free than the visual, but only within their expressed and formal limits—given our understanding that only within them may we be free and know them.

But, again, neither the visual nor the aural motive appears purely or isolatedly in serious fiction with much frequency.[27] The situation of mixed motives, visual-aural complexity, is in the novel the rule rather than the exception. This makes the novel a special form and a most problematic one so far as literary criticism and theory are concerned. But in terms of our reading experience, this problematic nature is the novel's richness and power as a form, for the obvious individual force of either visual or aural motives taken singly is most often in the novel emphasized and relieved by narrative conversion from one to the other. This is a conversion that normally, in aesthetic perception, happens only once in its obvious way. We walk up to a painting, or a conductor taps with his baton, and the quality of our entire imaginative experience changes, the world changes. But in the best moments of the novel as a form, this change may occur again and again, as visual and aural—or realistic and aesthetic—energies counter and generate each other and transform experience from reality to play and back again and again.

Yet this change is not infinite. Over the course of a narrative, decided conversions from visual to aural may reverse themselves, then to reconvert, and so on. But narratives in which this process is decided and sustained cannot end anyhow but musically: "When words and music come together in a song," Susanne Langer says, "music swallows words" (Feeling and Form, 152). As I see it, this is also true for the novel; when words as significant and words as musical come together there, the result can only be word-music. Fiction's aural aspect is compelling or, if we are choosing, doubly inviting. It is not—like the visual—exclusive, but allows us to have the fiction both ways, since the process of fictional music at the same time functions to secure and to reenergize the images of which the music is composed.

"I knew," Nabokov says at the end of *Bend Sinister*, of his hero, "that the immortality I had conferred on the poor fellow was a slippery sophism, a play upon words. But the very last lap of his life had been happy, and it had been proved to him that death was but a question of style" (241). Thus that hero and his story—and our engagement with them—are reasserted as the focus of real care even as they are discounted as imaginative play. And it is this voiced and present devotion to the fictional that distinguishes the aural motives of art and artist and defines the novel's music. So when another musical voice instructs us that "the final belief is to believe in a fiction, which you know to be a fiction, there being nothing else,"[28] we may indeed hear in it something other than a merely realistic resignation, for in the novel—and perhaps in all imaginative gesture—the final belief is in fiction as fiction just because there is nothing better, nothing that so embodies and binds the imagination's divided life.

Notes

CHAPTER ONE

1. Stephen Crane, "The Open Boat," *The Works of Stephen Crane,* ed. Fredson Bowers (Charlottesville: The University Press of Virginia, 1970), V, p. 68. Further references to Crane's stories are to this edition and are given in the text.

2. We not only assume the connection between seeing and knowing, then, but also usually conceive it as a matter of temporal sequence. This conception is crucial to our experience of reading narrative.

3. Ernest Hemingway, *A Farewell to Arms* (New York: Scribner's, 1969), p. 3.

4. In "Lexis and Melos," his introduction to *Sound and Poetry, English Institute Essays, 1956* (New York: Columbia University Press, 1957), Northrop Frye says that "the chief characteristics of musical poetry are continuity and stress accent" (xv), and thus suggests, as he goes on to develop this idea, that to be musical, poetry has somehow to counter its single- and even-lined layout, that it must be more continuous, en- jambed, and stressed than its separation into such microstructures allows. This may be relevant to my own concerns, in that we may infer from it that musical effects are more likely and indigenous in prose than in poetry, since prose has far less to work against to achieve these same effects.

 The prose that best fits the requirements of continuity and stress— oddly enough, considering the usual assessment of it—is prose like Hemingway's. In the same collection, Frederick W. Sternfeld, in "Poetry and Music—*Ulysses*," says that some of the "characteristics that mark the influence of musical procedures are lines of greatly uneven length and a prominent and extensive use of monosyllables" (35)— Hemingway again.

5. In *The Untuning of the Sky* (Princeton: Princeton University Press, 1961), John Hollander remarks this "Neoclassical" prejudice along with other conceptions of the force, in literary form, of "musical elements":

Throughout literary history, the "musical" elements of language have been assigned various purposes, from those of adornment, by Neoclassicism, to those of intrinsic irrational necessity, by the *symbolistes*. No matter what our view, or that of a poet whose work we are attempting to analyze, might be on this score, we would probably agree that because of this "musical" quality the language of a poem would affect us as readers in ways in which the words of a telegram would not. From a purely formalistic point of view, the "music of poetry" would be confined to patterns of linguistic redundancy, of those elements which, the poem being treated as a coded message, would be beside the point. But in any rational attempt to distinguish poetry from other utterances, it is precisely these elements which become of greatest concern.

It is also generally agreed that the materials of musical languages do not carry "meanings" either; in fact, the phrase "music of poetry" would generally be defended as useful because of the apparent similarity between the ways that music affects us and the manner in which formal, non-semantic poetic elements contribute to our experience of poetry. There are good overall reasons for likening the significance of music to the significance of literary form. (8)

But Hollander does not attempt that "likening" in *The Untuning of the Sky*, despite his grasp of the job that might be done. Instead he chooses to consider music and ideas about music as a poetic "concern" or as a "formal subject for poetry" (17). What he means by "musical imagery," for instance, is an aspect of music functioning as a poetic material (122 ff.). I am not faulting the critical course he takes, but only pointing out that it is very different from some of the questions he raises so pointedly in his "Introductory."

Perhaps more surprisingly, however, given his acknowledgment that "there are good overall reasons for likening the significance of music to the significance of literary form," he does not really attempt to do so in his later book, *Vision and Resonance* (New York: Oxford, 1975), whose title suggested to me that it would be about the radical differences between visual and aural motives in poetry. But this book is a collection of essays rather than a consecutive argument, and Hollander's concern with the function of sound in poetry, though both dense and delicate in his treatment of particular poetic effects, is itself essentially Neoclassical: he conceives that sound functions always as something that furthers communicative meanings (which include, of course, ambiguities) even by creating such meanings fictitiously. But his attitude on this issue is complicated. I shall return to it later.

6. Hemingway, *A Farewell to Arms*, p. 4.

7. "The Doctor and the Doctor's Wife," *The Short Stories of Ernest Hemingway* (New York: Scribner's, 1966), p. 97. The emphasis is mine.

8. For a simple demonstration of the limitations, in literary criticism, of this attitude that repetition in literary form is always liable to be "faulty," see Calvin S. Brown, *Music and Literature* (Atlanta: University of Georgia Press, 1948). Although ostensibly concerned with musical energies in literature, Brown supposes throughout that the motive of literature is to communicate intelligibly, and thus he considers that "music tolerates . . . far more repetition than does literature." He continues as follows:

> Repetition without variation is strictly limited in poetry by the fact that one remembers an idea even though the words in which it was embodied may have escaped the memory; *hence the idea alone is usually sufficient for the further purposes of the work,* and there is no need to repeat the exact wording until that has become established in the mind. It also follows from that principle that variation in literature does not, as a general rule, alter the feeling of redundancy which extensive literary repetition is likely to produce. The exact words are not established in the reader's mind as are the exact notes of a musical theme, and therefore when the idea is repeated in a different form he is not aware of—and hence not interested in—the difference. (111, my emphasis)

I would agree in part with this last notion, for it demonstrates the extreme liability of literary development to the action of repetition—its liability to aural or musical conversion. We may note, however, that Brown assumes that such a change would necessarily be for the worse. I have emphasized his phrasing concerning the "idea" and the "purposes of the work" to show that he assumes that such purposes are necessarily ideological, and therefore that "redundancy" must always amount simply to a formal lapse. This is the visual-intelligible bias, which grants to art only the same general motive as ordinary communication. Aestheticians have been strugglng with it ever since Aristotle—who was not, from the evidence that we possess, himself an aesthetician at all—first insisted on it.

When Brown considers fiction, therefore, his account of the repetitive formula—which he calls the "Leitmotiv"—presumes for this device an intelligible function: "in both music and literature the Leitmotiv has to be comparatively short and *must have a programmatic association— must refer to something beyond the tones or words which it contains*" (211, my emphasis). In short, his assumption that literature always "must communicate something outside [its] structural pattern" is exactly the attitude I shall argue against (270).

9. Ernest Hemingway, "Big Two-Hearted River: Part I," *Short Stories*, p. 215.

CHAPTER TWO

1. The particular discussion of "oral" versus "written" that I have in mind

is in Robert Scholes and Robert Kellogg, *The Nature of Narrative* (New York, 1966), pp. 17–56.

2. Ibid, p. 82.

3. John Hollander traces this conception to our view of the Greeks: "Behind so much Western aesthetics since Classical antiquity lies a nostalgia for what was believed quite naively to have been a perfect, mystical marriage, in Attic times, of musical mode and ethos, of form and the effect upon human behavior proper to that form; a nostalgia for what was thought to have been a perfect music-poetry that made of human sense an instrument whose own sound was human feeling. The myth of such a golden age in which communication was immediate, and guided only by the channel of suitable form, became in the Renaissance a myth of literature itself." *Vision and Resonance,* p. 160.

4. Scholes and Kellogg, *The Nature of Narrative,* pp. 83–84.

5. Ibid., p. 84.

6. "I was lately forced into the rather close examination of this book, for I had to translate it into French, that forcing me to give it much closer attention than would be the case in any reading however minute. And I will permit myself to say that I was astounded at the work I must have put into the construction of the book, at the intricate tangle of references and cross-references. Nor is that to be wondered at, for though I wrote it with comparative rapidity, I had it hatching within myself for fully another decade." *The Good Soldier* (New York: Vintage, 1955), p. xx.

What seems to me pretentious here is the implication that the novel, though written rapidly, was "constructed" together deliberately from a kind of minutely detailed outline that Ford had in his head. I am not taking exception to his estimate of the work that he put into it, then, though I would rather call it energy, but to his professed notion of the kind of work it was. For in my view, *The Good Soldier* is so intricate that no such deliberate and discursive process could have brought it about. It is relatively common for the authors of complex narratives to take credit for such processes—and thus to play to commonplace notions about how complicated work is done—and for some degrees and sorts of complexity this is perhaps justified. But again, anyone who knows the amazingly convoluted development of *The Good Soldier* may well doubt that it was planned as a matter of "reference and cross-reference."

7. Ralph Freedman, *The Lyrical Novel* (Princeton: Princeton University Press, 1963), p. 1. Further references to Freedman's argument are to this edition and are given in the text.

8. It may be worth noting, however, that—like so many models that treat unconventional narrative forms but assume the conventional motive of novelistic meaning—this one's emphasis must at some point, or at last, be negative. The model leads to talk about "imaginative failure": "It would not, then, be enough to say that [certain lyrical novels] represent failures of personal sensibility, constructs of pathetic minds unable to create concrete worlds. As compensations for failure they may indeed bear witness to the personal tragedies of writers. But the very ambivalence of novelist and poet which requires these compensations has often converted 'failure' into magnificent achievement" (Ibid., p. 17).

    This is the familiar doublemindedness that springs from considering irregular form in relation to regular motive, and it may occur to us that it is more than enough to label these forms failures on the one hand but successes on the other: it may occur to us that the whole notion of failure here, hinged as it is on the old unquestioned motive of the novel as realistically intelligible, may not be necessary. I shall say much more about this later, but for another such exercise in literary critical doublemindedness, see, for instance, James Guetti, *The Limits of Metaphor* (Ithaca: Cornell University Press, 1967).

9. Marshall McLuhan, *The Gutenberg Galaxy* (Toronto: University of Toronto Press, 1962). Further references are to this edition and are given in the text.

10. Louis Bouyer, *The Liturgical Piety*, p. 16.

11. Stephen P. Scher, *Verbal Music in German Literature* (New Haven: Yale University Press, 1968), p. 3. Further references are to this edition and are given in the text.

12. Wilson Coker, *Music and Meaning* (New York: Free Press, 1972), p. 158.

13. Ibid, p. 159.

14. Compare Susanne Langer: "The surprising thing is that long after art theory had passed the naive stage, and every serious thinker realized that imitation was neither the aim nor the measure of artistic creation, the traffic of the image with its model kept its central place among philosophical problems of art. It has figured as the question of form and content, of interpretation, of idealization, of belief and make-believe, and of impression and expression. Yet the idea of copying nature is not even applicable to all the arts. What does a building copy? On what given object does one model a melody?" *Feeling and Form* (New York: Scribner's, 1953), p. 46.

For a much subtler discussion than Scher's of onomatopoeia, however, see "The Metrical Frame" in Hollander's *Vision and Resonance*,
especially (p. 154): "By and large, the so-called imitative effects of
poetic rhythm will be seen to work in two ways: through those devices
which associate words or parts of words, and through those which
enforce re-groupings of them by more subtle means than simply those
of connection. . . . Assonance and alliteration link parts of words,
as well as syllables, and their operation is through what a linguist would
call a morphophonemic medium, creating momentary fictions about
the association of sound and sense in the language. The effects of
onomatopoeia in general can all be traced to these devices."

CHAPTER THREE

1. Susanne Langer considers that this sort of interrogation treats literature
    unaesthetically, and attributes such treatment to our assumptions about
    the "material" of which literature is made: "The reason why literature
    is a standard academic pursuit lies in the very fact that one can treat
    it as something else than art. Since its normal material is language, and
    language is, after all, the medium of discourse, it is always possible to
    look at a literary work as an assertion of facts and opinions, that is, as a
    piece of discursive symbolism functioning in the usual communicative
    way" (*Feeling and Form*, 208).

    How much this motive had to do with the inception of professional
    literary studies I do not know; but certainly it has much to do with
    their continuance. All of the common assumptions—no matter how
    apparently complicated or sophisticated—about how literature works on
    us and we on it are what I would call visual-realistic. They attempt to
    characterize literary energies by extending those energies to discursive
    processes outside them: we are used to thinking about the understanding
    a work brings us to, about its relations to kinds of statements different
    from its own, especially pseudophilosophical statements, which may
    seem so much more palatable when derived obliquely. In this way,
    reading literature becomes totally an act of translation, where the
    imagination shifts almost instantaneously from a text to the manipula-
    tion of that text within contexts external to it.

    The obvious counter-injunction—to describe literary processes as they
    are, to dwell upon them within their formal enclosure for longer than
    an instant—is not philosophically naive, for it does not suppose such
    description, and such concentration, a simple matter. On the contrary,
    it is the other activity that is easy.

2. Wallace Stevens, *Collected Poems* (New York: Knopf, 1954), p. 19.
    Further references to Stevens' poetry are to this edition unless otherwise
    noted and are given in the text.

3. *Opus Posthumous* (New York: Knopf, 1957), pp. 117–118.

4. Wallace Stevens, *The Palm at the End of the Mind*, ed. Holly Stevens (New York: Vintage, 1972). "Of Mere Being" is the last poem in the book's sequence, its own "final image."

CHAPTER FOUR

1. Anthony Burgess, *A Clockwork Orange* (New York: Norton, 1963), pp. 1–2. Further references are to this edition and are given in the text.

2. And it may be chicken and egg as to the motive of this "looking through": either one is hungry for sense and so ignores the particular aspect of the language itself and its music; or one is relatively unsusceptible to such music and so pursues intelligibility as the only obvious objective.

3. This is important in relation to those theorists and theories that contend that the interior meanings of literary form are distinguishable from more ordinary verbal meanings chiefly in that they are ambiguous or hypothetical or potential.

4. This notion may be compared to "fictional perception," which because we know it to be fictional always gives happiness, and yet that happiness itself encourages fuller and wider perception of the image, more patient and devoted articulation of its particular facets.

5. Even the most visual and unvoiced and realistic narrative, on the other side, may gradually acquire a voice and become fiction—through total formal repetition—if we read it over many times and begin to hear the words of it as such.

6. Compare the equally perverse use of music on Alex by the authorities to brainwash him (p. 113).

CHAPTER FIVE

1. Theodore Weesner, *The Car Thief* (New York: Random House, 1974), p. 3. Further references are to this edition and are given in the text.

2. Thus the most realistic forms are those in which the invitation or pressure to follow and account for and understand is most intense. Such forms occur in all literary genres, but that in which they are most common, perhaps oddly enough, is science fiction; that is the force of "science," in the phrase itself. But note that this is not so true of the genre we call fantasy.

3. Doris Lessing, *The Four-Gated City* (New York: Bantam, 1970), p. 3.

4. This suggests that form and voice in literature are the same thing.

5. John Barth, *The Floating Opera* (New York: Avon, 1967), pp. 65–66. Further references are to this edition and are given in the text.

6. John Barth, *Lost in the Funhouse* (New York: Bantam, 1969), p. 125.

7. Jules Siegel, "Who is Thomas Pynchon . . . and Why Did He Take Off with My Wife?", *Playboy*, 24, no. 3 (March 1977): 97. Later Siegel articulates the questions as follows: "Somewhere back of that pile of paper and ink there is a question mark named Thomas Pynchon, location unknown, of no fixed address, his biography a mere few sentences, physical description unavailable. Who is Thomas Pynchon, really? . . . Who is Thomas Pynchon and what does he mean" (122)?

8. Ibid., p. 172.

9. Thomas Pynchon, *V.* (Philadelphia: Lippincott, 1963), pp. 93–94. Further references to *V.* are to this edition and are given in the text.

10. For an exactly opposite effect in fiction, we may compare that of the "Singin' in the Rain" rape scene in *A Clockwork Orange*, where the imagining is all sound, and the violence or horror or whatever is completely muted and unfelt as such.

11. As Pynchon himself may have felt that he might never have to "write the answer," for the very life of his fiction.

12. Herman Melville, *Moby Dick*, ed. Luther S. Mansfield and Howard P. Vincent (New York: Hendricks House, 1962), p. 566.

13. This is something—it might be argued—that Melville himself attempted but could not achieve in *Pierre*, where his own self-conscious disassembly of his motives becomes patent and enervated.

CHAPTER SIX

1. From the "Preface" to *The Nigger of the "Narcissus"* (New York: Doubleday, 1914), p. xiv.

2. Joseph Conrad, "Heart of Darkness" (New York: Norton, 1963), p. 79. Further references are to this edition and are given in the text.

3. This is the image that Nabokov enacts so devotedly and ingeniously in *Pale Fire*. Here, from *Timon of Athens*, Act IV, Scene III, lines 438–451, in his title's own source; the text is that of "The New Cam-

bridge Edition," edited by Neilson and Hill (Cambridge [Mass.], 1942):

> *Timon.*
>
>   I'll example you with thievery:
> The sun's a thief, and with his great attraction
> Robs the vast sea; the moon's an arrant thief,
> And her pale fire she snatches from the sun;
> The sea's a thief, whose liquid surge resolves
> The moon into salt tears; the earth's a thief,
> That feeds and breeds by a composture stol'n
> From gen'ral excrement; each thing's a thief;
> The laws, your curb and whip, in their rough power
> Has uncheck'd theft. Love not yourselves; away,
> Rob one another. There's more gold. Cut throats;
> All that you meet are thieves. To Athens go,
> Break open shops; nothing can you steal,
> But thieves do lose it. Steal [no] less for this. . . .

4. Stephen Crane, "The Open Boat," *The Works of Stephen Crane,* ed. Fredson Bowers (Charlottesville: The University Press of Virginia, 1970), V, p. 69. Further references to Crane's stories are to this edition and are given in the text.

5. Again, I am not opposing words to reality here, but words as such, as fiction and even music, to words as signs, as representatives of the perceptual sequences of reality and of reality itself.

6. Bowers, ed., *The Works of Stephen Crane,* II, p. 316.

7. This last phrase, it turns out, may refer to the men in their march. It may be visual description of the army struggling through the mud. But it is oddly distanced: it sounds as if its relevance is to something— some body of thought and language—much larger than the story, something many have discovered. It is, again, an aphoristic rhythm superimposed on a realistic moment.

8. Ernest Hemingway, *A Moveable Feast* (New York: Scribner's, 1964), p. 91.

9. "The Art of Fiction XXI: Ernest Hemingway" (interview), *The Paris Review,* no. 18 (Spring 1958): 88–89.

10. Ernest Hemingway, "Big Two-Hearted River: Part I," *The Short Stories of Ernest Hemingway* (New York: Scribner's, 1966), p. 209. Further references to Hemingway's stories are to this edition and are given in the text.

11. Ernest Hemingway, *A Farewell to Arms* (New York: Scribner's, 1957), pp. 214–215.

12. "Three trout on a layer of ferns, then another layer of ferns, then three more trout, and then covered them with ferns. They looked nice in the ferns." Ernest Hemingway, *The Sun Also Rises* (New York: Scribner's, 1954), pp. 119–120. Further references to *The Sun Also Rises* are to this edition.

13. Ibid., p. 198.

14. William Faulkner, *As I Lay Dying* (New York: Vintage, 1964), pp. 165–166. Further references are to this edition and are given in the text.

15. Most of the time Vardaman says things like, "My mother is a fish," which seems to express his imagination in relation to his location within the progress, to express his character. But at another moment, in an italicized shift, his language is transformed: "*Then he comes up out of the water. He comes a long way up slow before his hands do but he's got to have her got to so I can bear it. Then his hands come up and all of him above the water. I cant stop. I have not got time to try. I will try to when I can but his hands came empty out of the water emptying the water emptying away*
    "'Where is ma, Darl?' I said. 'You never got her'" (144).

16. "I heard that my mother is dead. I wish I had time to let her die. I wish I had time to wish I had. It is because in the wild and out-raged earth too soon too soon too soon. It's not that I wouldn't and will not it's that it is too soon too soon too soon.
    Now it begins to say it. New Hope three miles. New Hope three miles. *That's what they mean by the womb of time: the agony and the despair of spreading bones, the hard girdle in which lie the outraged entrails of events* Cash's head turns slowly as we approach, his pale empty sad composed and questioning face following the red and empty curve; beside the back wheel Jewel sits the horse, gazing straight ahead.
    The land runs out of Darl's eyes; they swim to pinpoints. They begin at my feet and rise along my body to my face, and then my dress is gone: I sit naked on the seat above the unhurrying mules, above the travail" (114–115).

17. William Faulkner, "The Bear," *Go Down Moses* (New York: Random House, 1942), p. 331.

18. James Guetti, *The Limits of Metaphor* (Ithaca: Cornell University Press, 1967), pp. 158–163.

19. Frederick L. Gwynn and Joseph L. Blotner, eds., *Faulkner in the University* (New York: Vintage, 1959), p. 31.

20. Ibid., p. 32.

21. Ibid, p. 77.

22. Walter J. Slatoff, *Quest for Failure* (Ithaca: Cornell University Press, 1960), p. 261.

23. William Faulkner, *The Sound and the Fury* (New York: Vintage, 1954), pp. 411–412. Further references are to this edition and are given in the text.

24. Guetti, *The Limits of Metaphor*, pp. 69–108.

25. William Faulkner, *Absalom, Absalom!* (New York: Vintage, 1951), p. 303. Further references are to this edition and are given in the text.

26. For a fuller description of Sutpen's "progress," see Guetti, *The Limits of Metaphor*, p. 90 ff.

Chapter Seven

1. Aaron Copland, *Music and Imagination* (Cambridge: Harvard University Press, 1952), p. 9.

2. Leonard B. Meyer, *Emotion and Meaning in Music* (Chicago: University of Chicago Press, 1956), pp. 19–20. Both for considering the meaning of music and for possible analogies to meaning in literary process, this is a most useful book. It should be understood that in Meyer's terms "emotion . . . is aroused when a tendency to respond is arrested or inhibited," which occurs in the process of what he later calls "structural trouble," and that his distinction between "pleasant" and "unpleasant" emotions is a distinction between situations where such "troubles" are supposed by the perceiver to be either controlled (pleasant) or uncontrolled (unpleasant).

At times, however, Meyer appears at least momentarily to forget his early idea that what is important here is not actual control but expected control, in order to advance his conception that the aesthetic processes of music are basically the same as more usually intelligible processes of mind: "Problem solving and the aesthetic process are essentially one and the same thing except for this proviso: that in aesthetic thinking, the relationships between structural troubles and their resolutions are intelligible and resolvable" (88). This implication that control must be actually exercised by someone to be felt is rather too active and tense a model—not to say, in Meyer's phrasing, an illogical one—as Meyer appears to realize when later he returns to his initial idea, and prefers the term "structural gap" to "structural trouble," and then further modifies the conception: "In fact, it might be better to consider such a break as a disturbance in continuity rather than as a structural gap" (130). Here the emphasis is where he places it in the first place, and the assumed continuity both the ground and the control of its disturbances.

3. Ibid., pp. 73–74. The quotation within the quotation is from Ernst Kris, *Psychoanalytic Explorations in Art* (New York: International Universities Press, 1952), p. 42.

4. In *Vision and Resonance* (New York: Oxford University Press, 1975), John Hollander shows fully how perhaps a similar frame in poetry is generated by the poem's interior technical functions. And for his grasp of these functions, the entire chapter—"The Metrical Frame"—is to be recommended. But its ultimate drift, as I suggested earlier, seems both puzzling and contrary to my own attitudes. For when considering the special verbal dynamics generated by such "framing" in poetry, Hollander, rather than recognizing the aesthetic, and musical, force of such enclosure, seems to doubt it: "But the urging of a work of literature, perhaps accomplished by its formal frame, is no less an act of urging than any other kind of exhortation. The analysis of urging and exhorting can no longer be properly linguistic. And, finally, it is *as such* [i.e., as not linguistic?] that it lies outside the realm of poetics" (164).

That "no less" is curious. It would seem that Hollander is arguing for the unspecialness of aesthetic urging and exhortation and that the aesthetic frame is merely a special means of creating the same kinds of emphasis familiar to us in more ordinary sorts of usage. My own argument is exactly opposed to this, which seems to me so inaccurate that I become interested in the motive of Hollander's conception. "No less" suggests that this remark is an attempt to elevate poetry to the same status as ordinary language and to legitimize it in those terms. It suggests that the remark is an embattled one and an attempt to help poetry out. But I do not think it does that; nor does it serve the purposes of poetics. Aesthetic "urging" is not merely "no less an act of urging than any other kind," but much more an act of urging, a distinct form of urging, and so it would seem not "outside the realm" but precisely the subject of poetics.

Hollander's notion that it is not the subject of poetics, to be sure, arises from his conception and enactment of his own poetics. What he does is demonstrate with extreme nicety the radical modifications that energies of sound and music effect upon the sense of a poem's movement, with a fine sensitivity to and wide knowledge of musical dynamics. But he appears to consider that the music of a poem is always in service to meaning. Even when this music dominates, in his view, it does so by fooling us, by generating the illusion that it is a kind of sense. What Hollander shows us, then, is how sound embellishes sense, and such a demonstration—though often subtle and intensive—rests upon a theory of literary form that is Neoclassical and Aristotelian. It is to Hollander's credit that his poetics are a learned and complex way of making do with Aristotle. But such ancestry is too much of a handicap for any poetic to survive.

5. Wilson Coker, *Music and Meaning* (New York: Free Press, 1972), p. 32. For a thorough, though not unbiased, account of "extrageneric" meaning, see p. 60 ff.

6. If one feels, however, that the debate must be pursued, Coker pursues it very well and to conclusions that are—as I see it—inevitable. Despite his taste for extrageneric meaning, he allows, in his section called "Musical Metaphor," that "congeneric sign complexes may be regarded as metaphors for extrageneric meaning, the *primary* dimension of reference necessarily being congeneric and the *secondary* dimension being extrageneric. . . . But this is not to imply that extrageneric meaning is not itself a valid aesthetic dimension of musical meaning . . ." (152, his emphasis). The hedging at the end of this line later becomes explicit, when Coker asserts that not all extrageneric meanings are "derivative" (159). To support this, he cites extrageneric meanings in music that are fixed and obvious, like music imitating the sound of an engine, and so on. But he admits that such situations are "dead metaphors" and lack aesthetic force—if they are not downright offensive—and refocuses on more open metaphoric situations as more interesting. But I am afraid that, in theory, one cannot have this both ways, even if one wishes—if only for the sake of Coker's conscientiousness and tenacity—that he could: metaphoric meanings that are open are also arbitrary, and in gravitating to them, one is moving away from the primary and setting his imaginative agency against the music's own.

   We may compare Susanne Langer's attitude toward such metaphoric meaning: "Music must remain music . . . But where music is really music, though ideas of things or situations may underlie its forms, such ideas are never necessary to account for what one hears, to give it unity, or—worst of all—to give it emotive value." *Feeling and Form* (New York: Scribner's, 1953), p. 166.

7. Langer, *Feeling and Form*, p. 292. Further references to Mrs. Langer's aesthetic are to this edition of *Feeling and Form* unless otherwise noted and are given in the text.

   As we shall see in the case of Nabokov, there may be nothing apparently subtle or even technical about this process of "keeping it fiction," when the "manipulative" energy is extravagant.

8. We have seen that visual power may itself arise from the resistance created by such faults, and it should be admitted once more that, if the visual appetite is very strong, all musicalness may be ignored and the fragmentary visual pursued to ultimate satisfaction or frustration. But if we assume balanced motives in the reader, then the perceived relative weights of visual as opposed to aural processes in the form will decide the nature of the form, and one's response to it.

9. Leonard B. Meyer, *Music, the Arts, and Ideas* (Chicago: University of Chicago Press, 1967), p. 12.

10. One's purposes here are thus crucial, and Meyer's own insistence on the intelligibility of music becomes faulty when he fails to consider that such changes of fundamental motive make all the difference and so comes to ignore music's evident separation from ordinary cognitive process and to imagine that there is little difference between the activity and results of music and those of problem solving. This sort of mistake occurs most frequently in his later published book, *Music, the Arts, and Ideas*.

11. Gabriel Marcel, "Bergsonism and Music," in *Reflections on Art*, ed. Susanne Langer (Baltimore: Johns Hopkins Press, 1958), pp. 146–147.

12. Ibid., p. 150.

13. Basil De Selincourt, "Music and Duration," in *Reflections on Art*, pp. 156–157.

14. Earlier in *Feeling and Form*, Mrs. Langer has remarked that "music" is an "articulate but non-discursive form . . . in which the factor of significance is not logically discriminated, but is felt as a quality rather than recognized as a function" (32). "Non-discursive" I take to be the corresponding term in her scheme to the negative terms I have used in characterizing aural or musical processes in fiction—unintelligible or noncognitive—but it is unlike them in that it is not so apparently an intellectual dead end and yields more readily to the possibility of other kinds of knowledge or intelligibility within aesthetic processes: any other than the discursive. But I shall not surrender my more extravagant terms quite yet, for what the sense of aesthetic forms is remains to be seen.

15. Susanne Langer, *Philosophy in a New Key* (Cambridge: Harvard University Press, 1957), pp. 75–76.

16. Craig La Drière, "Structure, Sound, and Meaning," in *Sound and Poetry, English Institute Essays, 1956,* ed. Northrop Frye (New York: Columbia University Press, 1957), p. 97. The emphasis is mine.

    And earlier La Drière suggests that in this "non-aesthetic" usage sounds and even "natural" meanings themselves count for even less than he implies here: "In speech-constructs generated by non-poetic uses of language, the organizing principle by which these elements are related together into the cohesion of the construct is a principle derived not from the nature of the sounds or the meanings themselves—though some provision is always made to avoid doing violence to these natures—but a principle derived from their potential relation to some act or effect which is achieved or promoted by their construction thus together, *and might at least conceivably be achieved by similar use of quite other materials*" (92). I have emphasized here his implication that "non-aesthetic" processes are so disregardful of the elements that compose them that these elements could be, perhaps, anything at all. It would be hard to conceive, then, a greater neglect of words' quality than these processes exhibit.

17. La Drière gives, in a terminology somewhat different from mine, and with a slightly different emphasis, a nice account of this complex effect in his essay in *Sound and Poetry,* pp. 92–94. His insistence, however, that language's aesthetic potential derives from its prior aspect of social instrumentality—in my terms its visual-intelligible implementation—is not agreeable to me. For it is not necessary to consider the nonaesthetic use of language as its genesis, its original form, in order to recognize the potential presence of that form in aesthetic situations, or for the perception of its residue to occur. It is merely necessary for that nonaesthetic use to have itself occurred for an appreciable time and with an appreciable commitment—as La Drière says, "in language as we know it."

    Nor should he go so far as to restrict the "freer construction" of poetic and aesthetic usage to derivations from "the structuring they have taken in their instrumental use"; especially since he must grant a bit later, as most would, that this is a matter of complex mixture and balance and that an aspect that seems dominant at one moment will not at the next: "Not all their properties and relations, of course, are socially established, and in the character of these elements there remains a great deal that is not socially determined. But there is in the intrinsic nature of the sounds and meanings of language a *social aspect or element*" (my emphasis).

    But such disagreements do not seem crucial to me. La Drière's argument is acute and fruitful. In his terms, the residual instrumental property of aesthetic usage is reciprocal with another characteristic, which, in keeping with his conception that language's ordinary meaning is "social," he calls "natural," and which I would call "qualitative": "The semantic effect of a poetic structure as such is necessarily a 'natural' meaning, not a conventional meaning of the sort exemplified by lexical significations; apart from this, there is no theoretical reason why part at least of the total semantic effect (including of course the direct semantic residue of component lexical, logical, and rhetorical elements and structures) of a poem should not be of exactly the same character as some semantic and pragmatic effects of prose. When this is true, to 'read' the poem for these effects alone is to read it as prose; to read it as poetry is to prescind from these effects at least so far as to enjoy primarily the structure with which they are involved, and thus open the way to apprehension of the 'natural' meaning of the structure as such" (99).

I should add that I was delighted to find this essay, which seems to me both rigorous and suggestive as few treatments of its subject are. I was happy, also, to discover in the passage I have just quoted La Drière's parallel use—for I read his essay after I had devised this aspect of my own argument—of "residue" to suggest the signifying "potential" of language in aesthetic situations.

18. Marcel, "Bergsonism and Music," pp. 148–149.

19. S. Kierkegaard, *Repetition, An Essay in Experimental Psychology,* trans. Walter Lowrie (Princeton: Princeton University, Press, 1946).

20. Contrary to what Mrs. Langer's aesthetic model, in its particular relation to the novel, may lead her to suppose.

21. Vladimir Nabokov, *Bend Sinister* (New York: McGraw-Hill, 1974), p. 240. Further references are to this edition and are given in the text.

22. Compare Mrs. Langer's "a mere fancy by which the author entertains himself or his company" (*Feeling and Form,* 295).

23. Langer, *Philosophy in a New Key,* pp. 81–82.

24. All we need do to appreciate the special and artificial quality of time itself conceived as regular sequence and succession is to observe that succession operating in fictional contexts. If we think of narratives like Weesner's *The Car Thief,* such arrangement may appear strenuously artificial and mechanical as compared to the presumable potential of the life that it structures.

The point of observing that our ideas of time and sequence and the like are fictions—when this would appear obvious in the abstract—is to point out how insistently we hold to them as true in our practical experience. But even our notion of real time as regular sequence—upon which, as Meyer suggests, our ideas of causation seem to depend—is a clearly artificial conception: "The clock—metaphysically a very problematical instrument—makes a special abstraction from temporal experience, namely *time as pure sequence*, symbolized by a class of ideal events indifferent in themselves, but ranged in an infinite 'dense' series by the sole relation of succession. Conceived under this scheme, time is a one-dimensional continuum. . . . But for all its logical virtues, this one-dimensional, infinite succession of moments is an abstraction from direct experiences of time, and it is not the only possible one. Its great intellectual and practical advantages are bought at the price of many interesting phases of our time perception that have to be completely ignored. Consequently we have a great deal of temporal experience—that is, intuitive knowledge of time—that is not recognized as 'true' because it is not formalized and presented in any symbolic mode; we have only one way—the way of the clock—to think discursively about time at all" (*Feeling and Form*, 111).

And Mrs. Langer continues in a way that illuminates how this idea of time bolsters our faith in our free imaginative movement over and through our experience: "The underlying principle of clock-time is *change*, which is measured by contrasting two states of an instrument . . . and 'change' from one to the other is construed in terms of their differences . . ." (112).

25. One finds this prejudice acted out again and again in literary criticism and especially in criticism of the novel; and critics who would normally grant that any imaginative arrangement is, by definition, fictional nonetheless fall back upon sequential imagining as the real thing. In *The Sense of An Ending* (New York, 1967), for example, Frank Kermode considers normal temporal sequence, which he calls "chronicity," as the ground upon and the antagonist against which fictions must operate. And what that operation must yield, he argues, are fictions of "concord," in which the end is related to the beginning and so on, so as to make sense of a merely temporal succession. Of course, in such a case one is merely substituting one kind of succession or sequence—though a momentarily more comforting one—for another, and any attempt to deal *with* sequence will be a dealing *in* sequence. It will be to accept sequential imagining in general as justifiably dominant and to concede to the problematic succession of time in particular perpetual life as the antagonist, to be intermittently reinvoked so as to give one's "concord"—the sense that one has made of time—life. And Kermode is quite content with such a prospect: "So we may call books fictive models of the temporal world. They

will be humanly serviceable as models only if they pay adequate respect to what we think of as 'real' time . . . (54).

This assumption that fictions must always be in some service to our sense of reality is familiar by now as the visual-intelligible bias, in which "there *is* a simple relation between literary and other fictions" (36). As I have tried to show, such a relation indeed exists: it is the rule of realistic fictions. But Kermode does not seem to allow for any other sort; as I see it he is never speaking, in *The Sense of An Ending*, about what I have called aural or aesthetic fiction. Indeed, he seems to be saying that such stuff is illegitimate and that fiction must always be about something that he considers real.

But in my view, counter to Kermode's notion that the "critic's first qualification" must be a concern with "things as they are" (64), a critic should not commit himself to any such single fiction, even to the one most common in real life. His first qualification is not an interest in things as they are but in literature as it is, in fictions as they are—in fictions that are musical, if that is the way they are given— and not merely in the ways that fiction may or may not serve our presumably nonfictional, real interests. Our experience is full of ends other than The End, and for Kermode so to insist on the latter—and the accesses to it—is to declare that everything, literature included, is for him middle and means. But in aesthetic processes, which do occur in the novel, means are converted to ends, and the sense of any ultimate ending is beside the point. To deny this is precisely to trade fictions' inclusive power for their exclusive and dubious, and temporary, utility.

26. Perhaps the most sophisticated way we have of dealing with reflexive form—of maintaining our visual-sequential concentration, and dominance, when a linear form turns repetitively back upon itself—is to hold that it is thus about itself, that it makes itself the subject of its formal process. This is to consider reflexiveness itself as a kind of unreflexive, linear intelligence. Part of the satisfactoriness of this procedure is that it creates an "ironic" complex that is potentially limitless as a ground where critics may exercise their equally limitless hermeneutic appetites.

27. I use the phrase "serious fiction" here because the fiction with which the current market is glutted, and which must account for almost all paperback sales, except perhaps in colleges, is purely visual stuff.

28. Wallace Stevens, *Opus Posthumous* (New York: Knopf, 1957), p. 163.

Index